SHAKESPEARE
AND THE WORLD OF *SLINGS & ARROWS*

Shakespeare and the World of *Slings & Arrows*

Poetic Faith in a Postmodern Age

GARY KUCHAR

McGill-Queen's University Press
Montreal & Kingston • London • Chicago

© McGill-Queen's University Press 2024

ISBN 978-0-2280-2281-7 (paper)
ISBN 978-0-2280-2320-3 (ePDF)
ISBN 978-0-2280-2321-0 (ePUB)

Legal deposit fourth quarter 2024
Bibliothèque nationale du Québec

Printed in Canada on acid-free paper that is 100% ancient forest free (100% post-consumer recycled), processed chlorine free

This book has been published with the help of a grant from the Federation for the Humanities and Social Sciences, through the Awards to Scholarly Publications Program, using funds provided by the Social Sciences and Humanities Research Council of Canada.

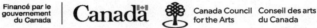

We acknowledge the support of the Canada Council for the Arts.

Nous remercions le Conseil des arts du Canada de son soutien.

McGill-Queen's University Press in Montreal is on land which long served as a site of meeting and exchange amongst Indigenous Peoples, including the Haudenosaunee and Anishinabeg nations. In Kingston it is situated on the territory of the Haudenosaunee and Anishinaabek. We acknowledge and thank the diverse Indigenous Peoples whose footsteps have marked these territories on which peoples of the world now gather.

Library and Archives Canada Cataloguing in Publication

Title: Shakespeare and the world of Slings & arrows : poetic faith in a postmodern age / Gary Kuchar.
Names: Kuchar, Gary, 1974– author.
Description: Includes bibliographical references and index.
Identifiers: Canadiana (print) 20240391780 | Canadiana (ebook) 20240391802 | ISBN 9780228022817 (paper) | ISBN 9780228023203 (ePDF) | ISBN 9780228023210 (ePUB)
Subjects: LCSH: Slings & arrows (Television program) | LCSH: Shakespeare, William, 1564–1616—Television adaptations. | LCSH: Television adaptations—History and criticism.
Classification: LCC PN1992.77.S62 K83 2024 | DDC 791.45/72—dc23

This book was typeset by True to Type in 10½/13 Sabon

For Edward Pechter

Literature remains alive only if we set ourselves immeasurable goals, far beyond all hope of achievement.

– Italo Calvino[1]

There's something very melancholy about doing something you love, because it will never be good enough, it will always break your heart … Or it will be fleeting.

– Susan Coyne; Mark McKinney[2]

Quod fere totus mundus exerceat histrionem
(Nearly All the World's a Stage)

– Motto of Shakespeare's Globe

Contents

Acknowledgments   ix
Abbreviations   xi

Introduction   3
1 Deadly Theatre and Holy Theatre   21
2 Poetic Faith   32
3 The Simulacra   53
4 Kingfisher Days   65
5 The Stage Is All the World   88
6 The Local and the Typical   116
7 Mimesis and Emotional Realism   127
8 Sold Out   140
9 Bardbiz   146
10 Being Darren Nichols   159
11 The Promised End   171
Conclusion   183
Coda: John Hirsch's *Tempest* (1982)   187

Notes   197
Bibliography   213
Index   227

Acknowledgments

This project began in 2019 when I was a fellow at the Centre for Studies in Religion and Society at the University of Victoria. I would thus like to thank all the members of the centre for making this time so inspiring and productive, especially Paul Bramadat, Rachel Brown, Scott Dolff, and Noriko Prezeau. Similarly, I would like to thank the students of my undergraduate course on *Slings & Arrows* at the University of Victoria for sharing their interest in this material, even if it had to be done over Zoom at times. The library staff at McPherson Library, especially the indomitable Erica Burns, also proved crucial for this project. James A. Knapp and Richard van Oort kindly offered comments on the article from which this book sprung, while Nola Accili shared many conversations and a wonderful idea with me, as I am happy to note in the apparatus. J.M. Richardson and Kim Fedderson sent me a copy of their article on *Slings & Arrows* during the pandemic when library materials were in short supply, helping to kickstart what would become this book. Kenneth Graham and other members of the Canadian Society for Renaissance Studies offered constructive feedback on a conference presentation version of the project. Lisa Surridge schooled me on some Victorian matters, while Jonathan Goldman, Matthew Huculak, Linda Morra, Emile Fromet de Rosnay, Daromir Rudnyckyj, and Lincoln Shlensky provided much-needed friendship and intellectual camaraderie during the composition of this book. There's nothing like a pandemic to remind one of how valuable friends are. I am also grateful to Erin E. Kelly for watching the series with me when it was initially released and for sharing her vast knowledge and deep love of theatre over many years. I would also like to thank Jonathan Crago and the team at McGill-Queen's for believing in this project when it was not much more than

x   Acknowledgments

an idea. Similarly, I am grateful to the editors of the journal *Shakespeare* for allowing me to reproduce material from my article "*Slings & Arrows* and the State of Play in Shakespeare Studies," *Shakespeare* 17, no. 3 (2021), 318–43, DOI: 10.1080/17450918.2021.1903980. And to Paul Thompson, I am grateful for permission to quote from the John Hirsch oral history at Library and Archives Canada. My greatest debt on this project, however, is to the late Edward Pechter. Along with his wonderful and much-missed friendship, Ed offered vigorous responses to the manuscript at various stages of development, making it, in many respects, the product of a two-decades-long conversation between the two of us. While Ed very much informed the sort of Shakespeare you will find in this book, and hopefully made me a better writer, he is not, of course, to blame for my shortcomings.

Abbreviations

AFS   Fraidie Martz and Andrew Wilson. *A Fiery Soul: The Life and Theatrical Times of John Hirsch*. Montreal: Véhicule Press, 2011.

BC   John Hirsch. "Father Courage: An Interview with John Hirsch." By Robert Enright. *Border Crossings: The Exiled Imagination* 7, no. 4 (Fall 1988): 80–5.

BTS   Michael Bristol. *Big-Time Shakespeare*. London: Routledge, 1996.

DG   Northrop Frye. *Divisions on a Ground: Essays on Canadian Culture*. Edited by James Polk. Toronto: Anansi, 1982.

EM   Sue Prideux. *Edvard Munch: Behind The Scream*. New Haven: Yale University Press, 2005.

ES   Peter Brook. *The Empty Space*. London: Nick Hern Books, 1968.

KD   Susan Coyne. *Kingfisher Days*. Toronto: Vintage Canada, 2001.

MM   Northrop Frye. *Myth and Metaphor: Selected Essays, 1974–1988*. Edited by Robert D. Denham. Charlottesville: University of Virginia Press, 1990.

MS   Terence Hawkes. *Meaning By Shakespeare*. London: Routledge, 1992.

NFMC   Northrop Frye. *Northrop Frye on Modern Culture*. Edited by Jan Gorak. Toronto: University of Toronto Press, 2003.

NFWE   Northrop Frye. *Northrop Frye's Writings on the Eighteenth and Nineteenth Centuries*. Edited by Imre Salusinszky. Toronto: University of Toronto Press, 2005.

NFWS   Northrop Frye. *Northrop Frye's Writings on Shakespeare and the Renaissance*. Edited by Troni Y. Grande and Garry Sherbert. Toronto: University of Toronto Press, 2010.

PM   Frederic Jameson. *Postmodernism, or, The Cultural Logic of Late Capitalism*. Durham: Duke University Press, 1991. Rpt. 2001.

Abbreviations

S&A   Peter Wellington, dir. *Slings & Arrows: The Complete Collection.* Acorn Media, 2019. Cited in text by season and episode.

SFSP   *Stratford Festival Souvenir Programme.* Given in text by year and page when paginated.

SO   Urjo Kareda. "Sold Out." *Toronto Life* 34, no. 11 (2000): 76.

SS   Jean Baudrillard. *Simulacra and Simulation.* Translated by Sheila Faria Glaser. Ann Arbor: University of Michigan Press, 1994.

TRV   Alasdair MacIntyre. *Three Rival Versions of Moral Enquiry.* Notre Dame: Notre Dame University Press, 1990.

WWP   Northrop Frye. *Words with Power.* New York: HarperCollins, 1992.

SHAKESPEARE
AND THE WORLD OF *SLINGS & ARROWS*

Introduction

Every year we take a play, and we sift it through our own lives, and our own
sensibilities, and our own sense of where the world is at, and we try to reflect
it in the story that we tell outside the play. There is an interpenetration of the
themes of the play and the themes of the lives of the characters.

Susan Coyne (*s&a*, season 3, disc 2)

A leading scholar of Hellenistic Alexandria named Aristophanes of
Byzantium once asked, "O Menander and Life, which of you took the
other as your model?"[1] By the eighteenth century, the issue had come
around again, only now the plays in question were not the comedies
of Menander but the dramas of William Shakespeare. Hence Goethe's
1771 exclamation in Strasbourg, "Nature! Nature! Nothing so natural
as Shakespeare's people," or Coleridge's subsequent claim that Shakespeare depicted the breadth of human nature with the precision of a
Dutch painter.[2] Behind such romantic convictions about the mimetic
power of Shakespeare's plays lie a range of critical assumptions and
practices, but none so powerful as the commonplace idea that "all the
world's a stage." If Shakespeare bequeathed this idea to the modern
world through Jaques's "ages of man" and Prospero's "our revels now
are ended" speeches, it was bequeathed to him by a rich, and oftentimes complexly anti-theatrical, tradition running from ancient Greece
(Plato) to Augustan Rome (Cicero) to the early Church Fathers (St
Augustine).[3] By Shakespeare's time, the idea that the vanities of
human life constituted a kind of cosmic drama was so familiar that a
playwright such as Thomas Heywood could reverse the moral direction of the metaphor to defend the stage from its Puritan critics: "If
then the world a theater present ... / He that denyes then theaters
should be / He may as well deny a world to me."[4] At such moments,

Heywood effectively asks with Hamlet: what access do we have to life, except insofar as it is reflected back to us through an embodied story? The play is indeed the thing.

These two interrelated contexts about the relationship between life and art – the mimetic power of Shakespeare's plays and the idea of the world as a stage – richly animate the critically celebrated but academically controversial three-season Canadian television series *Slings & Arrows* (2003–06). On one hand, the show's three writers (Susan Coyne, Mark McKinney, and Bob Martin) take these ideas seriously enough to incorporate them into the story's overall narrative structure. In formulating her basic design for the series, cited in the epigraph, co-creator and co-writer Susan Coyne explains how *Slings & Arrows* interlaces Shakespeare's plays, the fictional lives of the show's characters, and the real lives of the show's producers into one coherent narrative, thus interweaving the world of the theatre with the theatre of the world. On the other hand, however, the high romantic commitments animating this overall narrative conception are consistently undercut within the show itself, the wind rarely staying in the sails for long. The result is a dialectic of conviction and malaise that conveys the challenges of sustaining meaningful belief in classical theatre as a vocation in the proper sense of the term, rather than as simply a profession or worse yet, as we say today, a lifestyle. In this way, the show depicts the challenges of living up to legendary director Peter Brook's vision of theatre as "a complete way of life for all its members," or the one-time Stratford Festival artistic director Robin Phillips's conviction that "Theatre ... is a vocation. I believe that we do it for reasons other than just to entertain, and that if we do it well, we can make a huge difference to people's lives."[5] In structuring its televisual story as a dialectic of faith in and doubt about classical theatre as a vocation, *Slings & Arrows* tries to do what may now be impossible: communicate a genuine sense of shared artistic and existential purpose in a popular medium in an age of advanced capitalism, but in a manner that does not inadvertently become an instance of the commodifying culture it parodies.

If such an endeavour seems improbable, it's partly because it runs against the grain of what is sometimes said of television as a medium. According to Jean Baudrillard, television "cools and neutralizes the meaning and energy of events," operating through simulation rather than representation, through images without references and imitations without originals.[6] From this perspective, television induces an

Introduction

overly intimate immersion of receiver into transmission, preventing the viewer from gaining the distance required for any proper form of aesthetic understanding.[7] With television, so the argument goes, there "is no separation any longer, no empty space, no absence: you enter the screen and the visual image unhindered."[8] The televisual medium thus contrasts with the theatre because the world of late capitalism collapses the distinction of spectator and show; when "all are actors, there is no action any longer, no scene. An end to aesthetic illusion," as such.[9] From this bleak standpoint, television as a medium is inherently antithetical to theatre as a scene of ritual-like participation of audience with stage. Consequently, it is inherently hostile to the romantic idea of artistic vocation as, in Northrop Frye's words, "a total way of life," a calling that "has an importance for society far beyond" art itself.[10] After all, social reality has a strange way of disappearing behind the phantasmic flow of images on the small screen. From this general perspective, "a television program can only be understood by its relationship to other television programs, not by any relationship to the real," as a leading television critic says in a discussion of such postmodern theory.[11] Yet if the idealistic view of theatre in *Slings & Arrows* is necessarily hindered by the dynamics of its televisual medium, the show is nevertheless quite cognizant of the intermedial challenges inherent to its endeavour. Instead of blindly succumbing to such formal limitations, the series openly addresses them both thematically and formally, engaging such issues at the level of story as well as *mise en scène*. The result is a television series designed to make sense in terms of both its relationship to other texts as well as its relationship to life, particularly the dialectic of conviction and malaise that has often characterized twentieth-century classical theatre.

In this latter respect, *Slings & Arrows* remains self-consciously at odds with the cultural logic of postmodernism often associated with television as a medium. According to this postmodern narrative, the contemporary media-industrial complex no longer constitutes the cultural space in which human beings have an opportunity for self-realization, an opportunity to become more fully individuated, morally realized persons. Instead, it functions as a grossly autonomous sphere overwhelming humans with its excess of self-referring messages that are disarticulated from an increasingly inaccessible social reality, resulting in an orgiastic levelling of all values and hierarchies (*ss*, 1–43). While admitting the partial veracity of such dystopian claims, *Slings & Arrows* nevertheless resists blanket assertions that aesthetic illusions are no longer genuinely possible in an age of advanced capitalism, including on television. In place of such skepticism, it adopts a broadly post-romantic approach to Shakespeare and to classical theatre more generally, one in which drama is not simply a form of entertainment but a potentially dangerous, because transformative, form of artistic expression. This interlacing of art with life along broadly humanist lines is built into the three-season structure of the series, as each year's production moves the meta-dramatic story through the experiences of youth (*Hamlet*), middle age (*Macbeth*), and old age (*King Lear*). By stressing the dialectical relationship between life and art in this manner, *Slings & Arrows* holds the view that Romanticism constitutes a major imaginative revolution, the effects of which continue to unfold today, in however suppressed or dormant a fashion. From this perspective, culturally residual forces such as Romanticism, and the Shakespearean humanism that so deeply informs it, retain a degree of critical leverage over the mutually implicating forces of neo-liberal economics and postmodern culture.[12] At the same time, the show shares Baudrillard's early sense that in our consumerist society people tend to approach life with a vapidly "ludic curiosity" rather than a committed sense of "passionate play" in which there is a total involvement in the process of symbolic exchange.[13] After all, such an observation is a variation of Schlegel's romantic conviction that "the poetry of the ancients was that of possession; [whereas] ours is that of longing. The former stands on the ground of the present; the latter hovers between memory and anticipation."[14] From the standpoint of *Slings & Arrows*, then, recovering the view of classical theatre as a vocation means somehow overcoming the dehumanizing contexts in which we now read, study, and perform Shakespeare.

However comically unassuming it may be, *Slings & Arrows* invests deeply in the authority of Shakespearean realism to tell its story about the pursuit of artistic vocation in an age of advanced capitalism. But in doing so, it conforms to more updated accounts of Shakespearean mimesis than those expressed by Goethe and Coleridge. Throughout the series, the show self-consciously follows Peter Brook's high-modernist updating of romantic views of Shakespearean realism in his landmark book *The Empty Space* (1968), a heuristically suggestive account of modern theatre according to four potentially overlapping categories: deadly, holy, rough, and immediate. Adapting Brook's account of modern theatre to television, the metanarrative story of *Slings & Arrows* gives voice to a view of Shakespeare that not only reflects some of the challenges of post-millennial festival theatre, but also provides a meaningful context for understanding the pursuit of artistic and spiritual purpose in an age that seems increasingly hostile to the very possibility of vocation. In doing so, the show provides a privileged standpoint from which to reassess the current state of Shakespeare studies and the humanities more broadly. Bearing these local and general contexts in mind, the overall aim of this book is twofold. First, it provides a contextualized close reading of the dialectic of conviction and malaise in *Slings & Arrows*, explaining how the program's metafictional design operates, what it means, and why its execution has proven appealing to popular audiences and television critics but controversial to professional Shakespeareans working from anti-humanist perspectives. Second, it hazards that such a reading of the show might help literary and cultural critics rediscover a more sustainable sense of disciplinary purpose.

If the diagnosis of Shakespearean malaise in *Slings & Arrows* has a direct analogue in the academy, it is surely Edward Pechter's *Shakespeare Studies Today: Romanticism Lost* (2011). According to Pechter, Shakespeare studies is suffering from a complex process of cultural deracination that has stunted the discipline's sense of its own exigency. In his view, the general loss of conviction in Shakespeare studies is a consequence of the way Shakespeare scholars have lost sight of the discipline's origins in European romantic thought. This dislocation of past from present runs so deep, Pechter explains, that most accounts of romantic readings of Shakespeare miss the mark. Instead of stressing self-expression, formalist organic unity, or literary biography, key romantic figures such as Coleridge developed a critical practice that focused on the imaginative vitality of aesthetic experience and the way texts transfigure minds and persons. In making his case, Pechter explains the commonly heard refrain that literary studies has lost sight of why the aesthetic dimension of literature matters and is only now in the process of recovering this focus. In offering future directions, Pechter thus calls for modes of reading that revivify William Hazlitt's (1778–1830) emphasis on how the forms and patterns of Shakespeare's plays structure the range of possible responses, thereby stressing the importance of submitting to the play's designs on the audience rather than assuming a position of interpretive dominance over the text. So rather than taking the plays as a site in which readers and directors narrowly impose their own immediate preoccupations on the text, the plays are the site for a more dialectical encounter between text and readers, with the emphasis falling on the agency the plays have over their readers in different times and places. In turning to romantic aesthetics as a way of reimagining a shared sense of scholarly purpose, Pechter does in an academic context something very much like what *Slings & Arrows* accomplishes in the more popular mode of television.[15] At moments, his book even hankers after the purity of amateurism animating *Slings & Arrows*, especially its central character Geoffrey Tennant (Paul Gross). But rather than being isolated instances of a post-romantic recovery, these two works are part of a growing academic and popular response to the sense of declining purpose felt by those who study and perform classical literature in an age of advancing neo-liberalism and postmodern relativism. To fully understand *Slings & Arrows* as a cultural event, we need to see it within the broader and still evolving intellectual context of the wider Shakespearean world, especially as construed by critics who write in a self-consciously post-romantic vein, such as Jonathan Bate, Richard C. McCoy, Andy Mousley, and Kiernan Ryan.[16]

In other academic quarters, however, the cultural deracination Pechter laments is a consummation devoutly to be wished. For example, in her 2010 essay, "Close but Not Deep: Literary Ethics and the Descriptive Turn," Heather K. Love calls for a root and branch overhaul of literary studies designed to rid the discipline of its nagging residual humanism. Instead of basing literary study on forms of contextualized close reading that are attentive to the personal dimensions of aesthetic experience, scholars, she argues, should adopt a neutral ethnographic approach that gives a picture of the world not as "'fat and living' but [as] 'thin and dead.'"[17] Based on Erving Goffman's role-playing sociology in which human relations are voided of objective standards of success or achievement, this style of criticism rests on a social theory that places enormous stress on one particular form of moral transgression. According to Goffman's model, moral standards are often generated through a desire to sustain interpersonal role-playing relations in the face of charismatic or overly expansive individuals, those who get too loud or too passionate in any particular social practice, thereby upsetting the interpersonal balance.[18] Following this social model, Love calls for a style of criticism that consists of neutral, affectless description rather than impassioned redescription, a form of ethnography that disarms the "ethical charisma of the critic."[19] The stated advantage of such a form of analysis is that it ensures literary studies will remain rigorously empirical and materialist rather than residually metaphysical and

Introduction

hermeneutic. Moreover, it will void academic criticism of overly expansive, charismatic styles of writing that cast unhelpful enchantments on readers, especially those styles characteristic of romantic criticism. Whatever one may think of such avowed anti-humanism, viewers of *Slings & Arrows* will no doubt recognize in such postmodernism a sophisticated version of one of its primary satirical targets (the pseudo-Brechtian productions of Darren Nichols). To this extent, the show invites us to question the legitimacy of its response to ongoing debates about the legacies of humanist and romantic thought within the broader academy and the wider culture it serves. Viewed this way, we might ask if the show's parody of such affectless approaches to art and culture has any validity. Or whether we can dismiss it as, at best, entertainment or, at worst, retrograde humanism.

A major attempt to map the wider professional context in which these debates about literary humanism are now unfolding can be found in John Guillory's *Professing Criticism* (2022). In providing a wide-angle view of literary study as a professional enterprise, Guillory shrewdly observes that the "history of scholarship already knows much that our current practice has forgotten," not least of which is the "mundane yet mysterious process" of interanimation of reader and text, "which Coleridge described two centuries ago" and which is now being rediscovered among scholars dissatisfied with the hermeneutics of suspicion.[20] Returning us to Pechter's original insight, this crucial observation about the often forgotten richness of Western critical history tells us something important about a study of *Slings & Arrows*. It suggests that an analysis of the show in its cultural and intellectual contexts may not only be valuable in its own right, but may also deepen our collective sense that in the humanities critical innovation is often a matter of unacknowledged rediscovery. Hence my effort in this book to provide new directions from old.

RECEPTION

In a number of revealing ways, the general debates about literary humanism briefly outlined above have played out at a more local level in the notable differences between the academic and popular responses to *Slings & Arrows*. Originally aired in 2003–06 on three Canadian cable networks, *Slings & Arrows* presents a vision of the modern Shakespeare world that has been both celebrated and pilloried.[21] As far as its general reception is concerned, Peter Wellington's three-season series is one of Canada's most critically acclaimed television productions. Often described by TV critics as the best televisual depiction of theatre ever made, it is also seen by some as second to none in terms of overall quality.[22] According to the *Los Angeles Times*, *Slings & Arrows* is "as great a show as television has brought forth, in this or any other age – droll, poetical, satirical, sincere, allusive, immediate, romantic, unsentimental, thrilling, and incidentally informative."[23] Concurring with these assessments, David Simon, lead writer of HBO's *The Wire*, remarked that watching this "wonderful Canadian show ... about a Shakespearean theatre company" left him with "pure, distilled writer envy."[24] Most remarkably, Brazilian director Fernando Meirelles has adapted the series as *Som e Furia*, reaching eighteen million Portuguese speakers in the process.[25] Given this foreign reception, it is perhaps little wonder that the Canadian cultural establishment lavished awards on the show for its writing, acting, and direction, including thirteen Gemini and three Writers Guild awards. On the basis of such critical and popular success, the show's producers have begun work on a prequel titled *Amateurs*, which will focus on the founding of the New Burbage Festival, a storyline presumably inspired by the founding of the Stratford Festival in 1953.

And yet the program's reception among professional Shakespeareans has been less enthusiastic. Broadly speaking, the general scholarly consensus is that the show propagates an outdated humanist view of Shakespeare, one rooted in false notions of universalism and a deluded sense of transhistorical continuity. Worse yet, some think the series furthers heteronormative ideology and an indiscriminate anti-intellectualism, working, as one unimpressed critic puts it, to "cure the gays and the academics."[26] From this perspective, the show reproduces a conception of Shakespeare's authority that is more an ideological construction than the product of accumulated centuries-long critical and popular insight. Consequently, a primary scholarly goal has been to debunk the program's bardolatrous commitment to Shakespeare as an uncannily resonant writer and to expose the show's retrograde ideological commitments. Such a response to the show might thus be seen as a prime example of what led Canadian Shakespeare scholar and one-time Marxist critic Michael Bristol to ask of the discipline in 2011: "If Shakespeareans don't believe in Shakespeare's greatness, then who does?"[27]

Revealingly, ideological critiques of *Slings & Arrows* reproduce many of the same criticisms that have been levelled at the Stratford Festival three-season series is one of Canada's most critically acclaimed television productions. Often described by TV critics as the best televisual depiction of theatre ever made, it is also seen by some as second to none in terms of overall quality.[22] According to the *Los Angeles Times*, *Slings & Arrows* is "as great a show as television has brought forth, in this or any other age – droll, poetical, satirical, sincere, allusive, immediate, romantic, unsentimental, thrilling, and incidentally informative."[23] Concurring with these assessments, David Simon, lead writer of HBO's *The Wire*, remarked that watching this "wonderful Canadian show ... about a Shakespearean theatre company" left him with "pure, distilled writer envy."[24] Most remarkably, Brazilian director Fernando Meirelles has adapted the series as *Som e Fúria*, reaching eighteen million Portuguese speakers in the process.[25] Given this foreign reception, it is perhaps little wonder that the Canadian cultural establishment lavished awards on the show for its writing, acting, and direction, including thirteen Gemini and three Writers Guild awards. On the basis of such critical and popular success, the show's producers have begun work on a prequel titled *Amateurs*, which will focus on the founding of the New Burbage Festival, a storyline presumably inspired by the founding of the Stratford Festival in 1953.

And yet the program's reception among professional Shakespeareans has been less enthusiastic. Broadly speaking, the general scholarly consensus is that the show propagates an outdated humanist view of Shakespeare, one rooted in false notions of universalism and a deluded sense of transhistorical continuity. Worse yet, some think the series furthers heteronormative ideology and an indiscriminate anti-intellectualism, working, as one unimpressed critic puts it, to "cure the gays and the academics."[26] From this perspective, the show reproduces a conception of Shakespeare's authority that is more an ideological construction than the product of accumulated centuries-long critical and popular insight. Consequently, a primary scholarly goal has been to debunk the program's bardolatrous commitment to Shakespeare as an uncannily resonant writer and to expose the show's retrograde ideological commitments. Such a response to the show might thus be seen as a prime example of what led Canadian Shakespeare scholar and one-time Marxist critic Michael Bristol to ask of the discipline in 2011: "If Shakespeareans don't believe in Shakespeare's greatness, then who does?"[27]

Revealingly, ideological critiques of *Slings & Arrows* reproduce many of the same criticisms that have been levelled at the Stratford Festival

Introduction

hermeneutic. Moreover, it will void academic criticism of overly expansive, charismatic styles of writing that cast unhelpful enchantments on readers, especially those styles characteristic of romantic criticism. Whatever one may think of such avowed anti-humanism, viewers of *Slings & Arrows* will no doubt recognize in such postmodernism a sophisticated version of one of its primary satirical targets (the pseudo-Brechtian productions of Darren Nichols). To this extent, the show invites us to question the legitimacy of its response to ongoing debates about the legacies of humanist and romantic thought within the broader academy and the wider culture it serves. Viewed this way, we might ask if the show's parody of such affectless approaches to art and culture has any validity. Or whether we can dismiss it as, at best, entertainment or, at worst, retrograde humanism.

A major attempt to map the wider professional context in which these debates about literary humanism are now unfolding can be found in John Guillory's *Professing Criticism* (2022). In providing a wide-angle view of literary study as a professional enterprise, Guillory shrewdly observes that the "history of scholarship already knows much that our current practice has forgotten," not least of which is the "mundane yet mysterious process" of interanimation of reader and text, "which Coleridge described two centuries ago" and which is now being rediscovered among scholars dissatisfied with the hermeneutics of suspicion.[20] Returning us to Pechter's original insight, this crucial observation about the often forgotten richness of Western critical history tells us something important about a study of *Slings & Arrows*. It suggests that an analysis of the show in its cultural and intellectual contexts may not only be valuable in its own right, but may also deepen our collective sense that in the humanities critical innovation is often a matter of unacknowledged rediscovery. Hence my effort in this book to provide new directions from old.

RECEPTION

In a number of revealing ways, the general debates about literary humanism briefly outlined above have played out at a more local level in the notable differences between the academic and popular responses to *Slings & Arrows*. Originally aired in 2003–06 on three Canadian cable networks, *Slings & Arrows* presents a vision of the modern Shakespeare world that has been both celebrated and pilloried.[21] As far as its general reception is concerned, Peter Wellington's of the 1990s under the artistic direction of Richard Monette (1993–2007). One prominent Canadian theatre scholar, for example, excoriates the 1990s Stratford Festival as a "universalist, individualist, essentialist, and literary ... Ideological State Apparatus."[28] In other words, by the 1990s the festival had become little more than a corporatized entity serving the economic and social interests of elite, predominantly white male consumers who have a historical tendency to impose their view of the world on those who don't share it. Moreover, the festival had adopted a "literary" ideology in which individual performances were thought to be in service of an oppressively authorial intention, communicating forms, values, and meanings connecting the past to the present in a socially retrograde way. From this perspective, the festival's presentation of Shakespeare's plays as irreducible to any one local context was less an expression of accumulated critical awareness than a fabrication of a specific social group serving its own mercenary interests. Consequently, the festival's long-standing belief that Shakespeare's plays give expression to a commonly shared humanity had become conveniently reflective of its own material interests and particular social perspectives. Applying the same critical assumptions and interpretive habits to *Slings & Arrows*, scholars have rediscovered in the show the same problems they originally found in the Stratford Festival of the '90s.

Yet the situation is perhaps more complicated than such ready-to-hand parallels suggest. After all, if ideological criticisms of the '90s Stratford Festival were echoed in quarters beyond the academy, there were also more moderate voices reminding us not to paint with an overly broad brush.[29] As Peter Parolin has shown, Monette's artistically multifaceted festival "sought and often attained a much greater degree of aesthetic diversity" than critics who derisively labelled him a "populist" admit.[30] Moreover, such diversity is an expression of Monette's plausible belief in Shakespeare as cultural touchstone, as a resource for disclosing the time and pressures of the contemporary historical moment as experienced by a vast range of people in it.[31] Resting on many of the best aspects of Monette's view of classical theatre, while being implicitly critical of some of the more crassly commercial features of the festival under his leadership, *Slings & Arrows* does not easily reduce to ideological critique. For one thing, such criticisms do not explain the show's organizing dialectic of conviction and malaise so much as they repeat one half of it. Somewhat ironically, then, ideological critiques of the show go some way in confirming the program's diagnosis of our cultural situation. To properly account for the series as a cultural event, then, a more capacious approach is needed.

Such an accommodating approach might be found by adopting a more dialectical perspective. Instead of simply reading the show in its various contexts, we might also use the program to reconsider the state of play within Shakespeare studies more broadly. In doing so, *Slings & Arrows* begins to look remarkably like a narrativized version of the argument made in Bristol's *Big-Time Shakespeare* (1996). In his book, Bristol sets out to reconcile conservative and radical views of Shakespeare's legacy with a two-pronged thesis. On one hand, he acknowledges how Shakespeare's plays now often circulate in "an aggregate of commodities fashioned to offer distraction from the continuing pathos of Western modernity."[32] In this respect, he acknowledges how Shakespeare's authority has been eroded by a variety of social and economic forces, sometimes to the point of being reduced to a form of postmodern kitsch. On the other hand, however, he recognizes that Shakespeare's plays, and much of the broader interpretive tradition mediating them, remain irreducible to market and ideological forces. He thus concludes that "no one should presume that belief in Shakespeare's authority is either self-deluded or self-serving" (xii). And that demystifying Shakespeare's authority is just as likely to insult those who have had to struggle to gain access to great works of art as it is to placate their presumed grievances (viii).

For Bristol, the commodification of Shakespeare in popular culture may be frequent, but it does not exhaust the ongoing force of his work. After all, the ideology of commodification does not have a total grip on culture or the people who participate in it. "Even in the most vitiated and meretricious presentations" of Shakespeare's works, Bristol observes, "the semantic potential ... can 'break through' to a 'more intense and fuller life.' The possibility of 'breaking through' is what makes Shakespeare essential. Essential Shakespeare is a vital continuation of the past" (*BTS*, 94).

Such a view of Shakespeare's language is apropos of *Slings & Arrows* precisely because its televisual contrivances aim not only to entertain, but also to communicate why some people in the theatre world love classical literature enough to have made it an integral part of their personal and professional lives, sacrificing much for it. And yet, the show has few illusions about the challenges inherent in fusing horizons with the Shakespearean past in ways that meaningfully interpenetrate with the present. While such hope is built into the program's very narrative structure, the show repeatedly acknowledges the near impossibility of realizing such idealistic goals for any sustained period of time. The result is a broadly convincing, if comically and televisually stylized, depiction of the dialectic of conviction and malaise that has tended to characterize modern classical theatre and, by extension, early modern studies, across the last several generations.

Part of the exigency for this study, then, arises from the gap between the show's reception inside and outside the academy. Such a gap should concern academics for reasons that have been stated before, as they mark "the extent to which ... vanguard [Shakespeare] critics have separated themselves from, and alienated, a significant part of the public that used to be included in [its] audience and ... constituency."[33] In attempting to narrow this gap, *Shakespeare and the World of "Slings & Arrows"* is premised on the assumption that ideological critiques of the so-called Shakespeare myth, or the idea that his plays authoritatively disclose transhistorical realities, now accomplish little more than helping to "saw off the branch on which the humanities themselves are ever more precariously perched," as Michael Dobson observes in a parallel context.[34] And as the series effectively suggests, Shakespeare's greatness is not a fictionalized myth but an accomplished realization that each generation must make anew from its own perspective. Viewed this way, the Shakespeare myth is an attempt to account for Shakespeare's genius rather than being its originating source.

In advocating such post-romantic views, the overall narrative conception of *Slings & Arrows* also exemplifies a key thesis expressed in Jonathan Bate's *The Genius of Shakespeare* (1997): the view that Shakespeare's brilliance is "a truth-function of the difference it makes in the lives of those who maintain it."[35] From this standpoint, understanding Shakespeare's greatness means understanding how his works can be performed in different media over time in ways that prove consequential for those who participate in such performances, including actors, directors, audiences, and readers. At bottom, *Slings & Arrows* asks whether such a view is sustainable in the post-millennial age, or whether, as the terminally ill Charles Kingman (William Hutt) says in season 3, "the theatre ... is fighting a slow, undignified death."

MIMESIS AND THE SACRED

As I noted, if the show's depiction of the future of theatre has a degree of poignancy, it's partly because the program's resuscitation of a certain kind of post-romantic view of Shakespeare mirrors developments in literary and cultural studies over the last two decades. Both prior to and following the show's airing, a number of important works have appeared expounding the value of romantic conceptions of Shakespeare. At the same time, a growing body of criticism questioning the limits of ideological critique has gained force, revealing, at least in some quarters, a certain exhaustion with narrowly politicized approaches to culture criticism.[36] Particularly significant in this context is the show's ironized morality-romance structure and the way heroes and villains vie over the soul of the New Burbage Theatre Festival, especially in the first season. In constructing its narrative as an ironized morality play, the show presents a story that is broadly consonant with Shakespeare's late romances, most notably *The Tempest*, which is, among other things, a sustained meditation on the promise and precariousness of theatre as an art form. In reworking the metatheatrical themes of *The Tempest*, the show presents a focused and not altogether unsubtle example of the thesis that concepts of the sacred remain necessary to any proper understanding of rudimentary social and aesthetic dynamics generally. Put differently, *Slings & Arrows* rediscovers its own scaled-down version of Émile Durkheim's insight about the elementary forms of religious life. According to Durkheim, "Once a goal is pursued by a whole people, it acquires, as a result of this unanimous adherence, a sort of moral supremacy which raises it above private goals and thereby gives it a religious character."[37] The show provides a productively controversial window onto various concepts of the sacred in modern life – including the collective act of putting on a play – partly because these concepts are so often formulated with reference to Shakespeare, especially in the works of the eminent Canadian critic Northrop Frye (1912–1991) and the celebrated British director Peter Brook (1925–2022), both of whom influence the series in important ways. Routinely underestimated, both Frye and Brook can help us diagnose and thereby redress the cultural and scholarly impasses arguably characterizing Shakespeare studies and the humanities more broadly, hence their centrality to this book's overall argument, particularly its reassessment of the culture wars of the '80s and '90s (see chapters 9 and 10).

Taking the show as an occasion for reconsidering Frye's and Brook's influential but hotly debated accounts of Shakespeare, this book traces the show's depiction of how the stories we make make us in return. By exploring this reflexive process, the show responds to ongoing controversies about the nature of Shakespeare's plays and storytelling more broadly. In however modest a way, *Slings & Arrows* provides an occasion to reassess the question of Shakespearean mimesis, the question of how the plays' depiction of human experience helps render some of the defining features of social life more intelligible. In stressing the ongoing vitality of Shakespearean realism, the series, as I noted, explicitly follows Brook's *The Empty Space*, a work that combines heuristic suggestiveness with theoretical subtlety and sociological prescience, all the while being wholly unpretentious. Among other things, the show's reliance on *The Empty Space* provides an occasion to rethink the extent to which Brook's view of theatre exposes the limits of ideological critique and postmodern anti-realism at the very moment they began taking centre stage on the cultural scene. In this respect, the time is ripe for a reconsideration of Brook's major, and often misrepresented, theoretical work, not least because of his passing in 2022. For like Brook, the show does not simply explore the relationship between life and art. More subtly, it examines the relationship between living and dead illusions, between forms of artifice that convincingly intersect with life and those that do not. Moreover, in pursuing this agenda the show presents a compelling exploration of Coleridgean aesthetics, most notably his concept of poetic faith, which, in many respects, finds one of its most extraordinary rearticulations in Brook's critical writings.

Part and parcel of the show's response to Brook's *The Empty Space* is Northrop Frye's influence on the series and on the Stratford Festival more generally, which is especially evident in the show's metanarrative features. Throughout his career, Frye returned repeatedly to Shakespeare's *The Tempest* as paradigmatic of the literary imagination, a critical leitmotif that culminates in slightly modified form in his final major work *Words with Power* (1990). To understand the show's poignancy as a commentary on the relations between life and art is to understand it as a thoughtful response to the work of Brook and Frye. Moreover, in examining how these two figures illuminate the series, it will also become clear that they both benefit from comparison with the other, thereby disclosing how much they may still contribute to our understanding of the role that the humanities can and should play in contemporary culture. Important figures of the post-romantic Left, Frye and Brook were both early critics of some of the influential forms of anti-humanism emerging in the 1960s and '70s. Part of what accounts for the power of their response to these developments is that both men are in many ways quite close to and in certain limited respects sympathetic with certain aspects of post-structural or post-modern theory. In particular, both Brook and Frye are keenly sensitive to the way our shared sense of social reality is to some extent a by-product of the modes of representation by which it is accessed and, in certain limited respects, generated. As such, they provide some of the resources necessary for assessing the show's claim that post-romantic views of Shakespeare still retain some critical purchase in resisting the corrosively dehumanizing forces of advanced capitalism along with the more vitiated versions of postmodern anti-realism often coincident with it.

THE MIRROR AND THE LAMP

From at least the Romantic period on, Shakespeare's plays have been understood as both reflective and expressive at once, as both mirror and lamp. As a result, his plays have generally been viewed as providing particularly fertile ground for exploring questions about the interrelationships between life and art, and between reality and imagination. Viewed in such terms, Shakespeare's plays are thought not only to disclose the world as we know it, but also, especially in the late romances, to envision the world as we might collectively wish it to be. Working from such post-romantic assumptions, *Slings & Arrows* presents a coherent but routinely contested account of Shakespearean mimesis, including its more visionary dimensions, producing a productively controversial view of various elements of Shakespeare's plays, including questions of dramatic character, human personality, audience response, and authorship/directorship. Perhaps most significantly, the show is self-consciously concerned with the dynamics of commensurability between the local and the general, the culturally specific and the commonly human. This concern is an inevitable feature of television as a mass-market medium, an expression of the need to make local stories communicable to a general international audience. In the jargon of media studies, this process is called *glocalization*. However, the show pursues these questions in the context of an author who has proven remarkably

Introduction 17

resilient in showing how the local can fuse with the general, the specific with the transcultural, by sheer dint of good storytelling. In this latter respect, *Slings & Arrows* provides an occasion to revisit Frye's notion of the popular, with which it is tacitly sympathetic. In his book on Shakespeare's comedies and romances, *A Natural Perspective* (1965), Frye posits a view of the popular not in the sense of something trendy or commercially glocalized, but in the more robust sense that some narrative forms give poignant access to rich imaginative structures while requiring a minimum of cultural fluency. Bearing such a view of the popular in mind, it becomes clear that part of what is at issue in the series is what allows Shakespeare's works to be made new, be it on the stage, the page, or the screen, and why in being made new his works can continue to serve as equipment for living across a relatively wide swath of the population.

Like much of Susan Coyne's writing, *Slings & Arrows* is concerned with how creative processes develop a certain autonomy to which artists and audiences then become answerable, or what we might call the dialectics of poesis. Central to the show's concern with the way the stories we make make us in return is a sustained meditation on Coleridge's idea of poetic faith, the willing suspension of disbelief to participate in a shared illusion undertaken by both audience and actors during a performance. Over the course of its three seasons, the show repeatedly suggests that what turns a group of actors into a company, and what unifies a diverse audience with a diverse group of performers, is the activation, or living realization, of the exquisitely fragile yet strangely wondrous principle of poetic faith. In this respect, the series considers the extent to which poetic faith is an aesthetic phenomenon with important, if oftentimes fleeting, real-world consequences. In making its case, the show explores what occurs when poetic faith both fails and succeeds. At some moments, then, it depicts what happens when a dramatic illusion becomes too dangerously immersive and hence no longer consciously fictional, as it sometimes does for the show's tortured hero Geoffrey Tennant. While at others, it shows what happens when a performance becomes too contrived and hence insufficiently believable, as it does for more compromised figures such as Oliver Welles (Stephen Ouimette) and Darren Nichols (Don McKellar). In turn, *Slings & Arrows* also investigates what happens when poetic faith is fully realized, thereby making the theatre a space where a diverse group of actors and spectators become, as it were, one body, transfiguring all in the process.

The quasi-sacramental dimensions involved in the realization of poetic faith are even signalled in the show's recurring use of harp arpeggios, an aural sign that functions much like the ringing of a bell does in the Catholic mass to denote the shift to a sacramental level of reality. Only in this case the "miraculous harp" signals an aesthetic level of experience and not a literally sacramental one, though where exactly the line is to be drawn here is one of Coyne's recurring preoccupations as a writer. Indeed, the use of this non-diegetic sign is an example of the show's modest, yet earnest, engagement with the romantic experience of identification between human art and a larger power of creativity, a theme central to Coyne's 2001 memoir *Kingfisher Days*. As Frye explains, this numinous encounter with some larger source of creativity is sometimes symbolized in romantic literature by a rushing wind, as in Shelley's "Ode to the West Wind"; sometimes by a boat driven by a breeze or current, or "by more efficient magical forces," as in *The Ancient Mariner*; or by the "image of the Aeolian harp, or lyre" as in Shelley's "Hymn to Intellectual Beauty" and Coleridge's "The Eolian Harp" (NFWE, 84). But in each case, this encounter involves "a heightened state of consciousness in which we feel that we are greater than we know, or an intense feeling of communion, as in the sacramental corn-and-wine images of the great Keats odes" (NFWE, 84). In exploring the theatre as a vehicle for such experiences of communion and heightened consciousness, *Slings & Arrows* reflects on the differences between dramatic illusions that disclose reality and delusive illusions that obscure it, asking if the aesthetic revelations of art can still be communicated in an age of advertising simulacra and multinational capitalism. Part of the show's value, then, lies in its exploration of the aesthetic and existential consequences of the idea of poetic faith implicit in fictional narratives at the end of the millennium, especially, but not exclusively, dramatic and televisual ones. In short, it asks if poetic faith in Shakespeare is still truly possible in an age of advanced capitalism while meditating on what, exactly, poetic faith is as a phenomenon.

In posing such questions, the show asks how far the levelling forces of advanced capitalism now extend, and whether meaningful distinctions can still be drawn between entertainment and art, aesthetic truth and commercial advertising. In addressing such issues in the context of a semi-satirical television show, the program self-consciously asks whether the series can possibly address questions about mimesis without becoming a parodic instance of its own satirical energies and a victim of its elaborate formal contrivances. By doing so, the show offers an intelligent exploration of questions about art and life that philosophical sociologists are now addressing, as Charles Taylor does in *A Secular Age* (2007). Like Taylor, *Slings & Arrows* asks if the imaginative and intellectual resources of Romanticism and high modernism – those old-fashioned ideas about epiphany and artistic revelation – have any ongoing relevance for life in post-millennial North America. The relative seriousness of such an endeavour is further evinced by Margaret Atwood's *Hag-Seed: William Shakespeare's "The Tempest" Retold* (2016), which revisits many of the same themes and shares many debts with *Slings & Arrows*, including revealing references to Robin Phillips and Northrop Frye. As such, this comically unassuming Canadian show poses questions that continue to preoccupy not only literary and cultural critics, but anyone who cares about the role of the narrative imagination in society.

In terms of structure, *Shakespeare and the World of "Slings & Arrows"* has the following organization. The first three chapters place the series' dialectic of conviction and malaise in the context of Peter Brook's *The Empty Space* and the broader critical and cultural contexts animating it, including Coleridge's theory of poetic faith. This is followed by a chapter on Coyne's 2001 memoir *Kingfisher Days*, a work in which Coyne self-consciously participates in the Canadian visionary tradition most fully exemplified by Frye and further developed in *Slings & Arrows*. The subsequent chapter then examines the metafictional aspects of the series in the context of Frye's work and its reception, including his lifelong engagement with *The Tempest*, which, as I shall argue, played a significant role at Stratford while Coyne was there. Chapter 7 then places the show in the context of broader scholarly debates about mimesis, performance, and interpretation, while chapter 8 shows how Urjo Kareda's 2000 *Toronto Life* article on Richard Monette parallels the show's mythopoeic structures vis-à-vis patterns of faith and doubt. Chapters 9 and 10 then place the show's satirical energies in the context of the culture wars of the 1980s and '90s, specifically the so-called *Bardbiz* debate about Shakespeare's legacy in the *London Review of Books* as well as some of the relevant critiques of postmodernism from the period. Chapter 11, "The Promised End," then offers a close reading of the show's overall narrative structure, focusing particularly on the crucial role the final episode plays in its overall story and accompanying modes of characterization. In summarizing the book's general argument, the conclusion refutes accusations that the series is heteronormative, insisting that the show is a queer-friendly work of popular culture. In turn, the conclusion shows how the series reflexively addresses some of the ethical and compositional challenges inherent in the kind of satire it takes on. Following this, the book ends with a brief coda focused on John Hirsch's 1982 Stratford production of *The Tempest*. With more than forty years of hindsight, it should now be clear that Hirsch's production constitutes a significant event in Canadian cultural history. Both highly personal and poignantly contemporary, the production shows Hirsch grappling with two competing critical visions on the power of theatre, one exemplified by the moral and aesthetic idealism of Frye and one exemplified by the moral and aesthetic pessimism of Jan Kott. In the process, the production presents a visceral example of where the convictions about the power of theatre in *Slings & Arrows* derive. Among other things, Hirsch's 1982 production of *The Tempest* provides important context for understanding the complex humanist vision informing his 1966 answer to the question of whether theatre as a medium would outlast the century. He responded, in a manner that takes us to the very heart of *Slings & Arrows*, "Will the century last? If the century will last, then theatre will last."[38]

I

Deadly Theatre and Holy Theatre

When *Slings & Arrows* begins we are firmly on the malaise side of its organizing dialectic as we find ourselves in a world where not just art but death is commodified. The point gets made in the second episode by a Jaques-like mortician named Reg Mortimer (Julian Richings), who is preparing the recently deceased Oliver Welles for the last of his public performances, a gaudy funeral at the Rose Theatre of the New Burbage Festival where Welles served as artistic director. As oleaginous as he is quirkily comic, Mortimer delivers his platitude about the world being a stage in a manner that drains life of any possible urgency, like so much blood from a corpse. Having paid a bribe to get the festival's funerary business, the crow-like Mortimer approaches his profession with the same oily "solemnity" with which he treats Shakespeare. As such, this "King of Death" unself-consciously embodies the familiar *vanitas* motif implicit in the "world as a stage" metaphor, neatly exemplifying the banally sordid world of advanced capitalism in which the New Burbage Festival now swims. Thus rather than providing clarifying access to lived experience, as Heywood's theatre does, Mortimer's theatre of death is presented as an indistinguishable extension of the lifeless world that he inhabits, hence the vapid organ music and the comic, yet unnervingly counterfeit sensitivity associated with him. Little more than a simulacrum, or postmodern revamping of Plato's cave, the predatory, yet still pathetic, world to which Mortimer belongs discloses just how difficult it will be for those following in Welles's footsteps to resuscitate anything approximating Coleridge's level of poetic faith, let alone any collective vision of the theatre as a vocation. The overall result is a fictional snapshot of the real-world way in which Shakespeare's plays now often circulate in "an aggregate of commodities fashioned to offer distraction from the continuing pathos of Western modernity" (BTS, xiii).

Yet signs that a miraculous restoration of Shakespeare's authority might still be possible are intimated in the first episode, "Oliver's Dream." As the title suggests, this episode locates us in a world that vaguely recalls the promise of theatre experienced by Shakespeare's Bottom in *A Midsummer Night's Dream*, where traces of enchantment persist even after the dramatic illusion has been broken. Only now the dream takes place in a community that no longer believes in the potential for such a thing, as though almost everyone has internalized a post-millennial version of Duke Theseus's rationalist skepticism about the poetic imagination. The show thus begins in a world of unbelieving irony that is, nevertheless, haunted by the trace of enchantment, what Brook calls, without a shred of sentimentality, those "old impulses [which] stir in the marrow" (ES, 45). The show's opening scene both awakens and deflates such impulses, initiating the broader dialectic between faith and doubt that is developed in each season.

This dialectic begins in Théâtre Sans Argent, the edgy but impecunious double of the financially posh yet artistically stale New Burbage Festival, where a rehearsal of *The Tempest* is taking place. Set in a repurposed industrial building that looks somewhat like a mini version of the Tate Modern, the play is being directed by the show's morally ambivalent (anti-)hero Geoffrey Tennant, who is walking his youthful cast through the storm scene in act 1. With one hand on a toilet plunger, denoting material exigencies, and the other raised to the heavens, symbolizing the promise of a life-transforming theatre, the Prospero-like Tennant gives an inspiring homily on the power of the theatrical imagination. As we transition from the real-world rehearsal into the imaginative world of *The Tempest*, the plunger becomes a staff – making the analogies with Prospero unmistakable. The overall effect is that Tennant's physical posture comes to look like a mildly ironized version of Brook's description of Shakespeare as the poet who "has a foot in the mud, an eye on the stars, and a dagger in his hand."[1] In turn, the opening scene gives us the first instance of its broader concern with the art-life dialectic, the idea that, as Coyne says with respect to the series, "it's the moment of transformation from life into art that fascinates me. It's that tension that we are looking at for sure."[2]

Revealingly, Tennant begins his homily by subtly evoking the title of Brook's influential book *The Empty Space* (1968). According to Tennant, "A theatre is an empty space and as per the four-hundred-year-old stage direction we begin with a tempestuous noise of thunder and lightning" (*S&A*, 1.1). Over the course of the series, the show depicts its dialectic of conviction and malaise by oscillating between the enlivening and collectively transformative force of what Brook calls holy theatre and the soporific and superfluous effects of what he defines as deadly theatre. In both cases, Brook is speaking of a complex and hard-to-define phenomenon that transpires between audience and stage rather than anything reductively prescriptive. Speaking of the show in a 2018 interview, Coyne offers a cautious summary of Brook's conception of holy theatre, stressing the danger of sentimentality coincident with it. She explains how

> I'd often seen actors made fun of, and it's easy. It's easy to satirize actors. I think we do it to a degree in the show. It's also easy to sentimentalize. But between those two extremes I've never seen anybody try to really show what it's like, and that in some ways it certainly matters to the people who do it and it might even mean something to those of us who watch. It might have some value, it might have some weight to it, it might not be a silly thing to do with your life. And that these people might have some passion that has some dignity to it ... Even as I say that I'm always cautious not to give it more weight than it's worth, but I think that when theatre works well, everybody recognizes that there's something very powerful about it, transforming and ineffable and not silly at all. It's rare, but when you see it, there's nothing like it. You feel a little bit wrung out afterwards and your heart's beating faster and you feel chemically altered in some way.[3]

Coyne's stress on the transforming and ineffable qualities of theatre parallels the opening sequence of Brook's chapter on holy theatre. In it, Brook explains how he calls it

> the Holy Theatre for short, but it could be called The Theatre of the Invisible – Made – Visible: the notion that the stage is a place where the invisible can appear has a deep hold on our thoughts ... This is the notion, the true dream behind the debased ideals of the Deadly Theatre. This is what is meant and remembered by those who with feeling and seriousness use big hazy words like nobility, beauty, poetry ... The theatre is the last forum where idealism is still an

open question: many audiences all over the world will answer positively from their own experience that they have seen the face of the invisible through an experience on the stage that transcended their experience in life. (ES, 42)

So while deadly theatre wears comfortably on an audience like an old boot, as supercilious critic Basil Cruikshank (Sean Cullen) says of Welles's production of *A Midsummer Night's Dream*, holy theatre opens "a reality deeper than the fullest form of everyday life" (ES, 44). In waking rather than soothing an audience, holy theatre generates the possibility of a theatre whose purpose is holy in the sense that it "has a clearly defined place in the community," and that it responds to needs "the churches can no longer fill" (ES, 60). High aims indeed.

Appropriately enough, Tennant sets the show's dialectic of holy and deadly theatre into motion with a quasi-messianic reference to time, subtly preparing us to renew our faith in a re-enlivened theatre, while still giving us plenty of room for dubiety: "Andy has been working on the lights now," he declares, "for *three days and three nights*, and he assures me that there will not be another fire. Andy, the storm please" (1.1). This reference to the amount of time between Christ's death and resurrection is typical of the way the show both exploits and deflates archetypal patterns, infusing the narrative with poignancy and satire simultaneously. A typically Shakespearean strategy, this trick of deploying formulaic structures in surprising and effectively ironized ways contributes to the show's taut balancing of comedy and drama. The result is not dissimilar to Coleridge's sense of how *The Tempest* works through a series of "happy combinations of the highest and the lowest … the gayest and the saddest; [it is] not droll in one scene and melancholy in the other, but both the one and the other in the same scene: laughter is made to swell the tear of sorrow, and to throw, as it were, a poetic light upon it."[4]

ALL THE STAGE IS A SHIP

Providing us with a snapshot of the series as a whole, the show's opening scene compresses the overall story of New Burbage as the sinking ship returning from Tunis now becomes a metaphor for the collective tribulations New Burbage will undergo in the series. In deploying this analogy, the scene exploits the Jacobean commonplace of figuring playhouses as ships.[5] Important to *The Tempest*, this metaphor is explicitly evoked in Prospero's epilogue when he asks for pardon by describing the audience's approval as the gentle breath that must fill his sails so he may leave this "bare island." The analogy derives from a number of suggestive parallels. Like an early modern ship, a Jacobean playhouse is a wooden structure that, while in use, is densely populated with people who are generally working frantically and with intense concentration on a collective project. Moreover, confusions of authority and breakdowns in the required cooperation can result in chaos or even disaster. Exploiting these similarities, the opening scene of *The Tempest* parallels the confusion and authority on the deck of a sinking ship with the stress and strain of acting onstage at the Blackfriars Theatre, the private theatre known for its elite and uncooperatively disruptive audiences where Shakespeare staged his late romances.[6] When similar breakdowns begin to happen in New Burbage in season 3, Tennant and the festival's senior actress Ellen Fanshaw, his long-term love interest (played by Gross's real-world wife Martha Burns), find themselves comically belabouring the analogy until she finally drops it, saying, "Oh forget the metaphor" (3.4). The result is an example of how Shakespearean idioms generate both poignancy and irony in the story of New Burbage.

Reworking the Jacobean commonplace of the ship as theatre, the opening scene of *Slings & Arrows* has Prospero stand to Tennant as the usurping Antonio stands to the avatars of deadly theatre with whom Tennant will soon do spiritual and artistic battle, most notably New Burbage's executive director Richard Smith-Jones (Mark McKinney) and its resident faux avant-gardist Darren Nichols. Alluding to the opening stage direction of Shakespeare's First Folio (1623), Tennant calls up the tempest. Crucially, this invocation fosters an imaginative link between past and present. Stressing both the historicity of the play and its immediate incarnation in the living moment, he intones:

> A theatre is an empty space and as per the four-hundred-year-old stage direction we begin with a tempestuous noise of thunder and lightning … It is an unnatural storm … Sebastian, Alonso, and Antonio run below deck, "Let us all sink with our king," Antonio cries … the ship is torn apart by Prospero's magic … The mechanism of his revenge is set in motion. (1.1)

Momentarily consumed by darkness, Tennant is then lit with quick, violent flashes of light, only to emerge in a foggy mist interspersed with sharp thunderclaps. The result is a scene of raw intensity that effectively anticipates the directorial trials Tennant will undergo as he struggles to know when to push his actors as brutally as he pushes himself and when to back off and give them space. In Brook's terms, Tennant has to learn how "the director is there to attack and yield, provoke and withdraw until the indefinable stuff begins to flow" (ES, 109). In pursuing this challenge, it is not always clear whether Tennant, like Prospero, will finally emerge as a villain or a saviour, bringing vengeful destruction to New Burbage or life-giving renewal. For Tennant is a monomaniacal egotist with a gift for self-sabotaging conflict, while also being an exquisitely vulnerable man totally committed to his craft who possesses a gift for theatrical and erotic intimacy. Part John Hirsch, part Robin Phillips, yet fully fictional.

Tennant's wounded side emerges as we learn he is still suffering from a traumatic betrayal that he refers to as the "original sin" haunting his relationship to the New Burbage Festival (1.6). During their legendary run of *Hamlet* seven years earlier, the gay Welles slept with Tennant's passionately beloved girlfriend Ellen Fanshaw out of envy and an egotistical need for power, just as Antonio usurped his brother Prospero out of the dukedom of Milan. Tennant's use of the term "original sin" to describe this betrayal neatly captures how the show's story originates with the dynamics of mimetic rivalry, the strange way in which the people we admire become our competitors. According to Rene Girard's *A Theatre of Envy* (1991), it was Shakespeare who most clearly divined how the things people desire tend to become what their models/rivals desire. As Sonnet 42 has it, "Thou dost love her, because thou knowest I love her, / And for my sake even so doth she abuse me."[7] So here again the show is subtly following the plot patterns typical of Shakespeare. To be sure, though, such a triangulated economy explains how Welles's attraction to and envy of Tennant expressed itself as desire for Fanshaw. So rather than participating in the collective goal of an excellent *Hamlet* production, Welles inadvertently sabotaged the play's run by privileging his socially disruptive passions over the needs of the troupe as a whole. The result was the show's "original sin," a phrase that confirms the danger of undermining the quasi-sacred character of collectively pursued goals.

If the tension between Welles and Tennant hovers in the realm of the potentially tragic zone of Hamlet and his two fathers in season 1, and if it takes on some of the contours of Macbeth and Banquo in season 2, it moves into the more reconciling mode of *The Tempest* in season 3, only to finally reach a true apotheosis in the show's final episode, "The Promised End," where both men undergo a redemption of sorts in the sublimely tragic context of Lear, Cordelia, and Edgar. In this respect, the show is a relatively early example of how trauma narratives increasingly found their way into popular culture at the turn of the millennium, as Tennant's story involves overcoming a disabling mental breakdown. Consistent with his traumatic backstory, Tennant demonstrates far less mastery over events than Prospero, never gaining any secure degree of control over the festival's productions or its many interpersonal conflicts. This lack of control becomes clear at the end of the opening scene of "Oliver's Dream" when the energy of the storm crescendoes only to have the theatrical spell broken by the failing lights. The resulting effect is a movement from inspiration to deflation, apotheosis to derision, that will become one of the show's basic rhythms. Cinching this devolution, the scene segues into its first rendition of the first season's lighthearted theme song, sung by the show's main choric figure Cyril (Graham Harley): "Cheer up Hamlet, chin up Hamlet, buck up you melancholy Dane" (1.1–6). Taken as a sequence, the show's opening scenes translate the tempest-music (chaos-order) opposition that runs through Shakespeare's plays into a mood that is both serious and comic, setting up the show's exploration of the relationship between anarchy and creativity, and between destruction and renewal, as variations of the storm theme that will occur in each season, only to literally return, as we would expect, in season 3's exploration of *King Lear*.[8]

Yet these broader archetypal patterns are folded into a more culturally specific set of tensions between modern technology (such as phones, lighting effects, and television) and the empty space of the theatre. In this respect, the opening rehearsal updates Coleridge's view that the tempest scene "addresses itself entirely to the imaginative faculty," so "although the illusion may be assisted by the effect on the senses of the complicated scenery of modern times … this sort of assistance is dangerous," a point confirmed by the failing light system and then explored in the series as a whole.[9] Tempering theatrical idealism with the dramatic irony of failing technology, the opening scene sets the dialectic of conviction and malaise fully into motion, putting a wry smile on our faces in the process.

GEOFFREY RETURNS

Allusions to the organizing dialectic of Brook's *The Empty Space* occur again in the following episode, "Geoffrey Returns." But this time the dialectic of holy and deadly theatre finds expression during Tennant's eulogy of Welles in the Rose Theatre, after he returns to the site of his mental breakdown nine years earlier. During his celebrated performance as Hamlet, Tennant was overcome with terror after diving into Ophelia's grave. As a result of his breakdown, he stopped acting onstage and took up directing instead. Tennant's backstory thus echoes the experience of at least three actors: Daniel Day-Lewis, who had a nervous breakdown during a 1989 National Theatre run of *Hamlet*; Paul Gross, who describes having had hallucinations and near-crippling stress while performing the role at Stratford in 2000; and Richard Monette, who had to give up acting for directing after developing severe stage fright.[10] Terrified of returning to the site of his breakdown, the fragile Tennant finds the courage to both celebrate and vilify Welles during his eulogy. In doing the latter, he makes good on board chair May Silverstone's (Marcia Bennett) invitation to speak the truth rather than platitudes, thus setting into motion season 1's thematic (and self-consciously anti-postmodern) concern with integrity and authenticity. But in celebrating Welles, who gets hit by a truck advertising "Canada's Best Hams" at the end of episode 1, Tennant articulates a vision of theatre that more or less paraphrases the idealism of *The Empty Space*. According to Tennant, Welles taught his actors that

> The theatre is an empty box and it is our job to fill it with fury and ecstasy and with revolution. For a time … for a time there was a kind of electricity in this place that I've never experienced anywhere else. Because Oliver made us believe that what we did had meaning. He made us believe that love could be rekindled, that regimes could be toppled by the simple act of telling a story, with truth. A ridiculous ambition. But it was a beautiful idea. … Now it's all gone to shit now. I mean we all know that what really matters is that the cash register keeps ringing … that tourists keep streaming through the gift shop. (1.2)

In making his case, Tennant echoes the general sentiment that Stratford in the late '90s was no longer of artistic consequence, the view, as festival alum Urjo Kareda puts it, that it was "a tourist attraction, [and] no longer a temple" (SO, 76). Moreover, his use of the phrase "beautiful idea" subtly links this elegiac homily on holy theatre to Tennant's subsequent story-defining allusion to Coleridge's poetic faith in episode 5 when he defends his sense of purpose against Welles's accusation that he too has lost it.

Following Brook, Tennant suggests that New Burbage has fallen from holy theatre into deadly theatre, from a theatre that meaningfully transforms its audiences to one that briefly distracts or simply bores them. For Brook, holy theatre is a ritual-like event in which the "invisible currents that run our lives ... interpenetrate and animate the ordinary" (ES, 45, 57). Crucially, Brook's main model for holy theatre is Shakespeare because his "aim continually is holy, metaphysical, yet he never makes the mistake of staying too long on the highest plane" (ES, 62). Brook's Shakespeare thus sustains a balance between "apotheosis" and "derision," never "staying too long on the highest plane" (ES, 62) but also never presuming its absolute impossibility.[11] The result is an answer to Brook's adage, quite apropos for *Slings & Arrows*, that "to be too serious is not very serious."[12] Often applied to Shakespeare, this attitude is a guiding principle of Brook's dramaturgical vision in *The Empty Space*. After all, such delicate movement between "apotheosis" and "derision" is also, *mutatis mutandis*, the basic unit and the essential rhythm of *Slings & Arrows*. In all three seasons, the show cleverly oscillates between satire and drama, the comic and the affecting. In doing so, however, *Slings & Arrows* develops a more capacious frame for its exploration of the theatrical vocation than Kenneth Branagh's low-budget cult favorite, the 1995 film *The Bleak Mid-Winter*, which deploys a very similar structure. In Branagh's case, though, the film's story about a Christmastide production of *Hamlet* in a church errs so far on the side of satire that its poignancy becomes less consequential, making it more *Young Frankenstein* than *Pericles*.

In *Slings & Arrows*, on the other hand, the basic rhythm of apotheosis and derision is contained within a mythopoetic narrative that is, in essence, an ironized modern-day morality play about the crisis of faith in theatre as a living vocation. Here again, Brook helps explain how the show meets its challenges. Recognizing the near impossibility of realizing a view of holy theatre in the modern world, with its conviction in social revolution, anti-authoritarianism, and transcendence, Brook writes: "In fact, an expression of today's militant themes through traditional Catholic morality-play structures may well be the only possibility in certain regions of finding a lively contact with popular audiences" (*ES*, 83). Though Brook is not speaking here of the Anglo-American world, this is basically the wager laid in *Slings & Arrows*. Consequently, the show's subtle reworking of formulaic narrative patterns typical of film and television (as well as Shakespearean romance) fortuitously coincide with a desire to reassert the authority of classical theatre in the contemporary world.

Calling attention to such archetypal variation, the title of the second episode, "Geoffrey Returns," is a somewhat ironized allusion to the messianic hero's return that is now so familiar from popular media. On one hand, the title alludes to what has been described with reference to Stratford as "the absurdity of the saviour syndrome," the belief that a brilliant director can right the ship by the force of his solitary genius (*SFSP*, 1981). But on the other hand, the title subtly suggests that Tennant might be the answer to the funk New Burbage has fallen into, as displayed during the rehearsal scene for *Dream* in which Welles's key directorial dilemma is whether the sheep should be bleating. Exhausted with the pseudo-problem, the senior cast member Frank (Michael Polley) asks his wry partner Cyril: "How long can a man stare at a sheep?" To which Cyril responds knowingly, "If he's a shepherd, there's no telling" (1.1). The joke is a rich one. After all, it alludes to Welles's role as a struggling director, a shepherd who is losing his flock, while also intimating Brook's conception of holy theatre that Tennant will expound in the eulogy scene in the following episode.

As Welles's *A Midsummer Night's Dream* reminds us, deadly theatre can take many forms according to Brook, be it popular musical, high-concept avant-garde experimentalism, or tired remakes of the classics. Tellingly, *Slings & Arrows* presents deadly theatre in all three of these modes: in Welles's lame production of *Dream* (season 1), in Nichols's pseudo-Brechtian *Romeo and Juliet* (season 2), and in the earnest yet trivializing musical *East Hastings* (season 3). Brook's cutting assessment of deadly theatre is broadly indicative of his focus on questions of quality, and the principle that distinctions between good and bad theatre identify more than shifting fashions or irreducibly subjective judgments of taste. Every form, Brook explains, "once born is mortal; every form must be reconceived, and its new conception will bear the marks of all the influences that surround it. In this sense, the theatre is relativity. Yet a great theatre is not a fashion house; perpetual elements do recur and certain fundamental issues underlie all dramatic activity" (*ES*, 16). Brook admits that living theatre "is always a self-destructive art, and it is always written on the wind" (*ES*, 15), and so it

Deadly Theatre and Holy Theatre

should come as no surprise that "theatre's needs have changed" (*ES*, 37). Yet, "the difference is not one of fashion … today as at all times, we need to stage true rituals … that could make theatre-going an experience that feeds our lives" (*ES*, 37, 45). In other words, the patterns of creation and destruction that occur in the theatre are not random and without meaning, but disclose certain underlying forms and continuities, what Brook elusively calls "the invisible currents that rule our lives" (*ES*, 45). Hence his attempt to explain these patterns through a fourfold typology that would be impossible, or meaningless, were changes in theatre a matter of sheer contingencies. Part of what gives *The Empty Space* its ongoing relevance to our moment is its sustained attempt to overcome the malaise-inducing effects of cultural and aesthetic relativism, which Brook clearly saw as a much greater threat to theatre and culture than those critics now identified under the umbrella term of post-structuralism. Somewhat improbably, it is precisely this same desire to rediscover genuine aesthetic quality that *Slings & Arrows* renews.

As this brief summary suggests, *The Empty Space* provides a helpful commentary on the three-season series. After all, as well as depicting deadly theatre in each of the forms Brook analyzes, the show also translates his discussion of deadly actors through Henry Breedlove's overdone Macbeth, deadly critics through Basil Cruikshank's pompous self-regard, and deadly writers through Lionel Train's pusillanimous bad faith, not to mention deadly audiences like those more interested in the hockey score than Titania's blocking. Taken together, such features suggest that Brook's *The Empty Space* helped the show's writers tell a story that could rise above the limits of a televisual *roman à clef* about Stratford, Ontario to achieve much wider communicability about life in the theatre, especially the question of why such a life might genuinely matter to those living it.

2

Poetic Faith

As we saw, Susan Coyne noted in a 2006 interview that while it's conventional for fiction writers to depict actors and directors as slightly ridiculous, it is less common to stress why they are so deeply committed to their craft. So while the characters of *Slings & Arrows* can appear absurd at times, it's crucial, she insists, that what they love not be. This contrasts sharply with a show such as the Netflix series *The Chair* (2021), which depicts the dysfunctional side of contemporary English departments without giving any real sense of what motivates literary scholars in the first place. In stressing the question of conviction, Coyne attempts a response to Peter Brook's questions in *The Empty Space*: "Why theatre at all? What for? Is it an anachronism, a superannuated oddity, surviving like an old monument or a quaint custom? ... Has the stage a real place in our lives? What function can it have? What could it serve? What could it explore? What are its special properties?" (40). As I shall explain in this chapter, if Brook's questions about conviction are central throughout the series, they arise explicitly in episode 5 of season 1, "A Mirror Up to Nature," only to be repeated in an even higher-stakes mode in season 3's "Vex Not Thy Ghost," when the ghostly Welles laments how "Theatre is pointless. I see that now. It accomplishes nothing" (3.2).

Welles's vexation proves poignant partly because it occurs against the backdrop of a postmodern culture that is explicitly hostile to the principles of poetic faith and dramatic illusion on which the show's commitments are based. One vehicle of this broader cultural antagonism towards the conditions necessary to poetic faith is the advertising executive Sanjay (Colm Feore). Appearing in season 2, Sanjay lives in a world in which "truth is the new lie," a postmodern variation on *Macbeth*'s "fair is foul, foul is fair" (1.1.12). In one respect, then, San-

Poetic Faith   33

jay is a reincarnation of the meretricious sophists in Plato's *Phaedrus*, someone for whom opinion and persuasion matter more than truth or moral vision. In another respect, however, he encapsulates the world view lamented in Jean Baudrillard's elegy for aesthetic illusions in a postmodern age, an elegy that brings into relief the challenges those in classical theatre now face. According to Baudrillard,

> The impossibility of rediscovering an absolute level of the real is of the same order as the impossibility of staging illusion. Illusion is no longer possible, because the real is no longer possible ... There is no longer a stage, not even the minimal illusion that makes events capable of adopting the force of reality – no more stage either of mental or political solidarity. (*ss*, 19, 164)

What do tragic events come to matter, Baudrillard asks, when everything "comes to be annihilated on the television screen"? In such a time, he concludes, "We are in the era of events without consequences (and of theories without consequences)" (*ss*, 164). However overstated this cultural diagnosis may be, it helps bring into focus the challenges attendant upon classical theatre as depicted in *Slings & Arrows*. After all, part of what makes the opening five episodes of the series narratively compelling is the way they place romantic, modernist, and postmodernist values and perspectives in tension with one another. In doing so, the show does not simply explore the relationship between life and art; more subtly, it examines the distinction between living and dead illusions, between figures that interpenetrate with and illuminate social reality and those which do not. Following Brook, the show presents a convincing, if comically stylized, depiction of the theatrical possibilities and challenges that continue to characterize the contemporary Shakespeare world.

The question of artistic conviction first arises in the context of poetic faith in season 1 when Welles accuses Tennant of undue malaise as he struggles with the stage design for his *Hamlet* production, complaining to the younger man: "With that attitude, Geoffrey, why do the play at all?" (1.5). Surprised by the accusation, Tennant confirms his sense of purpose by passionately citing Coleridge's dictum: "Because ... drama is the willing suspension of disbelief for the moment, which constitutes poetic faith. Poetic faith, it's a beautiful idea" (1.5). As he cites Coleridge, Welles smiles warmly at him, clearly enjoying the affirmation of shared purpose.

34   Shakespeare and the World of *Slings & Arrows*

It is highly significant to the series that Coleridge developed his theories of poetic faith and dramatic illusion largely in the context of *A Midsummer Night's Dream* and *The Tempest*.[1] For on one hand, the show intersects with the three main tragedies performed each season reflecting the movement from youth (*Hamlet*), to middle age (*Macbeth*), to old age (*King Lear*). But on the other hand, its meta-theatrical and metanarrative dimensions interpenetrate with *Dream* and *The Tempest*. Consequently, the show's own storyline is really more a form of semi-allegorized comic romance than of tragicomedy. What is also crucial here is the underappreciated fact that Brook is essentially a Coleridgean on the question of theatrical illusion. He even goes so far as to suggest that Coleridge's conception of dramatic illusion is not incompatible with Brecht, so long as epic theatre is understood as a specific reaction against nineteenth-century naturalism rather than a universally applicable program. As coiner of the term *alienation effect*, Brook explains,

> Brecht must be considered historically. He began working at a time when most German stages were dominated either by naturalism or by great total-theatre onslaughts of an operatic nature designed to sweep up the spectator by his emotions so that he forgot himself completely. Whatever life there was on-stage was offset by the passivity it demanded of the audience. (ES, 72)

Contrary to Roland Barthes, who stresses the liberating promise of epic theatre's anti-mimetic strategies, Brook stresses the importance of reality implicit in Brecht's practices of demystification, his exposing of culturally specific illusions. In his chapter on rough theatre, Brook clearly worries about the long-term consequences of anti-realism, the way it could corrode our capacity to distinguish illusion and reality in exactly the manner Baudrillard argues has now happened. As Brook explains,

> In all communication, illusions materialize and disappear. The Brecht theatre is a rich compound of images appealing for our belief. When Brecht spoke contemptuously of illusion, this was not what he was attacking. He meant the single sustained Picture [of nineteenth-century naturalism], the statement that continued after its purpose had been served ... But when Brecht stated there was something in the theatre called illusion, the implication was that

there was something else that was not illusion. So illusion became opposed to reality. It would be better if we clearly opposed dead illusion to living illusion, glum statement to lively statement, fossilized shape to moving shadow, the frozen picture to the moving one. (ES, 73)

Consciously or not, Brook has here rediscovered Coleridge's key distinction between imitation and copy. According to Coleridge, the likeness of an effective theatrical imitation generates a process of interpenetration with social reality through its play of similitude and difference. But when theatrical illusion aspires towards identity or copy, it devolves into deceptive forgery, failing to sustain the distance from social life requisite to aesthetic illumination. Hence the difference between pornography and art. Rather than advocating an "ironic credulity" within aesthetic experience, Coleridge's poetic faith stresses the transformative potential of art, thus embracing its dangers as well as its promises.[2] From this perspective, Brecht's alienating techniques are historically specific strategies for establishing the tension of self-conscious illusion that Coleridge argued is intrinsic to the theatre as such. Thus when Tennant accuses Nichols of producing "postmodern, pseudo-Brechtian, leather-clad, school-boy thuggery," he is not being anti-intellectual or unpolitical. On the contrary, he is making the same point Brook does about misreadings of epic theatre. According to Brook, "The liveliest of theatres turns deadly when its coarse vigour goes: and Brecht is destroyed by deadly slaves" (ES, 76). A year later, a young John Hirsch made the same basic point when he railed against the oddly "Germanic" tendency among American directors to view Brecht in an overly theoretical manner, thereby losing the relation to life: "What does that have to do with the price of milk," he wryly yet passionately intoned of the North American appropriation of Brecht.[3] To be sure, the general point here still resonates. For just as Roland Barthes (who is the butt of parody in season 2) championed anti-mimetic modes of metafiction that seal themselves off from the illusions of referentiality, so Nichols creates a hermetically enclosed system of self-reference, one that is liberating in theory but often inconsequentially self-indulgent in practice. Hence the depiction of his hilariously abstracted approach to *Romeo and Juliet* as a morose form of middle-aged self-defence against its exuberantly adolescent passion. In keeping with the allegorical dimension of his character, Nichols symbolizes the ironic resistance to dramatic illusion implicit in the medium itself, but which, when taken to such anti-realist extremes, kills it. In this respect, Nichols embodies a threat to holy theatre that Brook identified as early as 1968, showing a degree of theatrical understanding and sociological prescience far in advance of the more influential Barthes.

SHADOWS OF IMAGINATION

In its original context from *Biographia Literaria*, Coleridge's dictum about poetic faith is an explanation of his contribution to the *Lyrical Ballads*, the fact that he agreed with his co-author Wordsworth

> that my endeavours should be directed to persons and characters supernatural, or at least romantic; yet so as to transfer from our inward nature a human interest and a semblance of truth sufficient to procure for these shadows of imagination that willing suspension of disbelief for the moment, which constitutes poetic faith.[4]

As the phrase "shadows of imagination" intimates, Coleridge's sense of the mode of illusion proper to poetic fiction derives in part from *A Midsummer Night's Dream*. The phrase recalls Theseus's response to the rude mechanicals, when he says, "The best in this kind are but shadows; and the worst are no worse, if imagination amend them" (5.1.211).[5] No less importantly, however, the phrase also echoes the play's epilogue, when Puck releases the audience from the compact between viewer and producer by which dramatic illusion is generated in the first place:

> If we shadows have offended,
> Think but this, and all is mended:
> That you have but slumbered here
> While these visions did appear.
> And this weak and idle theme,
> No more yielding but a dream. (5.409–14)

In episode 1 of *Slings & Arrows* this speech is badly delivered by the haplessly untalented Claire (Sabrina Gredevich), who is participating in a production that never successfully establishes the pact between audience and stage that Puck dissolves. Her epilogue thus reinforces our general sense that the New Burbage production of *A Midsummer*

Night's Dream works neither as illusion nor as a revelation but simply as deadly theatre. This point is further made by the sleeping audience members who are more in a state of half-slumber than shared vision, perhaps recalling Brook's reminder that in deadly theatre there is always "a deadly spectator, who for special reasons enjoys a lack of intensity" (ES, 10).

Crucial for Coleridge, poetic illusion is not a hindrance to truth but the very means by which it's communicated. Without a self-conscious sense of illusion from both audience and stage, the space requisite for revelation is foreclosed, either through over-immersion or excessive contrivance. Coleridge makes this point by distinguishing between *imitation* and *copy* in the manner outlined above. In drawing this key distinction, Coleridge sought a middle way between neo-classical

> French critics … who ground their principles on the presumption of an absolute *de*lusion, and of Dr Johnson, who would persuade us that our judgments are as broad awake during the most masterly representation of the deepest scenes of *Othello*, as a philosopher would be during the exhibition of a magic lanthorn.[6]

For Coleridge, both positions are too extreme because

> drama is an *imitation* of reality not a *Copy* – and that Imitation is contra-distinguished from Copy by this, that a certain quantum of Difference is essential to the former, and an indispensable condition and cause of the pleasure, we derive from it; while in a Copy it is a defect, contravening its name and purpose.[7]

In other words, dramatic illusion arises as the product of a shared agreement between stage and audience to suspend disbelief in what is fully acknowledged to be an illusion. Taken together, the willing illusion of the drama is born, giving life to what is otherwise sterile and dead. But part of what gives the illusion life is the implicit potential for a dialectical relationship with the world outside the play, a sense that the illusion somehow touches the reality of lived experience. Hence Coleridge's assumption that even romantic artifice must bear "a semblance of truth" to inspire the suspension of disbelief requisite to aesthetic experience as such.

From this perspective, the collapsing of dramatic illusion results not only in the loss of the dramatic or aesthetic effect, but in a disappearance of reality itself. Without some level of interpenetration between artistic illusion and lifelike reality, the aesthetic form devolves into self-indulgent fantasy or outright forgery. The danger of staging a forgery is thematized in season 2 of *Slings & Arrows* when Tennant begins taking Macbeth-like risks to elicit a vivifying performance from his complacent lead Henry Breedlove (Geraint Wyn Davies), who remains insufficiently immersed in his role, thus deadening the action of the play. Getting the right balance of illusion and reality proves a daunting affair, as Geoffrey pushes things dangerously far. In turn, the Geoffrey-Henry plot line is doubled by the Sanjay-Richard subplot as the deranged advertising executive makes no distinction at all between life and art, reality and representation, thus demonically perverting Geoffrey's artistic convictions and strategies. Fully revelling in a forgery-like existence full of excessive risk-taking, Sanjay, whose name is the Hindi equivalent of Nike (or victory), lives in a world of pure power relations in which all forms of expression are becoming absorbed by the depthless vacuity of advertising. In such a world, as Baudrillard says, "the question of 'believing' in [advertising] is no longer even posed" (*ss*, 90). After all, Sanjay confirms, "truth is the new lie." More than an allusion to *Macbeth*, the motto is also a play on Baudrillard's fraudulent non-quote from Ecclesiastes at the opening of *Simulacra and Simulation*: "The simulacrum is never what hides the truth – it is truth that hides the fact that there is none" (*ss*, 102). This collapsing of reality and representation even finds an opposing mode of expression in the elementary school production of *Macbeth* that Tennant experiences not as a challenging illusion but as a terrifying reality when Welles reappears, Banquo-like, to further haunt him. So rather than witnessing a play, Tennant finds himself staring into the possibility that he is losing his grip on reality. After all, he may have contributed to Welles's death, perhaps even inadvertently "murdered" him, as Welles is killed after Tennant refused to speak with him on the phone. It is thus highly significant that when Welles reprises his role as Banquo at the Rose Theatre for Tennant's benefit alone later in season 2, the dramatic illusion has been reinstalled and the effect is more warmly comic than unnervingly terrifying. As these subtly interweaving plot lines indicate, the collapse of dramatic illusion can occur when either side of the compact relinquishes its part in the bargain. At which point we find ourselves devolving from a healthy sense of the relationship between fiction and reality to a delusional one, be it through Tennant's old-fashioned, metaphysically verifiable insanity, or Sanjay's postmodern

Poetic Faith

simulacra, where the very distinction between madness and sanity loses its meaning.

Part of the show's poignancy, then, lies in how it communicates the risks of delusion inherent to the theatre, thus replaying the meta-dramatic ethics of *A Midsummer Night's Dream* and *The Tempest* in a postmodern age. But in using the medium of television to tell this story, the show must openly confront how postmodern culture is arguably characterized by a growing disappearance of reality into simulacra. As Fredric Jameson ruefully asserts, in the age of advanced capitalism "the past itself has disappeared ... [And] where its buildings still remain, renovation and restoration allow them to be transferred to the present in their entirety as those other, very different postmodern things called *simulacra*."[8] Somewhat paradoxically, it is the show's commentary on postmodern simulacra that gives it its mimetic force, for the series simultaneously reminds us that illusion and inauthenticity only make sense if we retain some implicit notion of truth and authenticity. As Peter Berkowitz remarks with respect to (mis)-readings of Nietzsche as the first postmodern philosopher: "distinctions between just and unjust, noble and shameful, and good and bad are the hallmarks of our humanity and cannot be sustained if their foundation in nature, reason, or revelation is altogether abolished."[9] Part of the pathos of *Slings & Arrows* lies in its refusal to take the abolishing of nobility and authenticity as a *fait accompli*.

THE INFLATABLE SCREAM

Importantly, *Slings & Arrows* pursues its post-romantic agenda not only at the level of character and plot, but also through *mise en scène* and subtle cultural reference. This returns us to the gift shop of the Rose Theatre. When we first encounter the New Burbage Festival, it appears very much the way Brook describes Stratford, England, in 1945, where he found productions of Shakespeare to be mired in a stiff, Victorian style that was reassuringly easy for many but increasingly deadening for those seeking something more vital (*ES*, 46). Rooted in a traditionalism that was "approved largely by town, scholar, and press" (*ES*, 46), the Stratford Festival of the period, Brook claims, played "comfortably to tourists in a reassuring way."[10] Conveying exactly this sense of cozy familiarity, the first shot in the series presents an idyllic little town. After the camera pans out, however, it becomes clear that the town is actually a Norman Rockwell–like painting in the gift shop of the Rose Theatre. This shift from apparent reality to evident unreality comes as a surprise. Rather than being the product of a Coleridgean pact between audience and show, it comes as the unexpected result of camera trickery. This subtly manipulative shot thus formally inscribes the larger questions regarding truth and illusion that will be explored in the series as a whole. In this respect, the show's opening shot is a shorthand way of signalling that the series is not simply an exploration of the relationship between life and art, but a more subtle exploration of the contrast between vivifying and deadening illusions. Put simply, this is Brook's *The Empty Space* translated into televisual terms.

Right after the Rockwell-like image of escapist unreality is disclosed, a customer walks by with a blow-up doll of the figure from Edvard Munch's *The Scream* (1893), known colloquially as "The Inflatable Scream." On one hand, the image is simply another pop culture reference to the commodification of high art so typical of the turn of the millennium, such as *Home Alone* (1990) or the slasher series *Scream* (1996).[11] On the other hand, however, Munch's proto-expressionist figure gets deployed as a shorthand way of signalling the series' uphill defence of post-romantic aesthetic modes in an age of commodification. As such, the image conspicuously recalls Fredric Jameson's reading of *The Scream* in his field-defining essay, "Postmodernism, or the Cultural Logic of Late Capitalism" (1984), which was then reproduced in a slightly truncated form at the opening of his hugely influential book of the same title (1991). For Jameson, the aesthetic categories of realism, modernism, and postmodernism are cultural reactions to three different phases of capitalism: market, monopoly, and multinational.[12] From this perspective, aesthetic and cultural practices change in response to shifting socio-economic relations, with each mode evolving its own symbolic logic in reaction to the evolving material modes of production. Remarkably, Jameson adduces Munch's *The Scream* as evidence for the shift from the second to the third cultural-economic phase and thus as an index of the turn from a modernist to a postmodernist cultural logic.

As a work of high modernism, Jameson notes, *The Scream* is an expression "of the great modernist thematics of alienation, anomie, solitude, and social fragmentation and isolation, a virtually programmatic emblem of what used to be called the age of anxiety" (PM, 11). At the same time, however, the painting apparently deconstructs its own modernist thematics in a manner that would come to define the postmodern. It seems evident, he intones,

> that *The Scream* subtly but elaborately deconstructs its own aesthetic of expression, all the while remaining imprisoned within it. Its gestural content already underscores its own failure, since the realm of the sonorous, the cry, the raw vibrations of the human throat, are incompatible with its medium (something underscored within the work by the homunculus' lack of ears) ... Such loops inscribe themselves on the painted surface in the form of those great concentric circles in which sonorous vibration becomes ultimately visible ... in an infinite regress.[13]

Viewed this way, the infinite regresses of *The Scream* constitute a visual parallel to postmodern metafictions based on rigorously anti-mimetic principles, presenting an aesthetics of self-referring absence and imprisonment characteristic of the postmodern as such. For Jameson, the image anticipates post-structuralism's eventual abandonment of the "very concept of 'truth'" as "part of the metaphysical baggage [with] which" high theory seeks to break (*PM*, 12). On this account, *The Scream* astonishingly signals the end of its own cultural logic and the beginning of another cultural phase, one more hospitable to Andy Warhol than Vincent Van Gogh (or Darren Nichols than Geoffrey Tennant). Among other things, then, Jameson's ingenious materialist reading offers an explanation as to why the image has devolved from modernist sublime to postmodern kitsch.

Viewed in these contexts, it becomes apparent that the cultural processes that have drained *The Scream* of its primal energies are the same processes at work in the Darren Nichols parody. That is to say, both are examples of the thesis that postmodernism is characterized by a flattening of emotional and hermeneutic depth. From a hermeneutic standpoint, Jameson argues, the postmodern consists of a deconstruction of at least four depth models of interpretation: the dialectical opposition of essence and appearance, the Freudian model of latent and manifest, the existential model of authenticity and inauthenticity, and the semiotic distinction between signifier and signified (*PM*, 12). For Jameson, the corrosion of such depth models is the consequence of capitalist ideology in its advanced, multinational phase. On this account, we are now living in a phase of advanced capitalism in which frantic change, ubiquitous commodification, and the generally impersonal character of a highly technologized life evacuates human beings of their ontological and affective moorings. For Jameson, this process has advanced so far that a return to such depth models in aesthetic modes of production risks looking quaint, if not fully retrograde. Against this cultural background the primordial energies of classic works such as *The Scream* and *Romeo and Juliet* are drained of life and authority.

In seeking to regenerate those dangerously creative energies, *Slings & Arrows* boldly harkens back to a more standard, archetypal reading of *The Scream*. For Munch scholars and art historians, *The Scream* is often said to depict "the fundamental starting point of the creative artist. It is the panic-chaos that is the starting point, the source and necessity of all creative inspiration."[14] From this standpoint, the sublime energies of the image express destruction while promising creation. For if the anguished cry voices a terrifying sense of anomie, it is only because the image's oscillating energy bears within it the promise of renewed meaning and creativity. In this respect, the painting expresses a primordial drama of the soul as Munch understood it. According to the artist, the painting emerged from a vision that struck him while he was walking in Kristiana (now Oslo) during "a time when life had ripped my soul open. The sun was going down – had dipped in flames below the horizon. It was like a flaming sword of blood slicing through the concave of heaven" (*EM*, 65). Feeling immense visual and aural oscillations, Munch then felt a great scream as the "colors in nature broke the lines in nature" (*EM*, 64). As this unsettling description implies, Munch understood his painting in terms that are both personal and apocalyptic, both psychological and biblical at once.

Despite the Shakespearean weight of Munch's biblical vision, the evocation of *The Scream*'s destructively creative cosmic energies in New Burbage does not begin with the puckish forces of *A Midsummer Night's Dream*, as might be expected. Instead, such cosmic forces are inadvertently and hilariously conjured during Welles's funeral by the wild-eyed homophobic ranting of a mentally ill priest who recalls William Prynne's anti-theatrical tirade *Histriomastix* (1633). Despite his distaste of Shakespeare's homoerotic theatre, the gay-bashing priest inadvertently engenders the most theatrical moment the Rose Theatre has seen in some time, certainly outdoing the deadening production of *A Midsummer Night's Dream* from the previous episode. Dramatizing the idea that chaos precedes renewal, the dialectic of destruction and creation becomes an explicit theme in the following episode, "Madness in Great Ones." In this episode, the repeated phrase "isn't life nuts" signals that the cosmic energies of destruction and chaos embodied by Munch's *The Scream*, and which are so crucial to romantic aesthetics, are now at work in New Burbage. The point gets cinched when even the mild-mannered octogenarian May Silverstone insists that New Burbage could "use a little madness." Hence her approval of Tennant's reintroduction of such electric energy. If such ideas resonate with viewers it's partly because they have deep roots in the Western tradition, going all the way back to Plato's idea in *Phaedrus* that some of best goods in life come to humans through a form of "divine madness," a sense of being taken over by forces of cosmic energy that underlie all patterns of creation and destruction. Even Shakespeare's neoclassical contemporary Ben Jonson – a man not normally associated with romantic cliché – was described just following his death as an example of the principle that "there's no great Wit without some Mixture of Madness."[15] That such ideas continue to resonate with popular audiences is something worth pausing over.

Importantly, the destructively creative energies associated with Munch's and Tennant's artistic risk-taking contrast with the neo-liberal version of risk ethics associated with Holly Day (Jennifer Irwin) and Richard Smith-Jones (Mark McKinney). In the first case, the recreative energy of risk-taking is in the service of aesthetic excellence and spiritual renewal, while in the latter case the absence of such artistic risk-taking is in the service of short-term profit and exploitation. The terrible irony of the neo-liberal case, of course, is that risk gets displaced from art to life, thus verifying the widespread sociological thesis that we now live in a globalized risk society, one in which we constantly have to mitigate the uncertainties and hazards generated by a cosmopolitan socio-economic system that has metastasized out of all human proportion.[16] Such a view of social reality is signalled in the opening episode at the headquarters of Cosmopolitan Lenstrex, New Burbage's major corporate sponsor, where the social violence of downsizing is subtly satirized. This opposition between neo-liberal and artistic risk-taking is made explicit when Tennant asks Smith-Jones if he would prefer a "garbage" production that sells out or a great production to an empty theatre, to which Smith-Jones exasperatingly replies: "Garbage! I want garbage!" (2.5). Following the show's ethical vision, the meaning of risk depends on its purpose and motivation, on whether it's humanizing or dehumanizing in effect. And yet, as the doubling of Tennant and Sanjay indicates, there is always a danger that the risk-taking drive for artistic and spiritual renewal will become more destructive and exploitative than recreative, something that comes close to happening during the staging of *Macbeth*, just as it does in the course of Shakespeare's *The Tempest*. After all, nothing guarantees artistic or moral success.

Bearing the double-plot pattern of season 2 in mind, we can see that the storyline in the show's second season does not inadvertently reproduce the neo-liberal ideology it critiques. On the contrary, it deploys the dialectical polarities typical of television and romance to signal the danger of precisely this kind of collapsing from art to exploitation. What results is not a mindless endorsement of completely undifferentiated forms of risk, but a thoughtful commentary on the phenomenon that closely parallels Simone Weil's discussion of risk in *The Need for Roots* (1949; 1952). In particular, season 2's counterpointing storylines recall her insight about the inadvertent dangers that arise from being overprotected from danger. According to Weil, "Risk is an essential need of the soul," precisely insofar as the

> absence of risk produces a type of boredom which paralyses in a different way from fear, but almost as much … The protection of mankind from fear and terror doesn't imply the abolition of risk; it implies, on the contrary, the permanent presence of a certain amount of risk in all aspects of social life; for the absence of risk weakens courage to the point of leaving the soul, if the need should arise, without the slightest inner protection against fear.[17]

The challenge, of course, is to discover forms of risk that are creatively enlivening rather than culturally and personally damaging, with art being the most privileged space in which to do so. If season 2 of *Slings & Arrows* proves affecting for many viewers, it's partly because of how it acknowledges the human need for risk without sentimentalizing or oversimplifying such a need in the process, especially given the realities of our contemporary "risk society."

Thus to suggest that season 2 of *Slings & Arrows* exemplifies the very neo-liberalism that it critiques is to assume an interpretive dominance over the series that is unwarranted. Such a reading claims to find a "political unconscious" unwittingly operating in the series, when, in fact, the series explicitly addresses these social and aesthetic issues at the level of the main plot's relation to the subplot. Properly understood, "The Inflatable Scream" is not only the show's shorthand way of expressing postmodern vacuity and neo-liberal near-hegemony. On the contrary, it is also the show's subtle way of insinuating the perennial energies still bubbling beneath our culture's supposedly depthless surface, leaving open the possibility that Romanticism and Shakespearean humanism still have the resources to inspire a wide cross-section of the populace. To be sure, Munch's *The Scream* is as good an index of the dialectical and archetypal forces at play in *Slings & Arrows* as one is likely to find in the post-millennial moment.

The relevance of Munch's *The Scream* to the conception of dramatic illusion orienting *Slings & Arrows* comes most fully into relief when we bear in mind the specific way it constitutes a stylized reaction against the conventions of naturalism. The painting is self-consciously painterly, a powerful example of the expressionist concern with inward states of mood and mind. Yet these painterly qualities do not undermine the effect of realism, but instead enhance it. The result is a striking visual parallel to Shakespeare's own combination of realism and artifice, his practice of giving us psychologically complex characters within the theatrically stylized world of highly structured, conventionalized stories. As Karl Ove Knausgaard explains,

> the brushstrokes [of *The Scream*] are visible, and the painting is sketchy, it has an unfinished air, not least the broad reddish-purple line running down along the entire right edge of the picture. In any other picture it would have broken the illusion, but *The Scream* is painted so wildly that it intensifies instead. Imagine what such a broad, closed brushstroke would have done to the precisely painted and realistic paintings from the same time – ... their entire magic, which lies in the credibility of the pictorial space, would have been ruined.[18]

What we have here, then, is a rather extreme visual reaction against naturalism broadly parallel to Brook's rejection of forgery-like mimesis in favor of Coleridgean dramatic illusion. The aim in both is not to break with reality, but to find a new way of expressing an illusion that will successfully disclose it.

These more standard, non-postmodern readings of *The Scream* bring further into relief another significant feature of "The Inflatable Scream" in *Slings & Arrows*. At bottom, the painting has "to do precisely with alienation, with seeing the world as if for the first time by

46 Shakespeare and the World of *Slings & Arrows*

creating a distance of non-familiarity," but since it has become one of the most overexposed iconic images of our age it is "in a sense ruined for us as a work of art."[19] So despite its widely acknowledged greatness, *The Scream* exemplifies how even genius can become deadening over time. As such, it is a striking parallel of Shakespeare. For as Brook makes clear, in the modern world deadly theatre applies more often to productions of Shakespeare than any other type of drama for the "greater the work, the greater the dreariness if the execution and interpretation is not of the same level."[20] Or as Holly Day says, "No one really *likes* Shakespeare" (1.3).

THE PRISON HOUSE

To communicate the sense of postmodern imprisonment that is first conveyed in *The Scream*, *Slings & Arrows* uses a recurring visual trope.[21] Throughout the series, repeated patterns of prison-like vertical lines are subtly associated with false or deceptive illusions, as opposed to the truth-telling illusions of authentic poetic faith. In turn, this image conveys what sociologists often refer to as the "iron cage" of modern life, the atomizing and instrumentalizing effects of the institutional and social structures of advanced capitalism. We first encounter this trope when Claire delivers Puck's epilogue, awkwardly fighting her way through cottony white stripes decorating the stage as she tries to find the audience literally as well as figuratively. We encounter it again in Darren Nichols's pinstriped suit jacket, which he wears during the rehearsal for *Romeo and Juliet* while making imperious allusions to the anti-realist philosophy of Roland Barthes in season 2. In this plot line, the pattern reaches its culminating image in the hilariously absurd hoop-like cages worn by the two lead actors during a key rehearsal of *Romeo and Juliet* in its original "avant-garde" mode. In turn, this visual trope associates Nichols with the even more wildly anti-mimetic Sanjay. In particular, it recalls a parallel scene in which Sanjay gives Smith-Jones a mesmerizing advertising pitch while standing in front of a large television screen showing the SMPTE colour bars visible when a TV station is not transmitting a signal, a subtle way of indicating that Sanjay is all style and no substance, all sign and no signified. The result is a spellbinding inversion of the pursuit for truth that Tennant expounds in his eulogy of Welles in the opening of season 1. The logic of the trope of imprisoning vertical lines culminates when Sanjay is finally sent to jail for fraud and the

Poetic Faith

bars become literal, thus concretizing the metaphorical prison that he both embodies and inhabits as a cipher of the postmodern simulacra. In the case of Nichols and Sanjay, the visual patterns of prison-bar-like vertical lines undermine the claims to authority paradoxically made by these avatars of the postmodern deconstruction of authority, harkening back, as they do, to the self-imprisoning absences of *The Scream*. As these visual patterns indicate, the show is structured according to a sustained defence of dramatic illusion as theorized by Coleridge and Brook.

STRATFORD THEN AND NOW

As a reflection of postmodern malaise, "The Inflatable Scream" suggests that we are no longer in the same modernist world that Brook described in *The Empty Space*. An iconic example of postmodern kitsch and hermeneutical flattening, the image is the very antithesis of Brook's view of holy theatre as the making visible of the invisible, a conception of theatre that rests strongly on distinctions between appearance and reality. In 1968, Brook writes, "the theatre of doubting, of unease, of trouble, of alarm, seems truer than the theatre with a noble aim." In turn, "Alienation is the language open to us today that is as rich in potentiality as verse: it is the possible device of a dynamic theatre in a changing world" (*ES*, 45, 73). In other words, even existential anxiety has apparently lost its hold on the affectively flattened, imaginatively foreshortened world of postmodern North America. In which case, Brook's distinction between vivifying and deadening illusions becomes difficult to sustain in practice, throwing into question the post-romantic underpinnings of *Slings & Arrows*. This helps explain why the world of New Burbage is less an echo of midcentury Stratford-upon-Avon than a reflection of how the Ontario festival appeared to reviewers in the late 1990s. Just prior to the show's production and release, the festival was getting reviews with titles such as "Saving Stratford from the Excesses of Success," "Stratford Needs to Take New Direction," "Troubled Times for Classic Theatre," and even the elegiac "Hail, Caesar, and Farewell."[22] The general contours of the theatrical world that Brook describes in postwar England effectively reappear in the world of '90s Stratford just as they do in New Burbage – to say nothing of the Royal Shakespeare Company of the time.[23] Such continuities suggest we are dealing not with sheer contingency, but with discernible patterns of conviction and malaise arising from the ongoing struggle to discover living illusions that convincingly interpenetrate with shifting, but not wholly unprecedented, social realities.

Remarkably, the opening episode of *Slings & Arrows* subtly alludes to the shared struggles of the two Stratfords, reminding viewers that the challenges of New Burbage are typical to classical theatre rather than unique to Ontario. As Brook writes in *The Empty Space*,

> Almost every season in most theatre-loving towns, there is one great success ... that succeeds not despite but because of dullness. After all, one associates culture with a certain sense of duty, historical costumes and long speeches with a certain sense of being bored: so, conversely, just the right degree of boringness is a reassuring guarantee of a worthwhile event. (11)

Importantly, the show's writers avoid potentially offending their colleagues in the theatre by carefully selecting the messenger of this wide-brush critique. Rather than making Tennant the voice of all such criticisms, they are also introduced by the buffoonish, faux-British theatre critic Basil Cruikshank. Comically played by Sean Cullen, Basil's unearned sense of superiority makes him appear like a pudgy King John from Disney's *Robin Hood* (voiced by festival alum Peter Ustinov). Standing at the bar following the final performance of *A Midsummer Night's Dream*, Basil smugly whispers to Ellen Fanshaw: "You see, Oliver isn't saying anything. He's just putting on the show. I've seen this show many, many times. When I say that, I don't mean *The Dream*. I mean, *this show*" (1.1). Again the point is a rich one. Basil is subtly indicating that New Burbage is facing the same challenges that Brook identified in post-war England, challenges that are in many respects intrinsic to classical theatre as an enterprise. But given the source of the insight, viewers are primed not to share his *schadenfreude*. After all, Basil is an example of the "critic who no longer enjoys the theatre," which places him in opposition to the "vital critic ... who has clearly formulated for himself what the theatre could be – and who is bold enough to throw his formula into jeopardy each time he participates in a theatrical event" (ES, 33). Nevertheless, Basil's point remains an important one, revealing that the show's dialectic of conviction and malaise goes back as far as the mid-twentieth century, if not to *A Midsummer Night's Dream* itself.

FRESH FROM THE VOID

This returns us to Tennant's defence of poetic faith from "A Mirror Up to Nature." Partly inspired by the ghost of Welles, Tennant decides to strip his production of *Hamlet* down and go with a bare stage concept. In making this decision, we begin to turn from Welles's over-cooked deadly theatre to Tennant's more simple, visceral staging. This decision to strip the production down is narratively meaningful precisely insofar as its underlying exigency is aesthetically and sociologically over-determined. To understand its appeal for mainstream viewers, we have to see it in the context of religious anthropology as well as in the highly specialized world of modern theatre directing. Unsurprisingly, the immediate source of Tennant's decision is to be found in *The Empty Space*, where Brook stresses how important it is for directors to "start afresh from the void," a phrase that neatly echoes the traditional meaning of *The Scream*. According to Brook,

> Deadliness always brings us back to repetition: the deadly director uses old formulae, old methods, old jokes, old effects; stock beginnings to scenes, stock ends; and this applies equally to his partners, the designers and composers, if they do not start each time afresh from the void, the desert and the true question – why clothes at all, why music, what for? A deadly director is a director who brings no challenges to the conditioned reflexes that every department must contain. (*ES*, 39)

In rejecting staging and elaborate costumes, Tennant hopes to return to a "radiant innocence," approaching the play as though it had "just been written and sent to him in the mail," as one critic said of Brook's legendary 1970 production of *Dream*.[24] Taking his production of *Hamlet* back to the "void" or "desert," Tennant hopes something exciting will happen, something that will help the cast make old things new. But when he reports his idea to the cast, Fanshaw is dismayed, perhaps paralleling the moment in rehearsing *Dream* when an actor asked Brook, "Will there be a set?" to which Brook replied, in characteristically gnomic fashion, "Why should there be a set?"[25] Narratively, this stripping down of the stage returns New Burbage to the originating point of creation associated with Munch's *The Scream* – the point at which chaos signals a new beginning. The storyline here broadly parallels Robin Phillips's first year at Stratford in 1975 when financial exigencies forced the festival to pare down the visually lavish productions of recent years and return "to essentials," something he thought was not "a hardship," but a potentially necessary lesson (*SFSP*, 1975). Yet in the context of *Slings & Arrows*, this return to the void, this radical setting of limits, is part and parcel with the show's overall search for the vocational dimension of theatre and concomitantly its openness to the idea of common humanity. The crucial question to ask is why this paring down of the stage effectively communicates with a popular audience, as it so clearly has?

An answer can be found in religious anthropology. As Durkheimian theorists often note, traditional cultural systems generate meaning and purpose by the setting of limits. So if modernity emerged as a rejection of the apparent arbitrariness of limit-setting symbolic systems, it arguably failed to see that such systems endow meaning and purpose on the finite and ostensibly meaningless nature of human experience. In doing so, modernity came to see the delimited conditions of human existence as the cause of alienation, oppression, and loss rather than a potential source of value and meaning. In turn, modern critical theory has tended to view the idea of universality based on commonly shared limitations as an ideological delusion, often one with colonizing implications. But as Andy Mousley notes in *Re-Humanising Shakespeare* (2007; 2015), universalism can be "an attempt to place some kind of *limit* on the human, a limit which counteracts the hubristic late capitalist belief in the infinite plasticity of human beings and their infinitely mouldable and remouldable desires."[26] Such newly recovered insights are implicit in Brook's stress on the common human needs that go unanswered in the failed rituals of modern life and in the deadly theatre of its culture. In returning to the void of the bare stage, Brook is attempting to revivify the reality of those needs. Similarly, when Tennant strips his production to the bare minimum, he is not simply "starting from scratch." On the contrary, he is tapping into the principle that the setting of limits constitutes the basic condition out of which meaning and purpose arise in the first place. So if Munch's *The Scream* continues to resonate as something more than kitsch, and if Brook's call to "return to the void" is not an artifact of a passing modernist fad, it's because they both speak to the perennial movement from nothing to something, from chaos to creativity, that defines the basic limits of human creativity as such. If viewers of the show find its depiction of Tennant's *Hamlet* moving, it's not simply because they have been manipulated by the televisual trickery of montage and non-diegetic music. It's partly because they are responding to these primordial and perennial features of human creativity. It may even be worth observing in this context that the renowned physiologist Denis Noble sees the exploitation of contingency or chance as the basic mechanism by which living organisms express agency and creativity. From this standpoint, the cultural exploitation of limits for the sake of generating purpose and meaning may, in the end, be nothing less than a cultural variation on a principle inherent to biological systems.[27]

And yet, a little camera trickery can go a long way. Indeed, the careful patterning of close-ups with distance shots deployed in the rehearsal scene of the "To be or not to be" speech in "A Mirror Up to Nature" is a reasonably effective way of translating the experience of an actor on a bare stage to television. In his account of rough theatre, Brook recommends something very much like this strategy for conveying the oscillation of lightness and intensity possible in the theatre. He thus explains how

> in an ideal relation with a true actor on a bare stage we would continually be passing from long shot to close, tracking or jumping in and out and the planes often overlap. Compared with the cinema's mobility, the theatre once seemed ponderous and creaky. (ES, 87)

Unsurprisingly, Brook then qualifies this momentary privileging of screen over stage, noting "but the closer we move towards the true nakedness of theatre, the closer we approach a stage that has a lightness and rage far beyond film or television" (ES, 87). Through the shifting pattern of long shot and close-up, television can convey some of the density of Shakespearean mimesis, the way it, as Brook says, presents

> man simultaneously in all his aspects: touch for touch, we can identify and withdraw. A primitive situation disturbs us in our subconscious; our intelligence watches, comments, philosophizes … Because the profound reaches past the everyday, a heightened language and a ritualistic use of rhythm brings us to those very aspects of life which the surface hides. (ES, 87)

What emerges here is a purposefully idealized vision of Shakespeare as achieving a mimetic density within a stylized, rhythmically structured, theatrical ritual. And while this performative density surpasses electronic media in its visceral intensity, its capacity for achieving certain effects of lightness and rage is not wholly antithetical to film and television. In trying to realize these dynamics in practice, *Slings & Arrows* aspires towards something like a "rough" vision in Brook's sense of the term, translating Shakespeare into a popular medium in which both mimesis and theatrical ritual, realism and artifice, work together in a way that speaks to ongoing aesthetic and spiritual aspirations in theatre as well as in life. In taking up this agenda, the show commits itself to the view that hermeneutic distinctions between surface and depth remain operative even as the relation between illusion and reality is increasingly problematized in the matrix of postmodern simulacra. In this sense, what is at stake in the show is not simply an "authentic Shakespeare," but the inevitability of authenticity as a post-romantic virtue.

3

The Simulacra

Often viewed as the postmodern philosopher par excellence, Jean Baudrillard warns that people in the West are now obsessed "with every real, with every real event, with every real violence, with every hyperreal pleasure."[1] But this obsession, he remarks, has something fake about it because "against this obsession with the real we have created a gigantic apparatus of simulation which allows us to pass to the act 'in vitro' ... We prefer the exile of the virtual, of which television is the universal mirror, to the catastrophe of the real."[2] This startling claim is a sociologically scaled-up application of Jacques Lacan's thesis that human desire always occurs against a background of fantasy. For Lacan, desire only works when it is placed within the coordinates of an imaginary *mise en scène* through which we gain safer psychological access to those with whom we are attached. According to Baudrillard, this individual process has taken on a new collective dimension, metastasizing to the point where modern culture as a whole has been swallowed up, as it were, by a hypermediated phantasmagoria of its own feigning. In such a world, the desire to break through the simulacra to arrive at a fuller, richer sense of the real is always-already co-opted by the culture's media-driven system. As a result, all efforts to touch the real become predictable symptoms of the cultural logic of postmodernism. What this means for popular culture is that disaster movies such as the Netflix production *Don't Look Up*, which parodies the loss of reality characteristic of our media-saturated world, are doomed to become an instance of the very thing they parody, inadvertently betraying their inevitable complicity with what they mock.

From this Baudrillardian standpoint, holy theatre in Peter Brook's sense of the term is neither aesthetically possible nor theoretically desirable. Such impossibility is particularly true of television, which is a primary means by which the simulacra perpetuates itself. After all, Brook defines holy theatre as arising out of a "hunger for the invisible, a hunger for a reality deeper than the fullest form of everyday life" (*ES*, 44). From this perspective, Brook's *The Empty Space* is one of those high modernist works that continues to haunt our postmodern experience of Shakespeare, unsettling but not fundamentally undermining the rupture-inducing effects of capitalism on the present's inevitably nostalgic relationship with the past.[3] Viewed in such terms, *Slings & Arrows* ultimately presents a safe way to experience a fake version of holy theatre through the medium of television, a predictably pusillanimous substitution of the real thing. One must admit that this sad state of affairs remains a distinct possibility, making all lovers of the show variations of Reg Mortimer. The very fact that I have been driven to reassess Brook's *The Empty Space* via a television show rather than the theatre may be the worst possible sign of our postpandemic times. But as I have been hazarding, there remains an alternative perspective, one intimated by a thespian blogger who goes by the name Ross.

According to Ross,

> When I see one of these four plays that exist inside *Slings and Arrows*, I can't help but reflect on the intense joy and serious love that exudes from Geoffrey Tennant when he digs into the meaning of some Shakespearean text. It has elevated my understanding of these *"difficult"* plays, and what it means to be enlivened by the attempt.[4]

Such popular reactions to *Slings & Arrows* answer to its somewhat improbable depiction of Brook's insistence that "it is only by searching for a new discrimination that we will extend the horizons of the real ... we need desperately to experience magic in so direct a way that our very notion of what is substantial could be changed" (*ES*, 96). In this instance, *discrimination* is another version of how vivifying illusions that are collectively experienced can generate enough exteriorization of the self to widen our shared horizons of possibility. In outlining this conception of dramatic illusion, Brook offered an early critique of the modes of anti-realism and materialism championed by postmodern theorists such as Roland Barthes. As such, *The Empty Space* is a striking example of how modernism remains vital and interesting precisely because it continually struggles for meaning and truth and in doing so is constantly driven towards classical styles of sense-making, if not its

The Simulacra 55

traditional forms. From such a perspective, traditional matrices of meaning continue to exert an irresistible force on the aesthetic imagination even as their authority is increasingly strained. So on one hand, Brook's semi-Brechtian approach to modern theatre is ruthlessly demystifying, as he stresses how "the period of necessary debunking [is not over] ... almost everything of the theatre still has to be swept away" (*ES*, 96). But on the other hand, he idealistically insists that "if we demolish a pseudo-holy theatre, we must endeavour not to bamboozle ourselves into thinking that the need for the sacred is old-fashioned and that cosmonauts have proved once and for all that angels do not exist" (*ES*, 96). Brook thus rejects teleological accounts of modern secularity in which all forms of the sacred will wither away in the wake of rationalizing modes of instrumental reason, or, alternatively, in the wake of an increasingly depthless culture wholly deracinated from the resources of the past. Adopting a more Durkheimian perspective, Brook insists that a desire for the sacred will continue to animate modern life. As such, the theatre will continue to be viewed as a vitally ritualistic space in which a collective experience of intense, potentially transformative, illumination remains possible, however difficult such a thing may be in practice. In maintaining the view that full secularity is not something human beings are capable of achieving, Brook presciently anticipates sociological accounts of contemporary culture expounded in recent critiques of postmodern theory such as Charles Taylor's *A Secular Age* (2007). For Taylor, the cultural logic of postmodernism is not fully characterized by the imprisoning dynamics of the dialectical operations of capital, which increasingly excludes us from the resources of the past. Instead, it is a site of conflicting and variegating modernities in which our contemporary moment is the outcome of multiple contradictory forces unleashed in Romanticism and high modernism. Such is the wager laid in *Slings & Arrows*.

And yet, like Taylor, Brook is hardly naive about the dangers implicit in the idea that contemporary life continues to be animated by a desire for forms of transcendence. Recognizing these dangers, Brook qualifies his discussion of the exigency for holy theatre by noting that its origins may lie elsewhere than in an authentic desire for reality. Perhaps it lies, he asks shrewdly, in "a hunger for buffers against reality?" (*ES*, 44). At such moments, Brook fully acknowledges the challenge that anti-humanism poses, just as he elsewhere wards off the countervailing threat implicit in the fascist potential of Artaud's theatre of cruelty, in which he was invested in complex and critical ways. In countering these dual challenges, however, Brook presupposes a cultural condition that does not fully reduce to a media-generated simulacra or the dialectical operations of capital. Instead of committing himself to a reductively Weberian thesis that no longer explains the return of religion that has occurred in post-9/11 culture, Brook anticipates Taylor's much more variegated picture of modernity. Viewed in the context of Taylor's theory of modernization, it would appear that we are only now in a position to properly evaluate Brook's theoretical writings. In turn, these writings can help explain why the pleasures of *Slings & Arrows* may involve something other than, at best, superfluous entertainment or, at worst, insidious gullibility.

Such a sociological reframing of *The Empty Space* reminds us that Brook the theorist tends to be far more idealistic and capacious than Brook the director, who has been described more than once as expressing "despondent nihilism" and misanthropy.[5] While such descriptions may be true of his *King Lear*, which was based on the Schopenhauerian pessimism of Jan Kott's *Shakespeare Our Contemporary* (1961; 1964), they do not begin to explain the capaciousness of *The Empty Space*. Brook's productions may sometimes express despondent nihilism and a commitment to so-called nomadic theatre, yet he is also a devotee of the highly disciplined spiritual tradition associated with G.I. Gurdjieff, who is the subject of Brook's 1979 film, *Meetings with Remarkable Men*. As a follower of Gurdjieff, Brook remains open to some of the higher reaches of human potential even as he is sharply aware of the Hobbesian realities in which we generally live. Such capaciousness instinctually primed Brook to be skeptical of exaggerated investments in demystification as a critical and aesthetic strategy, evident, for example, in his response to early critiques of "the author function." Ever aware of the Parisian scene, the fully bilingual Brook notes in *The Empty Space* that "French revulsion against the classic form of the novel was a reaction from the omniscience of the author" (34). In light of this growing wariness of omniscient authorship, Brook perceived an increasing sense that "the relationship between ... [Shakespeare] ... and the world of actors and stages is getting more and more tenuous, more and more unsatisfactory" (34). But unlike Roland Barthes, Brook did not see the critique of the author as providing sufficient resources for a renewal of modern theatre or a genuinely liberating form of aesthetic experience. Instead, he stressed a certain kind of historical consciousness. As he notes, it was still possible in the Elizabethan theatre "for a dramatist to wish to bring the pattern of events in the outside world, the inner events of complex men isolated as individuals, the vast tug of their fears and aspirations into open conflict" (36). So while Brook acknowledges that the narrative function of human experience is breaking down in light of the speed and fragmentation of the modern world, he does not see this process as a *fait accompli*. Consequently, he holds to the view that Shakespeare remains "a model of a theatre that contains Brecht and Beckett, but goes beyond both. Our need in the post-Brecht theatre is to find a way forwards, back to Shakespeare" (85–6). From this standpoint, Barthesian critiques of "the author function" express dissatisfaction with the models of the past, but they do not provide a lasting way forward towards a theatre (or by extension a critical practice) in which the richness of social and psychological dynamics can be expressed as successfully as in the Elizabethan theatre at its best. In hindsight, Brook had a keen eye for the limits of demystification and alienation effects, always calling for a positive hermeneutic as well as a critical one. Moreover, he foresaw the inevitable "return of the author," which has taken place in literary and drama studies over the last decade or two.

None of this, however, is to deny Brook's astuteness as a critic of bourgeois sentimentality. In exposing the desacralization of modern life, *The Empty Space* possesses the same desire to *épater la bourgeoisie* as Barthes's *Mythologies* (1957). Revealingly, though, Brook's analyses move in the opposite direction, which may help explain why some of his productions at the Royal Shakespeare Company (RSC) did not satisfy the exacting political standards of 1980s cultural materialists who complained that his work betrayed "political imprecision," meaning, I presume, that they were not polemical enough.[6] Rather than showing how bourgeois culture conceals its conventions under the guise of the natural, as Barthes did, Brook exposes the vacuity of their conventions to reveal the underlying need driving them in the first place. Barely requiring demystification in order to be properly perceived, bourgeois rituals and conventions, Brook shows, nevertheless momentarily touch on a deeply felt intuition of the need for something vital, something sacred, in human life. In explaining the loss of the sense for ritual that was so characteristic of modern bourgeois culture, Brook exposes the awkwardness of a Stratford celebration with some of the sharpness of insight that Virginia Woolf brought to a Cambridge luncheon just prior to World War I in *A Room of One's Own* (1929). According to Brook,

> it was at Stratford ... at the official luncheon to celebrate Shakespeare's 400th birthday, that I saw a clear example of the difference between what a ritual is and what it could be. It was felt that Shakespeare's birthday called for a ritual celebration. The only celebration anyone could vaguely remember was related to a feast: and a feast today means a list of people from *Who's Who*, assembled round Prince Philip, eating smoked salmon and steak.... If we understood more about rituals, the ritual celebration of an individual to whom we owe so much might have been intentional, not accidental ... However, we do not know how to celebrate, because we do not know what to celebrate. (ES, 47)

In conveying this story, Brook is evoking a larger world in which royalty and ritual have lost their aura more fully than in *Richard II* or *King Lear*. In doing so, he provides part of the context for the de-ritualization of culture animating the opening episodes of *Slings & Arrows*. By repeatedly depicting how awkward people become in the presence of Welles's corpse and by stressing the gaudiness of his funeral, the show relies on the widespread sense that modern life is grounded in a constitutive disavowal of mortality, expressed most clearly in the American cult of morticians and death parlours.[7] Concomitant with the rejection of limits noted in the previous chapter, this modern eschewal of death, as philosopher Catherine Pickstock has argued, "is at work on all occasions where artifice replaces the horror of impermanent reality, that is, where time is elided in favour of space."[8] From this standpoint, the postmodern simulacra of which Baudrillard speaks is the logical consequence of modernity's rejection of mortality and the limits that define the human as such, most notably time. It is thus no accident that the internet and other forms of modern technology and media give us the illusion of infinite synchrony. For such cultural dynamics are a symptomatic reaction to the loss of the principle of transcendence against which human culture has traditionally and necessarily measured its own limits. In subtle and not especially lugubrious ways, *Slings & Arrows* registers these dynamics. For instance, by structuring its narrative recuperation of holy theatre as a passage from youth to middle age to old age, the show sets itself against the necrophobic and de-ritualized tendencies of modern culture. Similarly, by culminating in a stripped-down production of *King Lear* in a multi-purpose room in a church, the show carves out a space for the sacred in and against the simulacra, however fragile and fleeting it may be.

The Simulacra , 59

While straddling the avant-garde, Brook nevertheless stresses the positive role classical drama and fiction need to play in keeping the horizons of possibility open within modern culture. Here again, we see why the writers of *Slings & Arrows* found in *The Empty Space* a meaningful way of communicating a dialectic of conviction and malaise vis-à-vis life in classical theatre. By narrativizing at least two of Brook's key categories, the show presents a story that rises above the status of a televisual *roman à clef* of '90s Stratford, presenting a convincing, if comically stylized, account of the challenges inherent in keeping art distinct from advert and time distinct from space.

SANJAY'S WORLD

As I noted, one of the central figures in the show's exploration of the distinction between vivifying and falsifying illusions is Sanjay, the advertising executive from season 2 who is played to great effect by Stratford icon Colm Feore. Even more than Darren Nichols, Sanjay embodies the forces threatening the mimetic convictions on which the show's commitment to theatre as a vocation rests. Presented as a false guru, Sanjay cheats, deceives, and manipulates others for personal profit and sadistic pleasure, aiming, as his pseudonym tells us, for nothing but "victory." More dangerously immersed in his own imaginative world than Glen Gould, whom Feore played in a 1993 biopic, Sanjay operates through deceit and bad faith rather than an open desire to reveal truth through fiction. In this respect, he stands to Tennant much as Spenser's Archimago does to Red Cross Knight. Figured as "con artist/image consultant" (*s&a* liner notes, 13), Sanjay stands as Tennant's double, a figure who embodies the ideology of commodification that threatens to swallow New Burbage, and everything else with it, whole.

Sanjay's association with the black arts of advertising is signalled by the *Macbeth*-like name of his company, Frog Hammer, a combination of the most famous early modern manual on witches, *Malleus Maleficarum* (*The Hammer of Witches*), and the "Eye-of-newt, toe of frog" line uttered by the witches for a "charm of powerful trouble."[9] Sanjay is so immersed in his own lies and persuaded by his own performances that he even seems to believe them himself. In this respect, he is a picture of unadulterated ideology at work, hence his odd practice of attributing all of his quotations to Richard Nixon. Here again Baudrillard provides helpful context. For not only do such allusions recall

Baudrillard's peculiar practice of wrongful attribution, they also echo his eccentric insistence that Watergate was a simulated scandal generated for the purpose of creating a false sense of moral regeneration within the political system. In Baudrillard's view, Watergate was not the archetypal scandal it has been taken to be, but a pathetic symptom of how ideology as such is now actually impossible because it presupposes a false picture of reality, and reality, Baudrillard insists, is no longer distinguishable from illusion: that is to say, truth is the new lie (*ss*, 14, 56). Viewed this way, Sanjay is not an embodiment of ideology in the old sense of being captured by a false picture of social reality; instead, he is an embodiment of the new idea that such a distinction can no longer be made in an age of ubiquitous commodification. That everything, in effect, is always-already ideology all the way down.

Recalling this sort of topsy-turvy world, Sanjay lives fully inside his own simulacra, somewhere beyond anything recognizably cynical or nihilistic. In this respect, he embodies a threat shared by Tennant, who, as the hero of the story, has a name that suggests "tenet" or "principle of belief." Unlike Nichols, who has no deep-seated convictions and so is always flip-flopping in his views, Sanjay is fully convinced by his own delusions. A kind of Baudrillardian nightmare, Sanjay remains beyond irony and anxiety. As such, he embodies the view that the postmodern age has disclosed the world as it has always truly been, a world in which rhetoric, appearance, and opinion form the underlying contours of what appears as the true and the good.[10] Through this reversal of traditional Western metaphysics, Sanjay becomes the perfect inverse of Tennant. Instead of using theatrical illusions to reveal and transcend what is already present in the social sphere, he uses pure illusion for sadistic thrills and material gain. Viewed in the context of *The Tempest*, Tennant and Sanjay embody the two sides or differing potentials within Prospero: his embodying of the promise of redemption through imaginative creativity and his threatening will to power through manipulative, self-aggrandizing delusion.

The twinned relationship between Sanjay and Tennant becomes clear during Sanjay's mesmerizing advertising pitch to Richard Smith-Jones in "Fallow Time." Narratively, the pitch, as I noted, is presented as a demonic inversion of Tennant's vision of holy theatre in his eulogy for Oliver Welles in "Geoffrey Returns." Perversely recalling Tennant's response to May Silverstone's advice that he speak the truth during his eulogy, Sanjay depicts an upside-down world in which "truth is the new lie." Dangerously mirroring Tennant's inspiring but

The Simulacra

potentially self-destructive description of theatre in his eulogy for Oliver, Sanjay hums with confident intensity as he makes his pitch for the New Burbage account:

> We at Frog Hammer ask ourselves very simple things. Is it wondrous? Does it move you? Is it culturally authentic? We believe that people are sick of being lied to. If you use truth, you can sell people anything. If you want them to react, to feel, to buy: tell them the truth. The truth is the new lie. (2.3)

With sorcerer-like charm, Sanjay casts a spell that is enriched with aural and visual trickery. Aurally, the scene is now backed with hypnotic synthesizer music that imperfectly parallels the harp arpeggios used to signal the revelation of holy theatre. So rather than moving deeper into truth through living illusion, we are moving deeper into the unreality of a dead illusion, a false imitation of social reality that is symbolized by the semiotically empty SMPTE colour bars. Captured by the pitch, Smith-Jones responds with the same faux-masculine intensity that characterized his troubled relationship with Holly Day in season 1: "Fuck it, you're hired" (2.3).

In the show's broader context, however, Sanjay's Baudrillardian desire for the hyperreal is itself a pathological reaction to the malaise of modernity. In this respect, the opposition between Tennant and Sanjay allegorizes the contrast between art and advertising that Northrop Frye delineates in *The Modern Century* (1967). In this strikingly prescient work, Frye clearly foresees the possibility of Baudrillard's simulacra but within the context of an alternative theoretical framework. Placing advertising in the broader context of mass media, Frye warned that

> if certain tendencies within our civilization were to proceed unchecked, they would rapidly take us towards a society which, like that of a prison, would be both completely introverted and completely without privacy. The last stand of privacy has always been, traditionally, the inner mind. It is quite possible however for communications media, especially the newer electronic ones, to break down the associative structures of the inner mind and replace them by the prefabricated structures of the media. A society entirely controlled by their slogans and exhortations would be introverted, because nobody would be saying anything: there

would only be echo, and Echo was the mistress of Narcissus. It would also be without privacy, because it would frustrate the effort of the healthy mind to develop a view of the world which is private but not introverted, accommodating itself to opposing views. The triumph of communication is the death of communication: where communication forms a total environment, there is nothing to be communicated.[11]

In that final sentence, Frye distinctly foresees the possible emergence of the simulacra and the highly polarized environment attendant upon a social field that is composed of minds that are incapable of accommodating themselves to opposing views, as is so often the case in today's world of social media. Only unlike Baudrillard, Frye does not think that the simulacra disabuses the world of its metaphysical illusions. Instead, he thinks it simply generates something like that circle in hell that is inhabited by people who do not know they are in hell.

For Frye, the "deliberately frivolous" attitude, so clearly embodied by Sanjay, finds a natural home in the world of advertising. As such, *The Modern Century* helps explain the outrageous hyperbole Sanjay deploys, first in his pseudo-inspiring pitch to Smith-Jones, and then in the actual campaign itself, in which the festival's ageing subscribers are ridiculed in a kind of hyper-Brechtian manner. In outlining the forms of hyperbole operative within this strategy, Frye effectively summarizes the broader social context in which Sanjay's manipulation of Smith-Jones is best seen. According to Frye,

The technique of advertising and propaganda is to stun and demoralize the critical consciousness with statements too absurd or extreme to be dealt with seriously by it. In the mind that is too frightened or credulous or childish to want to deal with the world at all, they move in past the consciousness and set up their structures unopposed ... A little study of the working of advertising and propaganda in the modern world, with their magic-lantern techniques of projected images, will show us how successful they are in creating a world of pure illusion. The illusion of the world itself is reinforced by the more explicit illusions of movies and television ... The prison of illusion holds all of us: the first important step is to be aware of it as illusion, and as a prison. (NFMC, 14–15)

The Simulacra 63

This self-imprisoning process very much describes Sanjay's stealthy attack on Smith-Jones, whom he emasculates and empowers in turns. The result is a striking example of how advertising "creates an illusion of detachment and mental superiority even when one is obeying its exhortations" (*NFMC*, 13). On Frye's account, then, the world of advertising produces ideological conformity by encouraging a self-protecting ironic distance from what is nevertheless being accepted. Such an attitude is particularly conducive to capitalism where consumption operates most effectively when life is an ironic game in which values, ethics, and subjectivity have the plasticity and changeability of a new fashion. Yet, as the show insists, such irony is unsustainable in the long run. Rather than being liberating, Sanjay's disposition towards life is a defensive posture against the solipsistic vacuity he eventually discloses as we learn that his real name is Morris Taylor and that he is a dentist from Halifax.

Sanjay's storyline culminates with him in prison as the barred windows behind him literalize the metaphor of vertical lines as signs of false or deceptive illusions noted earlier. We would thus be correct to associate Sanjay's final scene not only with Baudrillard's simulacra, but also with Roland Barthes's trivializing misreading of epic theatre. Like Nichols, Sanjay deploys pseudo-Brechtian strategies for reductively manipulative rather than revelatory ends. In doing so, he recalls Ellis Shookman's essay "Barthes's Semiological Myth of Brecht's Epic Theatre," in which Shookman shows how Barthes misconstrued and depoliticized epic theatre by stressing "its style more than its substance."[12] A demonic inversion of holy theatre, Sanjay is one example of how the show routinely acknowledges the dangers and pitfalls of approaching acting as a vocation, doing its best to communicate the promise and peril of its own idealism to a popular audience.

In the context of the series as a whole, Sanjay's Baudrillardian world view does not mark a radical rupture with a more typical modernist anxiety for purpose and meaning. Instead, it is the last psychosocial fold in the cultural logic of post-romantic modernism. On this score, anxiety and irony have not disappeared; they have simply retreated into the fantasy of the hyperreal, their last possible hiding place before they will eventually give way to a renewed drive for purpose, however faintly defined, terrifyingly authoritarian, or genuinely regenerative such renewed direction(s) may ultimately prove to be. What I am arguing in this book is that *Slings & Arrows* is one example of this growing cultural reaction to the limits of postmodern irony and critique, especially, but not only, as it expresses itself in Shakespeare studies. And the poignancy of the show's vision owes much to the vision of modern theatre expounded in the still highly valuable *The Empty Space*.

As we've seen, *Slings & Arrows* follows Brook in assuming that neither the stage nor the screen can present a direct opposition between life and art. But what they can do is oppose living to dead illusion. Hence his conviction that the aim of theatre "is not how to avoid illusion ... [for] the illusion that is composed by the flash of quick and changing impressions keeps the dart of imagination at play" (ES, 79). As Shakespeare's Touchstone says in *As You Like It*, "the truest poetry is the most faining" (3.3.17–18). Such insights form the background to the interlacing of life and art in *Slings & Arrows*, animating its depiction of the modes of poetic faith and truth-telling illusion with which it is concerned.

4

Kingfisher Days

Shakespeare's first major treatment of the dialectic between faith in and doubt about theatre as a vocation is *A Midsummer Night's Dream*. One exchange from the play at the opening of act 5 effectively captures this major feature of *Slings & Arrows*, along with its own depiction of the interrelations among love, poetry, and madness. After the four young lovers have retold the strange events of the evening prior, Duke Theseus expresses skepticism about the meaningfulness of their reports. Diagnosing love, madness, and poetry as variants of the same underlying irrationality, Theseus discredits their narratives by means of an Elizabethan medical commonplace. In expressing such conventional wisdom, however, he implicitly undercuts the value of the play in which he is a character along with the significance of his impending wedding to the Amazonian princess Hippolyta. Such dramatic irony suggests that a larger vision is coming into view, one that ultimately contains and transcends his blinkered skepticism:

I never may believe
These antique fables, nor these fairy toys.
Lovers and madmen have such seething brains,
Such shaping fantasies, that apprehend
More than cool reason ever comprehends.
The lunatic, the lover and the poet
Are of imagination all compact.
One sees more devils than vast hell can hold
That is, the madman. The lover, all as frantic,
Sees Helen's beauty in a brow of Egypt.
The poet's eye, in a fine frenzy rolling,
Doth glance from heaven to earth, from earth to heaven;

And as imagination bodies forth
The forms of things unknown, the poet's pen
Turns them to shapes and gives to airy nothing
A local habitation and a name.
Such tricks have strong imagination,
That if it would but apprehend some joy,
It comprehends some bringer of that joy;
Or in the night, imagining some fear,
How easy is a bush supposed a bear! (5.1.2–22)

Unimpressed by this exquisitely lyrical denunciation of poetry, Theseus's fiancée Hippolyta responds with one of Shakespeare's most suggestive descriptions of what it feels like to witness a play, especially a charming one like *Dream*. Given her status as a cultural outsider and one-time enemy of Athens, the vision of cultural unity she implicitly discovers in reflecting upon the evening's narrated events becomes particularly moving and generous:

But all the story of the night told over,
And all their minds transfigured so together,
More witnesseth than fancy's images,
And grows to something of great constancy,
But howsoever strange and admirable. (5.1.23–7)

Part of what makes Hippolyta's case appealing, but also, at a theoretical level, somewhat dangerous, is that it subtly implicates the viewing audience in the play's unfolding events, making the audience participants in rather than just witnesses to them. She thus voices a vision of theatre as a form of ritual, articulating a view that Tyrone Guthrie would reiterate at the founding of the Stratford Festival in 1952. The reflexive quality of Hippolyta's speech renders it a dramatically ironic defence of theatre as a form of collective dreaming, an aesthetic space in which even she, a one-time rival, is welcomed, however problematically, into communal wonder. Perhaps without realizing that she is doing so, Hippolyta presents a vision of unity in diversity. In this manner, she draws attention to the way that the Elizabethan theatre creates a unified audience out of a disparate and oftentimes quite conflicted group of individuals. By stressing the value of the story being told, Hippolyta unifies the people watching the play into a true audience. In the process, she justifies the conviction that the Lord Chamberlain's Men originally demonstrated in putting on *A Midsummer Night's Dream* in the first place, not to mention the time spent by those watching it. At this moment in the play, Hippolyta achieves greater moral authority than the patriarchal insider Theseus, disclosing, as she does, the very terms on which the play itself is forged. But things are further complicated later when they reverse roles during the performance of *Pyramus and Thisbe*. Dumbfounded by the actors' amateurism, Hippolyta snottily mocks the performers, thereby ingratiating herself with the Athenian aristocracy. In contrast, Theseus graciously thanks them, thereby earning our respect as an audience. Over the course of the play, then, our sympathies tend to oscillate in response to a dramatized action that is dense with the complexities of life itself, its exquisitely stylized movements only increasing our sense of morally complex involvement with the play.

This reversal of roles and sympathies reminds us that the unity achieved at the end of *Dream* remains hierarchically organized along class and gender lines. As a result, it might very well be viewed as one of those "golden fantasies of order and well-being, yoking together gentility and free-born earthiness within a deep dream of peace" that simply distracts us from real injustice.[1] At the same time, however, the play's comedy imperfectly gestures at the regulating ideal that is necessarily assumed when acts of injustice are recognized as inherently wrong across time and space. Viewed this way, *A Midsummer Night's Dream* presents a "prefiguration of true community [as] ruling-class lovers are elbowed aside and forced to give equal room ... to 'rude mechanicals / That work for bread upon Athenian stalls.'"[2] In doing so, the play arguably constitutes an example of what Kiernan Ryan calls Shakespeare's *revolutionary universalism*. From this perspective, Shakespeare's plays encourage viewers to imagine early modern England from the standpoint of a more just, equal, and less alienated future world. What Hippolyta momentarily reveals, then, is the role that imagined narratives play in making such a vision, or regulating ideal, a collectively orienting dream rather than a private delusion. If such a process requires a name, we might call it Hippolyta's faith. Part of what I am arguing in this book is that Susan Coyne's ambition as a writer can be understood as an attempt to elucidate what precisely is at play in Hippolyta's faith and the interlacing structures of art and life of which it is both cause and effect, including, to some extent, the fraught political dynamics inherent to it. And that in attempting this, Coyne is very much developing the tradition of Peter Brook and Northrop Frye.

Throughout her work, Coyne follows Shakespeare in repeatedly meditating on how the artistic imagination can delude as well as inspire, deceive as well as reveal. Theodor W. Adorno keenly identifies the positive side of this dialectic when he notes that "If art has psychoanalytic roots, then they are the roots of fantasy in the fantasy of omnipotence. This fantasy includes the wish to bring about a better world. This frees the total dialectic, whereas the view of art as a merely subjective language of the unconscious does not even touch it."[3] This modification of Freudian reductivism appears to be intrinsic to romance as a genre, finding fraught expression in *The Tempest*, which oscillates between Prospero's theatrical powers as redemptive and tyrannical, collectively revelatory and privately delusional. Even more clearly, fantasies of omnipotence orient fairy tales insofar as such stories are built on the power of fantasy to remould reality.[4] The reason magic is a perennial theme of childhood storytelling is that it's a metaphor for the power of imagination to transform reality. After all, if most children bring this intuition with them into the world, it tends to get confirmed once they learn how to "magically" change their world through language. Such assumptions allow us to see how adult aesthetic consciousness evolves as a necessary outgrowth of childhood make-believe, as in William Blake, rather than as a result of its rejection or suppression, as in Freud, or at least a certain reading of Freud.[5]

Coyne's first major exploration of the tension between artistic revelation and subjective delusion, both of which have psychic roots in fantasies of omnipotence, occurs in *Kingfisher Days* (2001). A mythopoeic parable about the modes of belief proper to aesthetic experience, Coyne's story is part memoir, part spiritual autobiography, part portrait of the artist as young child, part Blakean defence of the imagination, and part how-to manual for introducing children to Shakespeare. Carefully crafted, the memoir explains how a series of auspicious events in her childhood prepared her to experience the visionary themes of *A Midsummer Night's Dream* with unusual intensity and receptiveness. Appropriately enough, one of the guiding symbols in the memoir is Novalis's blue flower, that symbol of the longing, or *Sehnsucht*, for full reconciliation of reason and imagination, between the outward world perceived by the mind and the inward world of the psyche. Revealingly, this symbol is crucial to related forms of modern spiritual autobiography such as C.S. Lewis's *Surprised by Joy* (1955), which Coyne alludes to at the end of her work.[6] Adapted for the stage, a play version of the memoir was performed at the Tarragon Theatre in Toronto in March 2003 to glowing reviews.

The play version closely follows the basic story of the memoir: on summer vacation in Ontario's Lake of the Woods region in 1963, the five-year-old Coyne began receiving letters (written by a retired schoolteacher neighbour named Mr Moir) from the "delightfully self-involved" fairy princess Nootsie Tah that were interspersed with speeches, phrases, and names from *A Midsummer Night's Dream*, *The Tempest*, *Twelfth Night*, and later romantic and Victorian works, most notably Keats's lyrics and Lewis Carroll's Alice books. Consequently, when Coyne later played Helena in her first professional role as a young adult, she had the enchanting sensation of returning to her childhood world of fairyland letters from the standpoint of a mature person.

Taken as a whole, *Kingfisher Days* traces a movement involving three distinct moments in the development of a spiritually inflected form of aesthetic consciousness. First, there is literal childhood belief in magic and fairies. Second, there is the adult awareness of dramatic illusion as illusion, what Coleridge calls poetic faith. And third, there is a form of second naïveté or "as if" thinking in which artistic illusions, recognized as such, nevertheless serve as context for the hard business of getting on with life, offering frames of reference that further disclose otherwise inaccessible forms of possibility and potential within social reality. Robin Phillips coined the term *Shakespirituality* to denote this third phase of mature belief with respect to Shakespearean art, a term that nicely dovetails with Coyne's general approach.[7] The question of whether some form of this third stage of aesthetic consciousness is already implicit in the broader theological context animating Coleridge's concept of poetic faith is a matter of some debate, though Michael Tomko's *Beyond the Willing Suspension of Disbelief* (2016) makes a convincing case that this is indeed so. Nevertheless, Coyne's memoir narratively and temporally distinguishes between these two phases, as they can clearly be separated in principle if not in identity.

In telling its story about the evolution of aesthetic consciousness, *Kingfisher Days* raises some of the troubling questions about the popularization of Shakespeare's romances that Richard Halpern addresses in his dual critique of Charles and Mary Lamb's *Tales of Shakespeare* (1807) and Northrop Frye's *A Natural Perspective* (1965) in his formidable book *Shakespeare among the Moderns* (1997). According to Halpern, the

70   Shakespeare and the World of *Slings & Arrows*

simplification of Shakespeare's romances for children works by reducing the plays from complex dramas into commodifiable stories, something that could only occur after the rise of mass-market publishing. The end result of this simplification, he claims, is not an enriched understanding of Shakespeare's plays by adult readers, but a retrogressively nostalgic reexperiencing of the childhood versions one first encountered. Speaking of mass-market translations of Shakespeare for children popularized by Charles and Mary Lamb, Halpern writes:

> Almost all of these collections of tales present themselves as a way for children (or, in some cases, adults) to experience Shakespeare without needing to cope with the difficulties of language presented by the actual plays. That is, they pose as propaedeutic devices meant to anticipate and eventually give way to the richer and fuller experience of the plays themselves. But in the order of experience things work otherwise, and readers of such volumes almost certainly grew up to experience Shakespeare's plays as dramatic reenactments of the romantic 'tales' known in youth – that is to say, as mere elaborations or echoes of a more basic ur-narrative. Similar effects are produced by comic-book versions of the plays, which began appearing in the 1950s, only a few years before the publication of [Frye's] *Anatomy of Criticism*. (132)

The idea that childhood versions of classic literary works played a role in Frye's thought is keenly insightful. After all, he is on record as noting that in his lower-middle-class home there was "a whole shelf full of children's adaptations of the classics," including the Altemus editions.[8] It is thus entirely likely that this early childhood reading experience enhanced Frye's capacity to identify general narrative structures and patterns, locating forests where most other critics saw only trees. But the question Halpern poses is whether this Aristotelian dimension of Frye's thought amounts to little more than a critically retrograde means of reducing complex singularities to a simplifying Ur-narrative. Does Halpern offer a convincing account of how children's versions of Shakespeare work on readers? In turn, does he effectively demystify Frye's notion of the late romances as popular in the sense that they provide rich access to recurring imaginative structures with a minimum of cultural education, that they are, in a word, resonant rather than fashionable? And consequently, should his critique make us highly suspicious of Coyne's claim that her childhood expe-

Kingfisher Days

rience of Shakespearean characters led to a fully mature appreciation of the plays and their relationship to life in time, a claim that flies in the face of Halpern's account of how children's versions of Shakespeare operate in a commodified world?

To properly assess whether Coyne's *Kingfisher Days* verifies Halpern's thesis or not, it's helpful to recall Frye's definition of the popular in *A Natural Perspective* (1965). By popular, Frye does not mean what is "temporarily fashionable" but that which provides a "key to imaginative experience for the untrained. The popular in this sense is the continuing primitive, the creative design that makes its impact independently of special education" (53–4). For Halpern, such a notion of the popular rests on unacknowledged material conditions, most notably the rise of mass-market publishing. Surprisingly, however, Halpern's broad generalization about how all readers of childhood versions of Shakespeare encounter the texts as adults comes with no empirical substantiation or further explanation. Nor does it take account of Charles and Mary Lamb's insistence that the *Tales of Shakespeare* were especially intended for young girls who did not have the same access to their father's libraries as Britain's sons generally did.[9] With this in mind, Charles and Mary Lamb's versions of Shakespeare appear more politically progressive than regressively nostalgic. In turn, Halpern fails to mention that Charles and Mary Lamb encourage young readers of *The Tales* to move as soon as possible from the simplified version to parts of the original text, even before they are ready to tackle the actual play as a whole. But on the basis of this speculative claim about children's reading practices, Halpern concludes that Frye reduces Shakespeare's plays to decontextualized plots for the same reasons Charles and Mary Lamb did: to bring them in line with the homogenizing tendencies of a mass-market audience. On this basis, he "explains away" Frye's distinction between an enduring and a transient notion of the popular, claiming that such an idea could only arise in the capitalist context of mass-market commodification. Instead of literary resonance, such simplified versions of classic stories constitute a form of glocalization for children. Needless to say, such a view contrasts A.C. Hamilton's 1999 conclusion that "Frye is *the* cultural critic of our generation because he is the voice of that primary mythology expressed in poetry. What is special about him is his ability to awaken in us the mythology we already know."[10] Both views cannot be correct insofar as one rejects the principle of archetypal resonance that the other presupposes.

The closest Halpern's generalization about childhood reading practices comes to being empirically justified is by reference to Norman Holland's critique of mythopoeic criticism in *The Dynamics of Literary Response* (1968). Defending an old-fashioned Freudian universalism, Holland debunks the idea that myth-based narratives resonate with readers because of any innate features of the story by insisting that such stories resonate not because there is myth but because "I know there is myth. My conscious knowledge seems to be a *sine qua non* for that special feeling of resonance and sonority."[11] Like Halpern, Holland claims to be critiquing Frye's notion of the popular as something resonant and lasting rather than something fashionable and transient, a distinction Holland wrongly conflates with Jung's collective unconscious (which he derides as an "airy nothing … psychologists have long hooted at") (243). From Holland's and Halpern's perspective, then, Coyne's *Kingfisher Days* tells a story in which her childhood interlocutor, Mr Moir, plays Charles Lamb to her mystified, five-year-old version of Northrop Frye. Viewed in this skeptical manner, the story is less about the enchantments of art than it is about the falsely universalizing effects of commodification meeting with early childhood fantasies of omnipotence. On the face of it, Coyne's adulthood experience of Shakespeare may even confirm Halpern's sense that early exposure to the plays encourages a nostalgic reconstruction of them in mythic terms as expressions of a unified vision, or Urnarrative – something she arguably does in the book.[12]

But what if there are better ways of understanding the memoir than are allowed for by such Theseus-like reductions? For one thing, Coyne's childhood encounter with the plays as presented in the memoir did not come in the form of a narrative. Instead, they came through snippets of Shakespearean names, phrases, and characters expressed in the highly individualized language of private epistles. It is only from Coyne's adult perspective that the fragmentary childhood encounters with *The Tempest* and *A Midsummer Night's Dream* take on narrative unity and coherence. In this respect, her growing love and awareness of Shakespeare follows the route suggested by Charles and Mary Lamb, not by Halpern or Jameson. For another, Coyne's reconstructed adult story is rooted in a Blakean vision of Shakespeare that has its own internal philosophical and hermeneutic authority as a dialectic of innocence and experience. As such, Coyne's modest memoir does not easily reduce to materialist or psychopathological critique. On the contrary, its exploration of the three major phases involved in the development of Shakespirituality constitutes an implicit rebuttal of demystifying approaches to mythopoeic storytelling, particularly those involving Shakespearean romance. Rather than confirming Halpern's materialist reduction of Frye's concept of the popular, Coyne's book goes some way in challenging it.

As such, a much better psychoanalytic context for *Kingfisher Days* than Holland's 1968 study of literary response is Bruno Bettelheim's now classic work, *The Uses of Enchantment: The Meaning and Importance of Fairy Tales* (1976). A major influence on John Hirsch's productions of Shakespeare's comedies and romances at Stratford in the 1980s when Coyne was acting in the festival (*SFSP*, 1984), *The Uses of Enchantment* shows how fairy tales enact processes of psychological maturation, teaching children how to navigate the real and imagined dangers of separation anxiety, sibling rivalry, oedipal conflict, instinctual impulses, and the forms of ambivalence often generated by such familial trials. Through his studies with children, Bettelheim concludes that young readers of fairy tales intuitively recognize that while such stories are unrealistic, they nevertheless portray the inner struggles characteristic of early experience accurately enough to have therapeutic value.[13] Children, he claims, know intuitively that the stories are highly fantastical even while remaining true to psychic life, often portraying competing emotional impulses or drives through opposing characters, symbol, and magic so as to depict "the essential steps in growing up and achieving an independent existence" (73). What Bettelheim here identifies amounts to nothing less than the psychological origins of second naïveté, the recognition that a fictional story can be unreal or fantastical at the level of the world while still being true at the level of the psyche's relation to the world, thus providing meaningful context for rendering social and psychological reality more fully intelligible. Such imaginative experiences, he argues, are typical to childhood encounters with fairy tales and remain hugely valuable resources for integrating the competing pressures and potentials of the psyche in early development. Whatever poignancy *Kingfisher Days* possesses lies in the way it narrates the evolution from less to more mature conceptions of such aesthetic consciousness, as the pressures of reason and imagination vie for authority within Coyne's maturing psyche. But where Freud and Jung serve as the presiding geniuses of *The Uses of Enchantment*, Blake and Shakespeare do so in *Kingfisher Days*.

74 Shakespeare and the World of *Slings & Arrows*

THE WINTER'S TALE AND WILLIAM BLAKE

The dialectic of reason and imagination central to *Kingfisher Days* is signalled in its two epigraphs, both of which celebrate poetic faith. The first is Paulina's charge to Leontes in *The Winter's Tale*, said right before the "statue" of his long and apparently dead queen Hermione "comes to life": "It is requir'd / You do awake your faith" (5.3.118–19). Importantly, however, Paulina addresses this warning to the repentant king in the second person, thereby including the audience in her insistence that "It is requir'd *You* do awake your faith." Absent such faith, Paulina's priest-like illusion of bringing Hermione back into Leontes's life will look less like a miracle of renewed love and restored community and more like a hollow sham, something out of an old tale that might be hooted at. Taking place in Paulina's chapel, this meta-dramatic call to faith ostensibly blurs the line between the aesthetic and the sacramental, the theatrical and the miraculous. This double blurring of stage with audience and of sacred with secular grants the scene great imaginative scope. After all, Hermione's statue comes to life at the exact moment that the shaman-like Paulina tells the "dead" queen to bequeath to "Death her numbness," a ritual gesture that is metaphorical and fictional but which is nevertheless designed to interpenetrate and transform the reality of the kingdom's royal family and thus the kingdom as a whole. As a result, Hermione's "resurrection," or more precisely her "restoration,"[14] grants Leontes a second chance at loving the woman who he believed had died sixteen years earlier after his rash and foolish accusation that she had committed treasonous adultery. From the faithful perspective, then, the statue scene is an apparent miracle of "real presence," a ritualized sealing, or confirmation, of the king's penitent transformation from a stony heart into a supple one. In Frye's formulation, "the restoring of Perdita to her mother is an act of sacramental communion, but it is a secular communion, and the 'instruments' aiding it are the human arts" (*NFWS*, 120). From this perspective, the play very much endorses Coleridge's sense of poetic faith as a distinctly aesthetic phenomenon while, at the same time, keeping alive the view that literary art can transform our sense of reality, thereby expanding new horizons of awareness and possibility. On this latter point, the true miracle of *The Winter's Tale* remains an open question rather than a concrete reality depending on the audience's reaction. Either the offstage participants viewing the reconciliation scene incorporate its values of love and reconciliation, making them their own, or they simply walk away after spending a few distracting hours in the theatre. The possibility of such interpenetration between stage and audience is held out by the play in a way that strategically blurs the line between a poetic faith that is strictly illusory and a quasi-sacramental faith in which the possibility of love as a generally cosmic rather than a distinctly human phenomenon has emerged through the dramatic illusion. This tension helps explain why debates about *The Winter's Tale* tend to oscillate between those who see it in strictly secular terms and those who stress its sacramental aspects. In my view, the power of the play lies in the way it keeps both perspectives alive in the form of a dialectic, an oscillating tension between love as strictly human and love as ultimately divine. Nothing in the play prevents one from stressing either side of the human/divine tension should one be philosophically or temperamentally predisposed to do so.

As an epigraph to Coyne's memoir, Paulina's call to faith frames the book's own exploration of the interpenetrations of art and life in a way that sometimes enchantingly, sometimes dangerously, blurs the line between the imaginative and the imaginary, the aesthetic and the spiritual. If Coyne's book does not wholly foreclose the human/divine dialectic of *The Winter's Tale* on one side or the other, it nevertheless leans much more in a spiritual, if not fully religious, direction. This is because *Kingfisher Days* reinterprets poetic faith in light of William Blake's more openly gnostic view of the imagination as a creative source analogous to and in some mysterious sense participatory with God's creatively loving powers. For Blake, particularly as Frye presents him, God manifests through human acts of imagination that further primary human concerns, those underlying realities that freedom is better than slavery, dignity better than humiliation, and love better than hate. This Blakean dimension becomes clear in the book's second epigraph from *Auguries of Innocence*, Blake's sustained meditation on the modes of faith concomitant with the levels of developing awareness that occur over the course of a human life: "To see a World in a Grain of Sand / And a Heaven in a Wild Flower, / Hold infinity in the palm of your hand / And Eternity in an hour."[15] This quote clearly extends Coyne's interest in the creative imagination beyond a strictly aesthetic set of investments. As such, her central symbol of the kingfisher resonates with the themes of poetic inspiration and personal selving in Gerard Manley Hopkins's "As Kingfishers Catch Fire," if not T.S. Eliot's more depersonalized vision of eternity in *Four Quartets*

76 Shakespeare and the World of *Slings & Arrows*

where the kingfisher's wing answers the light "At the still point of the turning world."[16]

Most importantly, Coyne begins her memoir by suggesting that Blake's vision of interconnectedness struck her "with the force of something I had always known, but somehow forgotten" (1). This opening assertion indicates that the book's overall parable traces a complexly circular movement into the world of faith in which moments of "conversion" unfold as forms of *anamnesis*, a recalling of knowledge at a renewed and oftentimes higher level of awareness. In depicting the hermeneutic movements of anamnesis, Coyne's exploration of poetic faith leads to something very much like what Paul Ricoeur calls second naïveté, a mode of non-literal belief in the power of mythic narrative to metaphorically disclose levels of human potential and ultimate concerns that otherwise remain inaccessible. Neither literalist nor strictly aesthetic in orientation, second naïveté incorporates the lessons of ideological critique while still leaving space for a sense of the sacred within human life. Adopting this attitude, *Kingfisher Days* presents a spiritual journey from literal (childhood) belief to (adult) poetic faith to (mature) second naïveté. If the general pattern here broadly resembles C.S. Lewis's spiritual autobiography *Surprised by Joy*, it nevertheless lacks any obvious doctrinal component. Instead of focusing on her movement into a credal Christianity, Coyne stresses the story dimension of the Johannine vision of God as love, privileging mythos over logos, or narrative over doctrine.

Given its Blakean investments, it is perhaps unsurprising to learn that *Kingfisher Days* tells a story that closely corresponds with the general argument Frye derives from his study of Blake in *Fearful Symmetry*. According to Frye,

> Nearly all of us have felt, at least in childhood, that if we imagine that a thing is so, it therefore either is so or can be made to become so. All of us have to learn that this almost never happens, or happens only in very limited ways; but the visionary, like the child, continues to believe that it always ought to happen. We are so possessed with the idea of the duty of acceptance that we are inclined to forget our mental birthright, and prudent and sensible people encourage us in this. That is why Blake is so full of aphorisms like 'If the fool would persist in his folly he would become wise.' Such wisdom is based on the fact that imagination creates reality, and as desire is a part of imagination,

the world we desire is more real than the world we passively accept. (27)

Given her apparent Unitarian upbringing and literary theatrical training, Coyne demonstrates an unusual degree of receptiveness to Frye's visionary synthesis of post-romantic English literature. For all its self-conscious naïveté and childlike simplicity, Coyne's *Kingfisher Days*, like *Slings & Arrows*, suggests that the traditions at work in this post-romantic synthesis remain a popular part of the Canadian cultural landscape. Yet for her, these themes are very much tied to the experience of theatre and of acting. As such, they reinforce the commonplace belief that "if you scratch an actor you will find a child. Not that actors are inherently less mature than politicians, priests, etc. but actors must retain a child's appetite for mimicry; for demanding attention, and above all for playing. They must see with a child's heart, innocent of judgement."[17]

Given the importance of theatre to Coyne's visionary memoir, Peter Brook provides an important corollary to Frye's Blakean approach to the problem of how childhood make-believe evolves into adult aesthetic consciousness. In his own memoir, *Threads of Time*, Brook observes how the movement into adulthood involves discovering "that the imaginary is both positive and negative – it opens on to a treacherous field, where truths are often hard to distinguish from illusions and where both throw shadows."[18] This tension between competing forms of reality and the modes of illusion inherent in them are crucial to the dynamics of second naïveté. For one thing, second naïveté rests on the presupposition that religious language is essentially metaphorical in nature. As such, religious discourse involves the same sort of distanciation from literal reference that is proper to fictional discourse. Crucially, however, the theory does not propose that fictional discourse is fully autotelic or strictly self-reflexive in nature. On the contrary, fiction abolishes first-order descriptive reference to the world in order to open up a second-order, metaphorical connection with ordinary life. In this sense, as Ricoeur explains, fiction "constitutes a new sort of distanciation that we can call a distanciation of the real from itself. It is this distanciation that fiction introduces into our apprehension of reality ... Through fiction and poetry new possibilities of being-in-the-world are opened up within everyday reality."[19] From this standpoint, fiction and poetry generate new possibilities of being-in-the-world not by intending the world as it is objectively given, but by intending what remains strictly potential within it through the mediations of desire and imagination. In *Kingfisher Days* these distinctions are instantiated formally in the story's parabolic movement from childhood through to early adulthood and finally to parenthood where Coyne retells her story to her seven-year-old son. If this passing on of wonder from parent to child repeats the pattern of Carroll's *Alice's Adventures in Wonderland* (1865), Coyne's ending actually seems more convincingly integrated into the overall story rather than being tacked on as a kind of didactic safety valve as in Carroll's darker, yet somehow less true to life, story. As a result, *Kingfisher Days* reads more like a genuine parable than does the more wildly fantastic *Alice's Adventures*.

The movement across time explored in *Kingfisher Days* happens in and through the book's expanding vision of the kingdom of the imagination that R.C. Moir, Coyne's childhood neighbour, summarizes in more strictly synchronic terms in a passage that closes out the memoir: "How does it feel, Susan, when you put a few marks on a white sheet of paper, to have a new kingdom and all its people rise up in front of you?" (170). As I noted, this empowering meta-poetic insight unfolds in three distinct phases in the story. At first, the new kingdom occurs within the pristine world of five-year-old Susan's letters to Nootsie Tah, where no distinction between the imagination and the imaginary is made. The second occurs in a letter R.C. Moir wrote to Coyne on 1 December 1963, when the fictional story of Nootsie Tah is opened up beyond the world of *The Tempest* and *A Midsummer Night's Dream* to the imagined world of John Keats's fairy poems. Citing Keats's "Shed no tear – O, shed no tear!," a poem about the growing awareness of mortality in the mind of an innocent child, Moir asks Susan to do further research on the lyric, as he suspects Keats did not realize that the avian singer of the song he "recorded" was Ariel from *The Tempest*. In this second phase, the imaginary world generated the previous summer now begins to open up to the literary universe as a whole, as the stories of Ariel and Puck begin to intersect with Keats's lyrics and other poems. Through this expanding process, the distinction between the imaginative and the imaginary begins to form as one story interconnects with another story and one poem with another poem, moving in the direction of what Frye calls anagogic awareness, or the idea that any particular work of literature can serve as the center out of which one unifies the totality of one's experience with fiction and myth. The result is a widening of the horizons of both the imaginative and the real, along with the possible relations between them. In the third and final phase, signalled in a package sent to Coyne in 1974, the fictional world of Keats's poem enters into the real world of adult awareness when Coyne learns of Mr Moir's death. At which point, "Shed no tear – O shed no tear!" ceases to be a self-sufficient fiction and instead becomes a real-world confrontation with death and the challenges to faith concomitant with it. On one hand, then, this third phase completes the distinction between the imaginative and the imaginary by making it palpably clear through the experience of death and grieving. However, belief in the power of imagination to change the world for the better now intersects with mortality, thereby threatening the meaningfulness of the distinction in the first place. Put simply, Mr Moir's death raises the question of whether everything Coyne shared with him was simply "child's play" in the derogatory sense of the term, a passing illusion rather than a preparation for the mature expression of artistic creativity and aesthetic consciousness. Two differing views on the imagination thus compete for attention in the story after Moir's death. On one hand, there is the Freudian view that magical thinking is a passing phase of childhood experience, which must be given up on the basis of the reality principle, the result of which is a view of art that is necessarily tinged by the pathological. And on the other hand, there is the Blakean view that childhood make-believe forms the basis for aesthetic vision in adulthood, providing a means to test and reshape the reality principle on the basis of imaginative and visionary experience. If the first view conforms to the neo-Marxist claim that mythopoeic conceptions of the popular as resonant are a by-product of commodification and thus a misconstruction of the empirical data, the second view affirms the claim that certain kinds of stories resonate because they address widely shared desires and aspirations that are only achievable through the work of the imagination, starting with the commonly shared fantasy of omnipotence underwriting fairy tales as a genre.

The problem Coyne sets herself in the story, then, is to prevent the Blakean perspective from devolving into the skeptical view in a manner that does not feel excessively contrived or oversimplified. She does this in two interconnected ways. First, she admits to the demystifying effects that Moir's death had on her retrospective view of their epistolatory relationship. Second, she stresses the real effects that their shared fiction had on her eventual career choices and rich imaginative life. What prevents the latter view from feeling excessively contrived is that it was already articulated by Moir in one of the final letters he sent to the five-year-old Coyne. In the letter, the fairy princess reports how Ariel saw her transformed into a halcyon and so he sings to her a song that is the culminating vision of the summer's whole epistolary relationship, only to then release her, Puck-like, from the enchantment: "'Nootsie Tah, Susan says she loves you. Love is stronger than all of Queen Mab's spells. The difference between the fairies and the angels is love. God is love.' And all the birds bowed their heads. For a time, the spell that keeps you here is lifted" (KD, 138). In the Johannine tradition alluded to here, the idea that "God is love" is not so much a metaphysical claim made at the level of ontotheological speculation. Instead, it is a hermeneutic principle designed to prevent the collapse of mythos (story) into pure logos (reason), or if you prefer, imagination into what is already given as "reality." Crucially, it is out of this principle that Coyne's framing notion of anamnesis will find its eventual philosophical justification. To see how these two parts of the story – the claim about divine love and the claim about anamnesis – interrelate in this manner, it's helpful to note the parallel between Coyne's retelling of the Johannine myth with two complementary interpretations of it.

For Paul Ricoeur, the word

> "God" does not function as a philosophical concept, whether this be being either in the medieval or in the Heideggerian sense of being. Even if one is tempted to say – in the theological metalanguage of all these pretheological languages – that "God" is the religious name for being, still the word "God" says more: it presupposes the total context constituted by the whole space of gravitation of stories, prophecies, laws, hymns, and so forth. To understand the word "God" is to follow the direction of the meaning of the word. By the direction of the meaning I mean its double power to gather all the signification that issue from the partial discourses and to open up a horizon that escapes from the closure of discourse.[20]

In numerous places, Frye makes a parallel point with reference to the opening of the Gospel of John. In Frye's view, John does not depict God's Word as the servomechanism of his premeditated divine actions. Instead, he gives logical priority to the Word as a creative principle out of which reality is partly shaped and potentially redeemed vis-à-vis human imagination. In making this claim, Frye insists that John's use of the term Logos departs from the standard Greek usage that refers to an order of thought corresponding to a pre-existing order in nature. In contrast to this, he suggests, John infuses the Greek term with the Hebrew sense of *dabhar* or the idea of Word as event. In doing so, John links mythos to logos, and narrative to reason, in a way that distinguishes his use of the term from its ancient Greek meanings. *Truth* then becomes an explicit matter of storytelling, with *doctrine* becoming, in effect, a form of literary interpretation.[21] Importantly, this Johannine synthesis of story and truth provides the hermeneutic context from which Coyne's conception of anamnesis derives its philosophical coherence. After all, the basic story she tells is about how the creative imagination recreates a world in which love is continually affirmed over death on the grounds that love is the context in which one lives, moves, and finds one's being. According to this story, the imagination revivifies and reclarifies the context in which divine love acts and moves. But like Prospero, Coyne tells her story in a way that suggests she is the effect of her own story rather than its wholly sufficient cause. In other words, she wants us to believe that she has retrospectively unearthed the significance of her childhood relationship with Moir rather than fully contrived the meaning of it in advance. So if the memoir generates any sense of poignancy for readers, it's because this metaleptic reversal of the past transforming the future seems genuine. In which case, the memoir appears as a post-romantic revisioning of the Gospel of John that is being remembered or rediscovered even as it is being (re)created. Viewed this way, *Kingfisher Days* plausibly revises the Johannine creation hymn from the standpoint of a more Blakean notion of the creative imagination. But if the story irritates readers, or renders them indifferent, it's because this metaleptic reversal seems fake, as though it were tacked on after the fact.

In structuring her story as a form of spiritual memory, or anamnesis, Coyne recreates a commonly recurring but still poorly understood hermeneutic phenomenon: the oscillation, as Frye says in *Words of Power*, between a feeling that one "is part of a larger design and a feeling that a larger design is part of" oneself (*wwp*, 85). From this standpoint, the reader of a mythical metanarrative such as the New Testament is a whole of which the text is a part: the text is a whole of which the reader is a part: these contradictory movements keep passing into one another and back again. The Logos at the center, which is inside the reader and not hidden behind the text, continually changes place with the Logos at the circumference than encloses both.[22]

Among other things, this is Frye's rebuttal of the founding principles of deconstruction expressed in Derrida's breakthrough essay, "Structure, Sign, and Play" (1964). In Frye's formulation, interpretation of the biblical text does not involve a search for a lost origin that stands outside the text in the form of statically construed author, be it an unchanging God or an intentionally consistent John the Evangelist. But nor does interpretation primarily consist of an imposition of meaning on the text from a reader or community of readers. Resting in neither its textual or authorial origin (as in literalism or fundamentalism) nor its destination (as in Barthes's theory of reader response), the unity of a text, according to Frye, lies in the dynamic tension between origin and reader/viewer.[23] Such a view is consistent with Frye's sense of the Shakespearean text as open to a potentially infinite number of interpretations (*NFWS*, 233), but in a more delimited sense than that implied by Derrida's liberationist avowal of

the Nietzschean *affirmation*, that is the joyous affirmation of the play of the world and of the innocence of becoming, the affirmation of a world of signs without fault, without truth, and without origin which is offered to an active interpretation. *This affirmation then determines the noncenter otherwise than as loss of the center.*[24]

From Frye's standpoint, such unbounded interpretation cannot sustain joy for long, even if it's held in an irreducible tension with interpretation as the pursuit of an originary meaning as Derrida insists it must inevitably be in the realm of the human sciences today. After all, such free play quickly gives way to exhaustion and malaise, or even worse, a half-avowed worship of the self. For such a thoroughgoing critique of all values, including the self, inevitably reinforces an egocentric anthropocentrism, leading, eventually, to anxiety and loss of meaning. As Charles Taylor notes, popularized views of such antihumanism paradoxically leave people "with a sense of untrammeled power and freedom before a world that imposes no standards, ready to enjoy 'free play' or to indulge in an aesthetics of the self,' resulting not in liberation but malaise-inducing self-indulgence.[25] While Derrida's essay is oriented by a liberationist and egalitarian sensibility, this ethos floats free of any allegiance to a metaphysical concept of the good that would make sense of why liberation and equality are preferable in the first place, a point Derrida later tried to address by insisting that there are concepts that cannot be deconstructed, such as justice.[26] Frye, on the other hand, identifies a set of primary concerns that more clearly delimit the legitimacy of interpretive and ethical possibilities, thereby allowing for interpretive openness short of a full-throated "free play" in Derrida's more unbounded sense of the phrase. While the universal applicability of Frye's primary concerns might be questioned, the advantage of his theory is that it allows one to speak of a more or less faithful interpretation of the text, while still giving room to the way shifting contexts and emergent occasions illuminate, or even generate, unforeseen forms of significance.

This brings us back to Coyne's use of the term *anamnesis* as an orienting dimension of her account of spiritual and hermeneutic experience. By beginning her story with the claim that Blake's vision of the whole world potentially existing within one part of it struck her as something she always knew but had forgotten, Coyne implies that her story constitutes a form of repetition. And what is being repeated is the discovery that imaginative perception participates to one degree or another in remaking social reality according to an orienting vision of goodness, that art can interpenetrate with and transform life for the better. From this perspective, genuine creativity always involves a certain form of repetition, but a repetition which is "not the simple repeating of an experience, but the recreating of it which redeems or awakens it to life."[27] In rediscovering the power of imaginative experience to recreate social reality in more ethically realized form, one is interpenetrating with the source of that moral vision. If this story resonates for many readers, it's for some of the same reasons *Slings & Arrows* does. As Coyne reminds us, ideas of anamnesis have deep roots in the Western tradition, going back to Plato's *Phaedrus* in which the experience of spiritual recollection provides some assurance about the reality of goodness and beauty as, in principle, things that are discovered and given rather than fully constructed or contrived.

Like Frye, Coyne sees *The Tempest* and *A Midsummer Night's Dream* as the two plays in which Shakespeare depicts exactly this metaliterary experience of collectively enacted narrative self-exteriorization, the process of gaining perspective on oneself as a means of then becoming genuinely other than what one has previously been through a widening of vision. Viewed retrospectively, Coyne sees the summer of 1963 as her own simplified reprising of Miranda in light of Mr Moir's fully benevolent Prospero. She then takes up the role of Prospero in telling the story to readers and to her own children, neatly capturing Frye's conviction that *The Tempest* is the clearest depiction of the "interchange of illusion and reality which is what literature is all about."[28] The result is both more simple and more complex than anything Halpern's claims about childhood redactions of Shakespeare would lead us to expect. On one hand, Coyne presents a charming, if necessarily contrived, retelling of the Johannine story as reframed in Blakean terms, giving us a picture of how loving expressions of the imagination can produce greater forms of maturity and community. On the other hand, the story's parabolic dimensions expand outward in vision across time, resulting not in a commodifiable story but in a visionary framework that allegorizes how fictions can provide animating contexts for life through creative and enlivening acts of repetition. Rather than being an inadvertent allegory of late capitalism, the story is a self-conscious allegory of the interchange between reality and illusion that is implicit in the very act of telling a Blakean story about the overcoming of loss and death through love and faith.

By the end of *Kingfisher Days*, then, it becomes clear that Coyne is articulating in narrative terms something very similar to what Frye outlines in *The Double Vision* (1991). Outlining the same Blakean concept of imaginative faith animating *Kingfisher Days*, Frye writes:

> The Epistle to the Hebrews says that faith is the *hypostasis* of the hoped-for and the *elenchos* or proof of the unseen. That is, faith is the reality of hope and of illusion. In this sense faith starts with a vision of reality that is something other than history or logic, which accepts the world as it is, and on the basis of that vision it can begin to remake the world. (19)

While Coyne's aesthetic interests take her to the very edge of full-blown religious commitments, she tends, like Unitarians generally, to withdraw at the very moment when story becomes doctrine, when mythos freezes into logos. Like Frye and Blake, she stresses the quasi-gnostic powers of the imagination to partially create the reality in which it then lives and moves.

The ending of the play adaptation of *Kingfisher Days* makes this basic interchange of reality and illusion clear as the production concludes with a radio announcer reporting, in a manner that is both innocuous and miraculous, on Nootsie Tah's return home to Peru after a visit to Kenora. Such integration of fiction into reality marks the play's endorsement of second naïveté, which is the basis on which literature and myth become not just pastimes or forms of solace but equipment for living. As I noted, one immediate source of these values and her general sense of theatre as a vocation becomes clear in her 2018 documentary *Robin, Mark, and Richard III*. An homage to the late Robin Phillips (1940–2015), the documentary shows Phillips aiding Mark McKinney in mastering two scenes from *Richard III* as Maggie Smith and other veteran actors comment on Phillips's powers of intuitive and analytical insight. In turn, Phillips shares his general view of Shakespeare in a highly lyrical brand of prose-poetry. More than anything else, though, his concluding meditation on poetic faith bespeaks the delicate tension between aesthetic and spiritual commitments that animate his directorial practice even as they help convey the clear sense of purpose he sustained to the end of his life. With obvious parallels to Tennant's meditation on poetic faith in "Mirror Up to Nature," which was written and shot years earlier, the septuagenarian Phillips concludes the film by noting that Paulina's call to awaken faith stops one's heart because it is, in a sense, what all theatre is about: "You can't just go to the theatre and say 'entertain me.' You have to go the theatre and say 'I'm going to participate with you. I'm going to join you. But we won't do that, unless the actors are also asking us to join them.'"[29] For Phillips, Paulina's concept of poetic faith derives its full meaning from the possibility that once the dramatic illusion ceases, its effects are carried into the real world by the audience members who continue to resonate with it, thereby making it their own. This interplay between art and life stands at the centre of Coyne's preoccupation as a writer, no less in *Slings & Arrows* than in *Kingfisher Days*.

Halpern's suggestion that Frye's theory of recurring literary patterns and his accompanying concept of the popular constitute elaborate examples of bourgeois romance, a bad-faith attempt to escape from rather than intervene into historical injustices, was a perspective not unknown to Frye. More than a decade prior to the publication of Halpern's book, Frye warned that bad faith commonly lies in the contemplation of a timeless body of truth *in* itself, with none of the limitations of a specific temporal and historical conditioning *for* oneself taken into account. No human being is in a position to gain any benefit from that kind of vision, and the truths such a vision express soon shrivel into platitudes. (MM, 100)

Thus if Halpern's assessment of Frye's work as an overdetermined symptomatic reaction to advancing capitalism is correct, then *Slings & Arrows* is essentially a corroded form of bourgeois romance, with popular narrative simply mirroring the false consciousness at work in Frye's supposed ahistoricism. In which case, the show is less a critique of commodity culture's effects on the arts than an inadvertent affirmation of its culturally flattening effects. But if Frye's view of the popular does, in fact, identify a perennial phenomenon, then the show may be an example of the culturally revitalizing function often associated with demotic art. Indeed, we may even catch a glimpse of this revitalizing cultural dynamic at work in one blogger's enthusiastic response to *Slings & Arrows*. According to Sarah Bennett, the show "isn't just quintessentially Canadian, but universally great, and strange as it sounds to say about a TV show, it will make you feel like a greater person by watching it."[30] From Halpern's demystifying perspective, such a response is a symptom of false consciousness, a bogus fusing of the concrete and the universal, which is the very definition of ideology. From Frye's perspective, however, such a response is an intuitive affirmation that even popular modes of art can still prevent the vulgarization of culture through the contemplation of horizon-expanding art. Moreover, it is a sign that the show effectively communicates local experience to a wide international audience.

The potential for a television show to perform such a revivifying cultural function stands or falls with a view of the popular as resonant rather than as modish. When a popular work becomes resonant in Frye's sense, it provides audiences with access to a wider imaginative experience by generating a sense of value and meaning through connection with similar stories and experiences across time. When this happens in the world of multinational capitalism, stories sometimes become franchises, as with *Harry Potter*, *Star Wars*, or *Lord of the Rings* – the mythopoeic power of which is hard to deny. For Frye and Brook, Shakespeare's romances model such a concept of the popular as resonant. In contrast, Halpern's view of the late romances as laying the groundwork for a relatively vulgar bourgeois domesticity means that enthusiastic responses to *Slings & Arrows* must presumably be expressions of the same false consciousness apparently besetting Frye. At which point, it becomes very difficult to explain the show's success and poignancy as something other than the expression of a regrettable gullibility.

5

The Stage Is All the World

In *Slings & Arrows*, the interplay of life and art finds expression in the way several of Shakespeare's plays provide intersecting contexts for the show's story, especially the three tragedies that are performed in each respective season (*Hamlet, Macbeth, King Lear*). But as I also indicated, *A Midsummer Night's Dream* and *The Tempest* are arguably more central to show's overall framework as its self-reflexive storyline follows the conventions of comic romance rather than tragicomedy. Recalling that the Latin word *tempestas* means time as well as storm, the show's opening scene at Théâtre Sans Argent initiates a narrative structure in which the expansion of vision ultimately unfolds, as it generally does in Shakespeare's late romances, through a shift in conceptions of time. At the beginning of romances such as *The Tempest*, time is generally viewed as *chronos* or sequence, but by the end, it emerges as *kairos* or revelation.[1] By following this structure, *Slings & Arrows* opts for a traditional narrative patterning that is broadly amenable to moderated notions of the heroic and implicitly resists the collapsing of time into space (or diachrony into synchrony) so characteristic of postmodern culture, be it in the film trailer or the video platform TikTok.[2] In telling its story, the series updates the popular elements of Shakespeare's comic romances with an eye to the modernizing pressures of capitalism. In "Oliver's Dream," for example, this awareness is signalled by the central place given to New Burbage's gift shop as well as through architectural settings such as Toronto City Hall, which serves as the spatially discombobulating headquarters of Cosmopolitan Lenstrex, the festival's semi-evil corporate sponsor. Within their respective registers, both settings reflect the dehumanizing pressures of the market, disclosing how the economic realities of advanced capitalism are completely colonizing the world of artistic production.

The Stage Is All the World   89

Like *A Midsummer Night's Dream* and *The Tempest*, then, *Slings &
Arrows* is an exploration of the relationship between theatre and life,
one that is self-consciously in line with the view of Shakespearean
metanarrative espoused by Northrop Frye, whose influential writings
on Shakespeare form an important part of his broader post-romantic
conception of the literary imagination.[3] A significant presence at the
Stratford Festival of the 1960s, where he ran seminars and delivered
lectures,[4] Frye became an even more important influence at the festival under the directorship of John Hirsch (1981–85), when he delivered lectures on the interpenetrations of life and art in 1982 and
1985. An intellectual superstar by this point, Frye's writings on the
romances almost certainly informed Hirsch's unrealized desire to
stage all four romances in one season.[5] They also discernibly inform
Hirsch's critically celebrated 1982 production of *The Tempest*, as the
video of the performance begins with a prefatory address that glosses
Frye's stress on the interpenetration of the play and the audience in
his 1982 Stratford lecture and follows the broad contours of Frye's
reading of the play as an exemplary movement from exile and alienation to forgiveness and reconciliation through the powers of the theatrical imagination. As far as Coyne is concerned, then, the influence
of John Hirsch is closely bound up with and in some respects insepa-
rable from the influence of Frye.[6]

In a 2018 interview, Coyne explicitly identifies Hirsch as a significant influence on her vision of the theatre and thus one of the real-
life figures informing her characterization of Tennant.[7] Born in Siófok,
Hungary, in 1930, Hirsch was the sole surviving member of his
immediate family, who were all murdered in the Holocaust. Sponsored for adoption by the Canadian Jewish Congress in 1948, the
upper-middle-class and German-influenced Hirsch resettled with a
cultured, Yiddish-speaking, working-class Ukrainian-Jewish family in
Winnipeg's North End, leading him to later describe himself as a
member of four mafias: Hungarian, Jewish, homosexual, and Winnipeg, the latter category being, for a man of the theatre in twentieth-
century Canada, not much less deviant than the others (*AFS*, 10).
Crucially for Coyne, Hirsch overcame his shattered childhood by
finding a sense of purpose and meaning in the theatre, thus inspiring
her and many others in the Canadian theatre world. Such inspiration,
however, was not universally appreciated. Identified as a teenage
genius by a University of Manitoba psychology professor, Hirsch, who
has been called a "sacred monster," could be ferociously intimidating

to actors, sometimes folding in on himself with his legs up on the chair in front of him during a bad rehearsal (a posture imitated by Paul Gross as Tennant) (AFS, 127). Such intensity is discernible in a 1988 interview, given one year before he died of AIDS, in which he warns: "This is the thing that people are scared shitless of: that I take this seriously, serious to the point of being able to kill if the thing doesn't work. Isn't that how it's supposed to be? Haven't they read about van Gogh cutting off his ear?"[8]

Yet Hirsch's influence on *Slings & Arrows* extends beyond some of Tennant's character traits to the very narrative structure of the show itself. As artistic director of Stratford in 1983, Hirsch claimed that the festival's "goals are high, and risks, as ever, with us," while a year earlier he said that the festival welcomes "the challenge of sustaining these standards in a world where quality is constantly being eroded by the dictates of expediency" (SFSP, 1983, 82), sentiments that Tennant embodies. Most revealingly, though, Hirsch's high-stakes approach to art as a form of self-understanding finds expression in his 1984 article "A Sense of Direction." The article opens by expounding an existentially committed approach to Shakespeare's comedies and romances that broadly parallels Frye's writings on Shakespeare, including aspects of Frye's work that critics who mistake him as an anti-mimetic formalist fatally overlook. To be sure, the following passage from Hirsch neatly summarizes the view of Shakespeare animating *Slings & Arrows*:

> Directing, acting in, or even seeing a great play is like conducting a litmus test on yourself. After you've dipped into it and become absorbed by it, you come out, look at yourself and get a reading of who you are. Over the past number of years, I've been doing many of Shakespeare's comedies and romances because I'm interested in exploring mythologies, fairy tales and matters that have to do with my own spiritual development. Consequently, when I do one of Shakespeare's works, I'm investigating who and where I am at that particular moment as well as the play. A production comes alive – instead of becoming a dusty museum piece – when the people doing it undergo a process of self-examination through their total commitment to the play. (SFSP, 1984, 25)

In structuring *Slings & Arrows* as a movement from youth to middle age to old age, the writers of the show created a narrative structure

The Stage Is All the World　　　91

with sufficient capaciousness to explore the ways such a personally invested approach to Shakespeare, so typical of Stratford performers and directors, might play out at different points in a human life. Clearly, then, Frye's mythopoeic and existentially committed approach to Shakespeare's plays, especially the romances, forms a significant part of the shared background to Hirsch's ideas and the influence they had on Coyne in creating and composing both *Slings & Arrows* and *Kingfisher Days*. As Hirsch further said in his 1988 interview,

> I never was interested in formalism; my theatre is not boutique theatre ... My theatre and my literature deal with substance and that substance is the way we live and an investigation of who were are and what we are ... There is bad art and there is good art. And I firmly believe that there is a difference. I do believe that art, beauty, and truth are connected, and I do believe that at the centre of any art is a moral imperative. That's my credo. (BC, 82)

Coincidentally, the same year that the Canadian Jewish Congress was helping the seventeen-year-old Hirsch resettle in the North End of Winnipeg, a thirty-five-year-old Frye was finally seeing his long-awaited study of William Blake into print, a book that would later be described by an authority on the matter as perhaps "the most brilliant exercise of allegorical interpretation on record."[9] Written in self-conscious response to midcentury totalitarianism and global war, *Fearful Symmetry* presents one of the most profound anti-fascist statements of the period. This was apparently even clearer in earlier drafts of the book, which made its political intervention more explicit than the final version. Yet if the published version downplayed its immediate political context, it still made evident enough the sentiment Frye expressed more openly in a private letter to his future wife Helen Kemp: "Read Blake or go to hell. That's my message to the modern world."[10] Such early versions of the book indicate that Frye saw the exigency of *Fearful Symmetry* all around him in the Europe of the 1930s and '40s, perhaps even in his genial, but politically short-sighted, Oxford tutor, Edmund Blunden, who did not immediately recognize in Hitler what the younger Frye readily saw.[11] Readers of Frye's anti-fascist Blake book will recall that the study opens with an epigraph from *The Tempest*, the passage in which the good-hearted, if naively subservient, Gonzalo describes the island as lush and lusty while the morally depraved Antonio and Sebastian see it as tawny and barren.

In its epigraphic context, this ostensibly innocuous passage discloses how on Prospero's magical island, "the quality of one's dreaming is an index of character," making imagination revelatory of both existing as well as possible ethical realities (*NFWS*, 48). In other words, Frye saw this passage as disclosing the way in which great literature, as Hirsch says, functions as a "litmus test" on ourselves, with *The Tempest* being one of the most profound examples of a literary work testing and reflecting the furthest reaches of a reader's moral and spiritual vision.

Despite his very different background from the waspish, if working-class, Frye, Hirsch clearly recognized in Frye's criticism a breathtaking conviction in the power of the artistic imagination to keep open the horizons of possibility necessary for sustaining a free civilization through the production of individuals capable of sustaining the burden of freedom. Hirsch was thus understandably unconcerned that materialist approaches to literary study had begun to make Frye's post-romantic style of thought rather unfashionable in academic circles, making his final two Stratford lectures appear, at least to professional Shakespeareans, as ostensibly dated at the time of their delivery. Throughout the '80s and '90s, Frye's supposed irrelevance to contemporary critical theory was repeatedly proclaimed, and it was commonly said that his theoretical edifice stood in ruins.[12] Despite these rumours of death, however, he still remains one of the most cited and debated figures in humanities research, as his theories of genre continue to influence a wide range of scholarly fields in which narrative plays a role.[13] Moreover, his many studies of recurring plot patterns in Western literature provide significant purchase for understanding contemporary television and film writing.[14] Little wonder, then, that the basic dialectic of holy and deadly theatre in *Slings & Arrows* presents an ironized version of narrative romance as Frye defines it in *Anatomy of Criticism* (1957). Like *The Tempest*, *Slings & Arrows* complicates the basic pattern of romance as Frye first presented it while still recognizably reworking its basic conventions. The result is a satirically inflected and morally ambiguated mode of romance understood in Frye's general terms, with Tennant holding out the potential of the hero and the avatars of deadly theatre such as Darren Nichols those of the villain. According to Frye, the

> central form of romance is dialectical: everything is focussed on a conflict between the hero and his enemy, and all the reader's values

are bound up with the hero. Hence the hero of romance is analogous to the mythical Messiah or deliverer who comes from an upper world, and his enemy is analogous to the demonic powers of a lower world. The conflict however takes place in, or at any rate primarily concerns, *our* world, which is in the middle, and which is characterized by the cyclical movement of nature. Hence the opposite poles of the cycles of nature are assimilated to the opposition of the hero and his enemy. The enemy is associated with winter, darkness, confusion, sterility, moribund life and old age, and the hero with spring, dawn, order, fertility, vigor, and youth.[15]

On one hand, the clearly delineated polarities of romance fit neatly into established patterns of televisual coding, which often follow such conventionalized dichotomies.[16] On the other hand, the show morally and dramatically complicates its characters by mixing these conventions at key moments, sometimes demonizing its heroes, sometimes humanizing its villains. Such ambiguity is increasingly true as the series develops, with season 1 operating in the most clearly polarized manner and season 3 the most ambiguated. Yet such complications have their limits, especially with characters who are endowed with allegorically inflected names, such as the desacralizing figures of Reg Mortimer and Holly Day. It is precisely these allegorical inflections that generate the show's loose morality play structure in which characters vie over the soul of New Burbage. The result is a narrative pattern that makes good on Frye's claim that in every play Shakespeare wrote "the central character is the theater itself" (*NFWS*, 409).

Among other things, the show's narrative structure reminds us that Shakespeare's plays are often complexly rooted in the morality tradition, especially in the comedies and romances in which one or more characters undergo a journey that closely resembles that of the morality hero. Figures such as Pericles and Leontes undergo transformations of a more or less miraculous nature through a complex and anguishing process of self-discovery.[17] Even *King Lear* has romance-like distinctions between moral and immoral characters as Lear and Gloucester undergo terrifying spiritual journeys due to the actions of their villainous children. The romance form of such journeys helps explain why popular retellings of Shakespeare's plays often follow such quasi-morality patterns, as the putting on of a Shakespeare play is routinely figured in mainstream culture as having redemptive power. Viewed this way, the popular practice of depicting

Shakespeare's plays as having regenerative authority is not primarily a consequence of method acting or emotional realism. On the contrary, it constitutes a popularized reworking of morality themes that are operative within the plays themselves, however ambiguated they may often be. In turn, the ongoing presence of the morality pattern in Shakespeare's plays make it possible for directors such as Hirsch to approach the plays as a form of spiritual discipline in which unpredictable forms of personal transformation may take place. For this to happen, though, a director must presumably allow his or her vision of the play to emerge organically from rehearsal, as Tennant does in each season. By giving way to such a relatively open-ended process, Tennant undergoes a journey similar to Prospero in one key respect: in directing plays at New Burbage, and in partly overseeing the actors of the festival, Tennant is transformed by the very aesthetic forces he puts into motion. Like Prospero and Oberon, Tennant stands at the centre of the dialectic of poesis, making and being remade by the creatively destructive forces he unleashes.

In the course of the series as a whole, Tennant undergoes a journey from near-despair to a renewed joy in the beauty of theatre for its own sake. Despite this regenerative movement, however, he is not, in the end, able to save New Burbage from aesthetic and spiritual corrosion. *Slings & Arrows* thus infuses a strong degree of skeptical irony into romance and morality conventions as they play out in the world of contemporary classical theatre. One might even discern a distinctly Canadian fatalism in the show's ending,[18] as though it concludes by conveying Hirsch's melancholic "feeling that we are at the tail-end of a civilization" (*AFS*, 183). From this perspective, *Slings & Arrows* leaves open the distinct possibility that the promise of holy theatre remains too fragile, or simply too notional, to be sustained for any degree of time within the institutional circumstances of festival theatre in a commodified age. In which case, the heroes are always on the verge of being not so much vigorously renewing as anachronistically delusional, while the villains are not so much sterile and moribund as either pusillanimous or mercenary.

By acknowledging but never fully succumbing to such cultural corrosion, *Slings & Arrows* may ultimately appear less like romance in Frye's archetypal sense of the term and more like a historically belated form of bourgeois romance that Fredric Jameson identifies in *The Political Unconscious* (1981). Translating Frye's genre theory into a neo-Marxist register, Jameson follows a Weberian view of modernity as the increasing secularization and instrumentalization of a market-driven culture to argue that medieval and renaissance modes of romance undergo a radical change in the "great period of bourgeois hegemony."[19] In the wake of the atomizing and alienating effects of capitalism, he argues, romance loses its original exigency and social authority. As a result, it becomes more a reflection of bourgeois complacency than convincingly collective or creative energy. So where

> Shakespearean romance ... opposes the phantasmagoria of "imagination" to the bustling commercial activity at work all around it ... the great art-romances of the early nineteenth century take their variously reactive stances against the new and unglamorous social institutions emerging from the political triumph of the bourgeoisie and the setting in place of the market system.[20]

This apparent rupture in the genre is discernible, Jameson claims, in the way that romance substitutes a new set of purpose-endowing sources of value for the old patterns of magic and enchantment. In lieu of magic, bourgeois romance infuses theological, psychological, and theatrical forces into the narrative mix (134). Jameson even identifies allusions to Bottom's dream as one favourite example of how this repurposed form of romance works in the nineteenth century (134). Through this substitution, Jameson concludes, bourgeois romance allows itself the delusion that the forms of epiphany characteristic of traditional romance can continue "in the secularized and reified world of modern capitalism" (135). In making this case, Jameson maintains that Marxism is not an ideological expression of romance as a pre-generic myth (as Frye claimed), but the means for explaining the otherwise inexplicable persistence of romance at a time when all idealist illusions have been exposed by the material conditions of advancing capitalism. Such a debunking of bourgeois romance thus provides one possible genealogy for, and neatly prepackaged interpretation of, *Slings & Arrows*. From Jameson's perspective, the show stands within a longer line of distinctively bourgeois reaction formations against the dehumanizing powers of the market.

While such a demystification of modern romances needs to be taken very seriously, Jameson's literary sociology has not aged particularly well. First, it is an overstatement to suggest that nineteenth-century romance substituted an entirely new conception of theatre for an older traditional thematics of magic. After all, the romances Jameson discusses continue to celebrate the enchantments of theatre and poetic faith already present in *Dream*, suggesting that Shakespeare's romances are already more modern than such a distinction permits. In this sense, Jameson finds wholesale rupture where a more complicated pattern of narrative adaptation seems to have taken place. Second, and more significantly, Jameson's general conception of secularization has been superseded in recent years. Ex-Marxist Alasdair MacIntyre did a much better job of anticipating post-millennial sociology back in 1968 when he rebutted Engels's predictions about secularization by noting that the phenomenon

> has not resulted ... in the working classes – or indeed any other social group as a group – acquiring a new and more rational set of beliefs about the nature of man and the world. Rather, men have been deprived of any over-all view and to this extent have been deprived of one possible source of understanding and of action.[21]

For MacIntyre, the inability of modern Western society to wholly discard Christian morality is a function of its incapacity to provide any post-Christian means of rendering social experience properly intelligible in moral and ethical terms.[22] In his account, modern moral discourse is riven with internal contradictions as traditional idioms and frames of reference continue to provide tacit conceptual and ethical support despite having been officially abandoned. The result is an increasing awareness of the need for what metanarratives and metaphysics originally supplied. Such insights about the inescapability of metanarratives and metaphysics to moral practice and virtue theory find their fullest articulation in Charles Taylor's *A Secular Age* (2007) and *The Sources of the Self* (1989), both of which refute Jameson's thesis that history is inexorably moving in a secularizing direction and that spiritual impulses and non-materialist modes of analysis are thus legible as so many forms of false consciousness.

In this light, the mode of romance operative in *Slings & Arrows* does not appear to be radically discontinuous with *The Tempest* and *A Midsummer Night's Dream* – one more nostalgic attempt to recover a past that was never really present as such. Instead, it is a story that moves over questions of ethical, aesthetic, and spiritual meaning in a manner that is creatively, if somewhat formulaically, continuous with its Shakespearean sources, especially as they define the terms of poetic faith within which dramatic aesthetics are still best understood.[23]

The Stage Is All the World   97

From this perspective, *Slings & Arrows* does not inadvertently register
a radical rupture between Shakespearean and bourgeois romance.
Instead, it self-consciously navigates the question of historical continuity in the Shakespearean tradition across romantic, modern, and
postmodern modes, revisiting the same modes of aesthetic enchantment and poetic faith explored in the late romances in the context of
new electronic media.

Aware of the immense challenges involved in this temporal and
intermedial translation, the show's final season poses something of a
conflict between theatre and television as forms. As Laurie E. Osborne
observes, season 3 opens with a phalanx of onstage television screens
blasting commercialized endorsements about the successes of New
Burbage, thereby signalling the mutually implicating threat that TV
and neo-liberal economics pose to the festival's artistic integrity.[24] The
point is cinched in the season's opening shot by a roving camera that
moves over the audience much more quickly than anything we've
seen thus far. So instead of being made to feel part of a diverse yet unified audience, as we are during scenes of holy theatre, we now hover
over the theatre's spectators with the dominance and power of tech-
nologically enhanced speed. In staging these intermedial challenges,
the series asks whether Shakespearean drama can survive as drama in
the digital age, or whether it will inevitably give way to the sort of Dis-
neyfication dreamed of by the Holly Days of the world. In responding to these questions, the show develops the post-romantic views of
Peter Brook, John Hirsch, and perhaps most notably, Northrop Frye.

So how, then, does the series stand with respect to Frye's broadly
archetypal view of Shakespearean romance? Is Frye's generic approach
to Shakespeare not even more outdated than the cultural materialism
that replaced it in the '80s and '90s? And so is the show's endorsement
of his approach not a clear sign of its aesthetically and socially retrograde qualities? To address these questions, we need to take a fresh
look at Frye's career-long engagement with *The Tempest*, particularly
as it culminates in his 1985 Stratford lecture, "The Stage Is All the
World," and his 1991 study of the Bible's influence on Western literature *Words with Power*. By examining how *The Tempest* functions as a
leitmotif throughout the whole of Frye's works, we can gain a much
fuller sense of what is at stake in Coyne's claim that in *Slings &
Arrows*, as in *Kingfisher Days*, "It's the moment of transformation from
life into art that fascinates me. It's that tension that we are looking at
for sure" (*s&a*, 3.2). After all, at the most fundamental theoretical

level, what is at stake in this tension between the transformation from life into art is the dialectic between created and revealed meaning that must be at play in storytelling if human culture is capable of forms of repetition that are adaptive, creative, or liberating. Viewed this way, the following passage from Frye's *The Secular Scripture* hits on what it is precisely that drives Coyne's writing, helping to account for the power of fascination inherent in it:

> if there is no sense that the mythological universe is a human creation, man can never get free of servile anxieties and superstitions, never surpass himself, in Nietzsche's phrase. But if there is no sense that it is also something uncreated, something coming from elsewhere, man remains a Narcissus staring at his own reflection, equally unable to surpass himself. Somehow or other, the created scripture and the revealed scripture, or whatever we call the latter, have to keep fighting each other like Jacob and the angel, and it is through the maintaining of this struggle, the suspension of belief between the spiritually real and the humanly imaginative, that our own mental evolution grows. (60–1)

What Robin Phillips's term *Shakespirituality* designates is faith that this play of created and revealed meanings still operate in Shakespeare's works fully enough for his plays to function as a context for life. Consequently, to understand Coyne's ambitions as a writer is to understand her own approach to the tensions between created and revealed meanings, not least in terms of how they are given paradigmatic expression in *The Tempest*.

FRYE ON *THE TEMPEST*

In the 1960s and '70s, Frye stood near the centre of a general, if increasingly contested, interpretive consensus in which *The Tempest* was understood as a romance concluding in forgiveness and reconciliation. Looking back on his contribution to this consensus after it had given way to more skeptical readings of the play's colonial and dynastic politics two decades later, Frye summarized his long-standing interest in the play. Writing in an essay called "Auguries of Experience" (1991), Frye claimed that he knew of "no other work of literature that illustrates more clearly the interchange of illusion and reality which is what literature is all about" (7). Such an approach shows Frye

The Stage Is All the World 99

stressing *The Tempest*'s meta-dramatic elements, the way it comments on how theatre not only reflects social reality but can serve as context for it. In drama, Frye explains,

> the illusion on the stage is the reality, and *The Tempest* is a play about the creation of a play through Prospero's magic, where illusion becomes the raw material for a new creation, while the old objective reality turns into illusion in its turn and disappears, leaving not a rack behind. (7)

However overstated this formulation may be as a description of the ending of *The Tempest*, the specific interpretation here could not be more central to Frye's general project. After all, this interchange between fictional hypothesis and given reality constitutes his understanding of how human beings are capable of recreative forms of repetition rather endless repetitions of the same, meaninglessly random variations on existing conventions, or repetition as a means of self-aggrandizement. What is thus at stake in the ending of *The Tempest* for Frye is not the transmission of one dynastic power to another and certainly not the right of one people to colonize another, though both dynastic and imperial power are operative within the play to varying degrees. On the contrary, what is at stake is how through the work of the imagination the vindicative logic of *realpolitik* that routinely passes for common sense can be outwitted by a gracious disposition of reconciliation that, in the long run, better serves the ends of human liberty. As he writes in the introduction to his Pelican edition of the play (1959, repr.1969):

> Dramatists from Euripides to Pirandello have been fascinated by the paradox of reality and illusion in drama: the play is an illusion like the dream, and yet a focus of reality more intense than life affords. The action of *The Tempest* moves from sea to land, from chaos to new creation, from reality to realization. What seems at first illusory, the magic and music, becomes real, and the *Realpolitik* of Antonio and Sebastian becomes illusion. In this island the quality of one's dreaming is an index of character. When Antonio and Sebastian remain awake, they show that they are the real dreamers, sunk in the hallucinations of greed. (NFWS, 48–9)

On this account, what emerges at the end of *The Tempest* is the sort of disposition Kierkegaard identifies in *Works of Love*. According to

Kierkegaard, while "love believes everything and yet is never to be deceived," cynicism mistrusts everything and is nevertheless thoroughly duped.[25] For what the cynic overlooks is that the ultimate horizon of truth does not emerge once all our illusions are dispelled. Beyond the bitter lucidity of skepticism stand dimensions of faith and hope that are only revealed through the illusions of good faith, through the ostensibly mad belief that "love's best habit is in seeming trust," meaning that love becomes a shared reality when grace is bequeathed even when unmerited.[26] On this basis, Kierkegaard asks: "Which is more difficult, to awaken one who sleeps" (like Gonzalo), "or to awaken one who, awake, dreams that he is awake" (like Antonio)?[27] The many ambiguities of *The Tempest* notwithstanding, Frye never ceased seeing it as Shakespeare's most highly distilled form of holy theatre and thus his major work of love.

What most distinguishes Frye's reading of *The Tempest*'s comic conclusion is his insistence that it constitutes a distilled expression of the structural logic inherent to dramatic romance as a narrative form. From this self-consciously transhistorical perspective, the play ends with a transfer of authority from Prospero as onstage playwright to the reconciling action of the play itself, a transfer symbolized by Ariel, who brings Prospero to the realization that "The rarer action is / In virtue than in vengeance" (5.1.27–8). In turn, this reversal of authority crystallizes the movement towards a regenerated community that Frye sees as inherent to romance as a structural form. Through this reversal, Frye suggests, we witness a staging of the commonly experienced but poorly understood dimension of literary composition in which elements within the story take on their own agency, thereby talking back to the author. On this account, *The Tempest* doesn't just dramatize Prospero's renunciation of magic; instead, it also shows Shakespeare renouncing his own personality to such a degree that he allows the form itself to speak through him, disappearing into the "abysmal objectivity of his characters and situations," as Henry James observed.[28] Revealingly, though, Frye insists that this is primarily an artistic achievement and only secondarily a moral one. In his view, Shakespeare's emphasis on reconciliation in the romances "is a technical emphasis rather than an oozing through of personal benevolence" (*NFWS*, 196), a counterintuitive claim that rests on Frye's belief in the impersonal agency of literary conventions. In accomplishing this effacement of the author, the ending of *The Tempest* not only collapses distinctions between actors and spectators, stage and world, but

The Stage Is All the World

also playwright and play, taking us, Frye declares, beyond drama to a space where "reality is what the word itself creates, and after creating, sees to be good."[29] Seen in the context of the play as a whole, then, Prospero's resigned declaration that "We are such stuff as dreams are made on" need not confirm the pessimistic view that we live only to be the stuff of other people's self-aggrandizing stories, nor that the creative forces humans unleash are necessarily disarticulated from larger structures of reality.[30] Despite the flaws and compromises to which Prospero is subjected, the play, for Frye, nevertheless affirms that his interventions have disclosed an imaginative power that is the basis on which greater human liberty and creativity can be realized.

Given this meta-dramatic account of the play, *The Tempest* depicts a social form of what Hegel calls "self-exteriorization," the way that human societies find ways of acting on themselves through some kind of external agency, traditionally identified, as King Alonso repeatedly insists on doing at the end of the play, with some kind of supernatural power or divinity.[31] Indeed, orthodox Christian readings of *The Tempest* effectively endorse Alonso's perspective of the action when they insist on identifying the exterior power acting through Prospero with divine providence. Yet Prospero explicitly rejects this supernatural reading of the play's action when he insists that Alonso not infest his mind "with beating on / The strangeness of this business" (5.1.246–7). "At pick'd leisure," Prospero says, he will reveal the secrets of his tricks (perhaps further revealing that he is not the shrewdest of political minds) (5.1.247). Rejecting this orthodox, Alonso-centred, reading, Frye is adamant that *The Tempest* is "not a religious play" because it "keeps entirely within the order of nature: there are no gods or oracles" (*NFWS*, 340). Instead, Frye centres his reading of the play's conclusion on Gonzalo's summary of the action, where the faithful servant says, in a moment ostensibly free of his previous obtuseness, "O, rejoice / Beyond a common joy, / ... in one voyage ... Did ... Prospero [find] his dukedom ... and all of us ourselves, / When no man was his own" (5.1.206–12). Frye implicitly takes Gonzalo's summary of the action to be authoritative when, in his Pelican edition of the play, he concludes that "Each character in *The Tempest*, at the beginning of the play, is lost in a private drama of his own. This is true even of Prospero ... Through the action of the play, a communal dramatic sense gradually consolidates, in which all the characters identify themselves within the same drama, a drama which the audience is finally invited to enter" (*NFWS*, 342). Clearly, then, the deepening of meta-dramatic awareness that Frye describes at work in *The Tempest* should not be confused with orthodox Christian interpretations of the play.

From a strict Christian perspective, Prospero's moral transformations are an expression of his "grace-bestowed human characteristic," a formulation in which a strictly theological view of *grace* explains the exteriorizing force requisite to self-transcendence.[32] In Frye's heterodox view, however, the dramatic space of the play-within-the-play is sufficiently self-exteriorizing to initiate the vision requisite to a genuinely recreative act of repetition. So where orthodox Christian readers identify God as the force of moral transformation in the play, the Blakean Frye identifies the imagination, or more precisely the collectively shared space of theatrical illusion. On this score, the ostensible resurrections that occur at the end of the play, as Alonso rediscovers Ferdinand and Ferdinand Alonso, "are those of a natural, and therefore also a moral and intellectual, renewal of life" (*NFWS*, 47). Insisting that the play is not a "religious drama," Frye stresses how highly significant it is that the vision of a "brave new world" that momentarily opens at the ending of the play is "attained only through some kind of theatrical illusion" (*NFWS*, 340). Crucial here is the principle that Prospero is morally transformed by the creative energies he puts into circulation, even to the point where they momentarily overrule his potential desire for vengeance and mastery. Rather than being the absolute master of the play-within-the-play, Prospero becomes subject to the agency of his own creative actions. Hence his carefully ritualized renunciations of revenge and magic.

To understand how Frye's reading of *The Tempest* dovetails with Coyne's preoccupations as a writer is to understand the specific sense in which he thought it a highly peculiar type of mystery play, a strange rite of theatrical initiation. For Frye, *The Tempest* is a work in which "the restructuring of the lives of the characters ... is ... a deeply serious operation, with an application in it for ourselves" (*NFWS*, 338). In viewing a performance, he continues, "We have not merely been watching a fairy tale, we feel, but participating in some kind of mystery" (*NFWS*, 338), one in which "there is no longer tragedy or comedy, but an action passing through tragic and comic moods to a conclusion of serenity and peace" (334). Coyne's mentor John Hirsch adopts this reading in his 1982 production of the play when he interprets Prospero's concluding remark that "every third thought shall be my grave" (5.1.312) in the context of the play's theme of freedom rather than in terms of power politics or disillusioned resignation. By interpreting these lines as the culmination of a journey into spiritual maturity through a confrontation with mortality, Hirsch sees Prospero anticipating "his own ultimate freedom."[33] From this now relatively unfashionable standpoint, Prospero's allusion to his grave is not primarily angst-ridden. Instead, it's a terse variation on the sentiment expressed in the Latin psalm or anthem, "In Pace," sung at compline or vespers in both Catholic and Anglican traditions: "In peace and into the same I shall sleep and rest. If I give slumber to my eyes drowsiness to my eyelids, I shall sleep and rest."[34] Needless to say, this view of Prospero as having undergone a kind of *ars moriendi* is light years away from the more skeptical view that his forgiveness of his unrepentant brother Antonio is a vindicative move to set Antonio up for moral failure and thereby legitimate his own power. In which case, Prospero's lines about mortality sound glumly resigned rather than maturely poignant, a confirmation that his ending is, as he momentarily appears to say, much closer to despair and disillusionment than joy in authentic freedom.[35] But this interpretation also differs from the orthodox Christian view that God is the direct and supernatural source of moral transformation in the play.

Both the speculative audaciousness and the spiritual exigency of Frye's interpretation of *The Tempest* come into full relief in a striking passage from *A Natural Perspective*. Frye sees the play as rehearsing the supposed origins of theatre in the renunciation of sympathetic magic, the desire to act on the natural environment by means of verbal and ritual actions. After identifying these origins, Frye immediately qualifies the point, explaining the general difference that fictional storytelling makes in society:

> However, drama, gets back the magic it renounces in another way. Once it becomes a part of literature it enters into the function of literature: This is to use words, not to operate on the nonhuman world, but to assimilate it imaginatively to the human world, which it does mainly in the two archaic forms of identity and analogy.[36]

So if drama is born of the renunciation of sympathetic magic, Frye concludes, then *The Tempest* remembers its inheritance to creatively renew it. In this sense, *The Tempest* is about nothing less than the origins and possible futures of theatre as a space in which the recreation of culture might be envisioned in imaginative form. Such an interpretation sees in Shakespeare's final romance an allegory of both theatre's ritualistic and recreative elements, a variation, in effect, on what Brook calls holy theatre.

If Frye's reading of *The Tempest* as reconnecting with the ritual sources of theatre tells us more about his theory of the imagination than it does about Shakespeare's response to Renaissance power politics, it has nevertheless proven enormously influential in both academic and theatrical circles, suggesting that its appeal may have less to do with its apparent "blandness" than it does with the enormous intensity underwriting Frye's brand of visionary criticism. Here too it is Hirsch's 1982 production that most fully realizes the theatrical potential of Frye's reading, as the playbill for the production offers a simplified version of his vision of the play, noting that "Every great work of verbal art celebrates an ancient ritual. *The Tempest* is the supreme variation of this ancient ritual – man's journey toward self-knowledge" (*SFSP*, 1982).

Needless to say, many materialist interpretations of *The Tempest* reject Frye's optimistic reading of the play's aesthetic and ethical vision out of hand. After all, since Antonio does not undergo a genuine repentance at the end, the world of *realpolitik* (to say nothing of imperialism) continues to impinge on the questionable authority of Prospero's rough magic. At which point, we might conclude that the late romances are more about the failure of art to transform the political realm than their capacity to do so.[37] One critic who saw the play very differently than Frye was the influential Polish writer Jan Kott, who also had an important impact on both Brook and Hirsch at specific moments in their careers. Not mincing words, Kott sees *The Tempest* as "the most bitter of Shakespeare's plays," an aggrieved expression of the "lost hopes of the Renaissance."[38] On this account, *The Tempest* presents a vision in which theatre is not only a bare "repetition of the real world, [but] the entire world is an image and a duplication of *Theatrum Mundi*," or the world is a vain stage play.[39] From this grandly nihilistic perspective, Prospero's "great globe" is a theatre "in which everything is repeated but nothing is purified," making the play a strikingly pure expression of the social impotence of drama, a lament for "the very end of Elizabethan tragedy."[40] We might very well conclude from these two readings of *The Tempest* that Kott and Frye each give us one half of a moving dialectic, two extremes of a more subtle and complexly dynamic whole. After all, Kott sees the play as exposing how Shakespearean drama mirrors the world without interpene-

The Stage Is All the World

trating it enough to make any meaningful difference. While for Frye, *The Tempest* interpenetrates and transforms the world in a manner that seems too credulously idealistic. As we have seen, these are precisely the dialectical energies animating *Slings & Arrows*, one key source of which is *The Tempest*.

At the end of his career, however, Frye modified this overall view of *The Tempest*, somewhat eschewing the Johannine formulation used in "Romance as a Masque" and adopting instead the revolutionary terms of Saint Paul. In this later formulation from *Words with Power*, he simply notes that at the end of the play, "for an instant there has been an epiphany, when how things should be has appeared in the middle of how things are" (86). What emerges here is not a triumphalist apocalyptic vision so much as a fragile yet sublime hope in human solidarity and liberty, a momentary glimpse of transcendence through the interchange of illusion and reality that forms the basis for moral action. Like Frye, Coyne is primarily interested in exactly this interchange of art and reality, taking into account, in various ways, the ethical, imaginative, and political dangers inherent in the dialectics of poesis. No less importantly, her writing also seeks to take simultaneous account of the ritualistic and recreative aspects of theatre and the theatrical imagination more broadly.[41]

Importantly, the metaleptic reversal of illusion and reality that Frye sees as pivotal in *The Tempest* involves two contrasting uses of art as a form of magic: an escapist form associated with Prospero's esoteric studies in Milan and a more dialectical form associated with the play-within-the-play. In Milan, Prospero's fascination with magic isolated him from the world as he became "transported And rapt in secret studies ... thus neglecting worldly ends" (1.2.76–7, 89). Preoccupied with magic for magic's sake, the pre-play Prospero indulges in self-absorbed fantasizing.[42] On the island, however, Prospero's illusions are now directly aimed at widening the moral horizons of the royal party. In the process, however, his magical art metaleptically transforms even him as he discovers an ethic of forgiveness and reconciliation rather than revenge, particularly through the agency of Ariel's alienating techniques. The overall effect, in Frye's formulation, "is of an audience being taken inside a play, so that they not only watch the play but, so to speak, see it being put on" (*NFWS*, 337). What *The Tempest* presents, then, is a kind of Pygmalion effect in which the audience both onstage and offstage find themselves initiated into a vision of the world in which the egotistical impulse for control and domination eventually gives way to a shared vision of reconciliation.

If such a view of the play strikes some as blandly sentimental, it's important to bear in mind that excessively skeptical reactions to the play run the risk of reproducing Antonio's world view, thereby occluding the play's broader, if ambiguated, moral vision. At the same time, however, it simultaneously contains Gonzalo's well-meaning but somewhat self-refuting utopian fantasizing, thus modifying the more optimistic strains that are otherwise discernible in the play's denouement. Viewed this way, it would appear that the play somehow manages to contain both Kottian pessimism and Frygean idealism simultaneously. Such capaciousness helps explain Frye's career-long attempt to obtain a perspective on the play that the play itself doesn't already both contain and refute. Thus if it's true to say that there has long been two strains of dissenting interpretation of *The Tempest* – an authentically utopian tradition beginning with Percy Bysshe Shelley and a blandly idealist tradition beginning in the Victorian period – Frye may justifiably be said to oscillate between both, ultimately landing, in *Words with Power*, on a Shelleyan view that is at once sober yet visionary.[43] Coyne's ambition as a writer can be understood as an attempt to negotiate these oscillating tensions, avoiding Victorian sentimentality but without wholly disavowing the enchantments of poetic faith or even second naïveté.

FRYE AT STRATFORD

To understand how Frye's lifelong approach to *The Tempest* animates Coyne's work, it's helpful to bear in mind that his reading of the play's meta-dramatic elements occur within the context of a notion of mimesis that comes from Aristotle through post-romantic aesthetics. This means that for Frye, the criterion of literary mimesis is the "conceivable, not the real, and it expresses the hypothetical or assumed, not the actual" (*wwp*, 22). From this perspective, literary mimesis does not simply reflect pre-given realities, but opens channels for interpenetrating and transforming what is already given. One of Frye's most highly distilled explorations of this life-art dialectic that he associates with *The Tempest* occurs in his 1985 Stratford lecture "The Stage Is All the World," the same year Coyne played Laura in John Hirsch's production of *The Glass Menagerie* and two years before she joined Robin Phillips's Young Company (1987–88). In his talk, Frye notes how the

The Stage Is All the World

creation of verbal fictions often gives rise to a reversal of agency from creator to created. In producing a work of verbal art, he observes, writers and actors often feel that fictional characters begin to take on a life of their own, thereby exercising the sort of willfulness explored in a play such as Pirandello's *Six Characters in Search of an Author* (1921). According to Frye, the sense of objectivity that attaches to fictional characters confirms nothing less than a particular understanding of human personality and a particular conception of literary mimesis, both of which find paradigmatic expression in *The Tempest*.

In Frye's view, the feeling that a character is coming to life within one's mind suggests that our personalities arise from the limits of our persona, from the limited repertoire or "masks" that we bring to different social situations, as is apparently the case with lifelike persons such as Hamlet, Falstaff, and Rosalind. This theory of personality goes all the way back to *Fearful Symmetry*, in which Frye notes that "The imagination in Blake *is* the personality, the Selfhood routine that we usually think of as the personal life of the artist being to him purely generic" (321). This idea of personality as a set of congealed habits limited by the horizon of the imagination as the self's coordinating principle contrasts with the idea that it arises from an underlying essence, as in Jonson's comedy of humours. The key difference lies in the degree of freedom and unpredictability that attaches to each kind of character in any given situation. If personality is an expression of habituated patterns, the likelihood of predictable action combines with an unpredictable sense of spontaneity, whereas if personality is an expression of underlying essence, a character is more likely to be predictable and is thus less likely to "talk back" in surprising ways to a writer in the process of composition or to an actor during rehearsal. In her metafictional narrative about Dicken's composing of *A Christmas Carol* (1843), Coyne's *The Man Who Invented Christmas* (2017) shows Dickens moving from a fixed to a more Shakespearean notion of character as he revises his story through a series of imagined encounters with his own creations. In the process, Coyne's Dickens discovers the dialectics of literary world-making or *poesis* that Frye sees crystallized in Shakespeare's mode of characterization. As Frye explains,

> To a professional dramatist, the axiom that the world's a stage suggests the way he works. I said that there is no solid essence or identity behind the various dramatic roles we assume in life. If there were, the dramatist's creations would be what Theseus, in *A*

Midsummer Night's Dream, thinks they are: shadows, purely subjective entities dreamed up out of nothing. But in practice the dramatist finds a fully inhabited world of impulses, moods, even things like personalities, inside his mind, and sees an objective social world outside him with counterparts of these things. Whenever we start to create, the creation hooks on to something objective and autonomous, something with a life and character of its own, so that we never know when we are creating something and when we have invoked or summoned something that is starting to recreate us. The drama is the most obvious form of the objectivity of creation in words, because there the fictional figures are taking the form of actual people on a stage. (*MM*, 201)

Here we see Frye directly articulating the self-exteriorization that he sees as definitive of fictional storytelling as an engagement with both created and revealed meanings. Properly understood, this process involves writers, actors, and readers in a process that is neither neutrally objective nor purely solipsistic but participatory and dialectical, one in which meaning, structure, and purpose are discovered as much as they are invented.

By identifying Shakespeare as the one writer who most fully achieved what we might call a "personhood effect" vis-à-vis character, Frye rediscovers a point William Hazlitt made in his 1818 essay "On Shakespeare and Milton." According to Hazlitt, "In Chaucer we perceive a fixed essence of character. In Shakespeare there is a continual composition and decomposition of its elements, a fermentation of every particle in the whole mass, by its alternate affinity or antipathy to other principles which are brought in contact with it."[44] Crucially, this sense that characters are irreducible to their stories comes very close to violating the Aristotelian principle that ethos (or character) is an effect of mythos (or narrative). Often taking this principle to the breaking point, Shakespeare gives us characters such as Hamlet who appear to be logically prior to the stories in which they find themselves. Hence his unsolvable mystery. One of the ways Shakespeare's legacy is felt today lies in the widespread assumption among screenwriters that character is logically prior to story, an axiom stressed in writing manuals in the field but which is alien to many narratological theories, including, to some extent, Frye's own.[45] Indeed, Frye runs the risk of contradiction when he insists that Shakespeare's plays can be analyzed according to the Aristotelian principle that narrative is logically prior to character (*NFWS*, 152–3). After all, his view that Shakespeare most clearly expresses the realization that personality is a set of performances rather than a set of essences would seem to put significant pressure on Aristotelian narratology, thus calling into question his sharp distinction between Chekov's character-centred and Shakespeare's plot-centred approach to drama (*NFWS*, 137).

To be sure, though, the theory of personality animating Frye's account of Shakespearean dramaturgy coincides with the dynamics of self-exteriorization that he sees as inherent to the very act of telling an old story in a compellingly new way. Importantly, then, the romantic origins of Frye's theory of personality indicate that he does not radically question the notion that the imagination is the coordinating principle organizing the experience of the self over time (*NFWE*, 48). However determined the ego may be by the operations of discipline and power, the self nevertheless exercises varying degrees of freedom according to the force of its own imagination and rationality, both of which, of course, come to it through culture and language. Without assuming such a transcendental principle, it is very difficult to account for the modes of self-exteriorization characteristic of human culture, especially literature. For all its political and psychological realism, *The Tempest*, according to Frye, is principally about how this dynamic of self-exteriorization expands the range of human possibility through collective illusion.

Frye's conception of Shakespearean character is concomitant with nothing less than a particular understanding of literary mimesis and an accompanying view of the powers of imagination as such. For him, literary mimesis is as an imitation not of social reality per se but of the mediating nature of thought as it operates when reference to the external world is momentarily suspended. He calls this self-referential mode of aesthetic language *centripetal* as opposed to the *centrifugal* direction of externally descriptive modes of reference. Similar to Ricoeur's distinction between fictional and non-fictional linguistic modes, these two forms of verbal communication dialectically mediate private and public realms, creating the social space in which self and other become legible to one another as characters in a contested narrative rather than expressions of a fixed and unchanging essence. Moreover, the distance Frye identifies between the centripetal direction of literary mimesis vis-à-vis social reality accounts for its capacity to resist as well as endorse social conventions.[46] In short, we rely on the world-generating dynamics of narrative to create a sense of coherence and continuity across time in what we call our "real lives."[47] Hence Frye's reversal of the adage "the world is a stage." In reversing the adage, Frye signals Shakespeare's stress on the way social life depends on narrative forms of representation for its intelligibility, but without such modes of representation necessarily constituting or fully mediating the givens of the world. Hence the possibility that imaginative illusion can interpenetrate and thereby transform social reality. Though in the case of Shakespeare, especially his comedies, this process is often indirect. For Frye, a Shakespearean comedy often "does not hold a mirror up to nature, but it frequently holds a mirror up to another mirror, and brings its resolution out of a double illusion" (*NFWS*, 196). In other words, we only know social reality through the projection of fictions that form the context by which shared realities are both revealed and generated. This is Frye's variation on Brook's distinction between living and deadening illusions, a position that looks in many respects "postmodern" but which should not be confused with more fully self-referential theories of metanarrative that presuppose that there is no such thing as revealed as opposed to created meanings.

On Frye's account, then, Shakespearean drama does not reduce to something called "the metaphysics of classical theatre." According to post-structural thinkers who describe Western drama in such terms, the theatre is too often a site in which actors and directors are "interpretive slaves who faithfully execute the providential designs of the [author as] 'master.'"[48] Following Frye's account, such a position oversimplifies and thereby misconstrues the dialectics of agency that necessarily arise in Shakespearean modes of characterization and storytelling. As Frye explains, the agency in a Shakespearean play does not emanate from a providential notion of authorship, but from the dialectics of character, plot, and story as such dialectics operate in relation to the shifting contexts of other stories and from the past, present, and future. This hermeneutic principle lies behind his 1964 lecture for the CBC, in which he observes that Shakespeare's

> plays are structures that contain infinite meanings. They can be read and acted and interpreted forever, but no reading or interpretation is ever definitive; at no point can we say that this and this only is what Shakespeare really means. There is no "real meaning" in Shakespeare because there is nothing to be abstracted or pulled out from the total experience of the play. (*NFWS*, 233)

The Stage Is All the World

This does not mean, however, that the plays are void of moral or aesthetic vision. Nor does it mean that contrasting readings cannot be rationally adjudicated with reference to the internal structures of a play or in relation to their relevant social contexts. On the contrary, what Shakespeare's plays present for Frye is nothing less than the possibility of a classless vision of society, a necessary vision for preventing the world from being reduced to a set of pure power struggles on the model of Hobbes's *Leviathan*. According to Frye,

> Shakespeare is detached from his society but not removed from it; he deals with all of it at once, not with a part against another part. That society was a class structure in his day and it appears as such on his stage; but his own point of view, and the one he hands on to us, is classless. There are social and moral differences between Prospero and Caliban, Henry V and Falstaff, Ulysses and Thersites, but each articulates something essential to the situation he is in: we must have both sides of the difference. His is a detachment that is totally involved, an impartiality that brings everything equally to life. (*NFWS*, 234)

In other words, it does not follow from the world-creating dialectics of *poesis* that truth is structured like a fiction, if by fiction we mean something that cannot, in principle, be rationally or morally adjudicated. For Frye, the way to avoid the corrosive force of moral incommensurability is to imaginatively postulate a possible point of synthesis and agreement. So while "disagreement is as essential and as creative as agreement is … Nonetheless the vision of a created order where, in Blake's phrase, 'no dispute can come,' is essential to the total picture" (*MM*, 91–2). For it is only from the standpoint of a metanarrative vision of order in diversity that we can "see ourselves capable of creation as well as destruction, with reason a means to an end of ultimate consensus, however distant" (*MM*, 92). Without projecting a hypothetical metanarrative that is expressive of the fullest possibility of human realization, both life and art risk becoming foreshortened, potentially losing their sense of coherence and purpose. Once diminished in this manner, they run the risk of devolving into, at best, parochialism, at worst, nihilistic relativism. At which point, the realms of art and social life can be easily translated back into a world consisting entirely of commodities and exchange value where pointless signification and material profit fit hand in glove. After all, from such a relativistic perspective hierarchies of value are either disguised power relations or indisputable matters of taste, not revelations of what makes for better and worse forms of art and life. In such a world of pure subjectivity, entertainment easily subsumes and eclipses edification, easily dissolving art into commerce.

As we've seen, such a collapsing of artistic construction into commodified illusion is precisely what characterizes the malaise-induced world of New Burbage, a world that *Slings & Arrows* diagnoses even as it, perhaps all too idealistically, seeks to transcend. Viewed in this light, it becomes clear that the dynamics and challenges of *poesis* in a postmodern age are as much the stuff of Frye's theorizing as they are, *mutatis mutandis*, of Coyne's storytelling. Hence their shared fascination with what *The Tempest* might still mean today. Viewed as a whole, Coyne's body of work appears very much like an offspring of the tradition of visionary Canadian writing that B.W. Powe has identified in his study of Frye and Marshall McLuhan. According to Powe, these two ostensibly antithetical thinkers nevertheless embody a broader visionary tradition that is discernibly Canadian in sensibility even as it aspires towards the generality of the transnational.[49] Like *Kingfisher Days*, *Slings & Arrows* can be understood as participating in something very much like this tradition of visionary Canadian writing, particularly as it descends from Frye's view of literature as the site of an interchange between illusion and reality.

ANTI-REALISM

The metanarrative structure of *Slings & Arrows* rests on an important difference between Frye's reading of *The Tempest* and the forms of self-reflexive narrativity Roland Barthes champions with reference to the French *nouveau roman*. To understand this distinction is to appreciate why the show takes Barthesian metanarrative as a cipher for depoliticized, pseudo-liberatory postmodernism. As viewers will recall, Darren Nichols makes imperious references to Barthes during an exercise for his *Romeo and Juliet* in which he gives a lesson in gender fluidity while nevertheless behaving like a petty patriarch. Describing the play as being composed of signifiers rather than characters, Nichols uses an archly structuralist approach to the play not so much as a way of undoing patriarchal hierarchies (on which he openly avows his own directorial dependence), nor as a way of sensually engaging with the pleasures of the text (as Barthes does in *Le Plaisir du texte*), and cer-

The Stage Is All the World

tainly not as a way of clarifying the narrative trajectory of the story (as Frye does). Instead, Nichols deploys anti-humanist theory as a way of resisting the visceral elements of the drama, as a means of standing aloof from its passion and violence. In context, the parody is not directed at gender theory per se, as the gay actor playing Romeo describes playing Juliet as his lifelong dream, thus indicating the potential legitimacy of gender-reversed casting and the undeniable joys of gender-bending. Instead, the parody is directed at the excesses of anti-realist theory, in which language colonizes social reality in ways that oddly reinforce the very egotism and anomie it is supposed to counter. That the real target of the satire is the failure to dialectically intersect with the play is further conveyed by Nichols's insistence that Romeo and Juliet not look at one another during the balcony scene, a choice based on the assumption that the play is about words rather than people, signs rather than affects. Fairly or not, the show participates in a broader tradition of parodying Barthes, beginning with *Le Roland-Barthes sans peine* (1978) and, more recently, Laurent Binet's *The Seventh Function of Language* (French 2015; English 2017). Among other things, such parodies inevitably target Barthes's somewhat reductive view of mimesis. For Aristotle, mimesis is defined as *eikos* (or natural probability). From this perspective, mimesis refers not to what happens in life but to what is likely to happen given a certain situation, what, in a word, is typical. For Aristotle, probable naturalism is what distinguishes literature from history, giving it its cultural and philosophical authority as a practice. For Barthes, however, mimesis is strictly *doxa* (or opinion/ideology). On the basis of this reduction in meaning, Barthes was led in the opposite direction than Plato in *The Republic*. While Plato rejected mimesis on the grounds that it's socially subversive, Barthes rejects referentiality on the grounds that it is inevitably oppressive.[50] In lieu of mimesis, he sees fully self-reflexive fiction as socially liberating insofar as it openly acknowledges what is ostensibly implicit but systematically repressed in all forms of classic realism. Writing in 1966, Barthes proclaimed that "What goes on in a narrative is, from the referential (real) point of view, strictly *nothing*. What does 'happen' is language per se, the adventure of language, whose advent never ceases to be celebrated."[51] Responding to this theory in *The Order of Mimesis* (1986), Christopher Prendergast notes that the semiological critique of reference obscures the fact that in the very act of identifying a code one necessarily presumes a minimal degree of reference, namely the act of designating the elements of a code as belonging together in a sequence.[52] So to articulate a critique of reference one must inevitably assume it. Prendergast thus concludes that in his critique of mimesis Barthes "mobilises his combined semiological artillery and rhetorical infantry to fight what appears to be an imaginary enemy in a phony war."[53] Such assessments constitute the cultural and intellectual background to the show's parody of Barthesian postmodernism.

Properly understood, the satire in *Slings & Arrows* operates by pitting two forms of metanarrative against one another. On one hand, there is the metanarrative of the series itself, the interweaving of the story of New Burbage with Shakespeare's plays and the actual history of the Stratford Festival. In this form of metanarrative, fiction and reality interpenetrate in a way that is designed to mutually illuminate both, giving rise to some level of widened or intensified awareness. On the other hand, there is the more strictly self-reflexive and anti-mimetic form of metanarrative associated with Darren Nichols's avant-garde production of *Romeo and Juliet* in which the story refers only to its own "galaxy of signifiers" as a way of resisting the oppressiveness of bourgeois life. In the first, more dialectical, mode of metafiction, self-reference is designed to move outwards to the audience beyond the play. Consequently, the artifices of fictional self-reflexivity work in combination with mimesis and realism for the sake of widening hermeneutic horizons. Mixing realism with self-reflexive contrivance, such dialectical modes of metafiction achieve some of the mimetic density of Shakespeare's plays. This is the sort of effect aimed at in Shakespeare-inspired novels such as Iris Murdoch's *The Black Prince* (1973) or Margaret Atwood's *Hag-Seed* (2016). In both metafictional works, stylized artifice and characterological realism work together to create a level of internal complexity and multiple vying perspectives that achieves something like the density of lived experience.

The same dialectical view of meta-drama/metanarrative informs Peter Brook's view of *A Midsummer Night's Dream*. According to Brook, his legendary production of the play was conceived as a celebration of the theatrical imagination, a celebration of "the play-within-the-play-within-the-play-within-the play."[54] For Brook, however, these intersecting mirrors are not purely self-reflexive. On the contrary, they are aimed to harness emotion and thought in order to get the "audience to see more clearly into itself."[55] So where Brook sees celebratory, theatrical reflexivity as a means of collective self-discovery, Barthes conceives of metafiction in more purely formalist terms, as language freed from the illusions of reference. In one case, then, metafiction interpenetrates social reality as a means of enhancing social intelligibility, while in the other case we are told that aesthetic discourse always-already withdraws from it for the sake of liberating release. In this way, one might reasonably suggest that Barthes bears a passing resemblance to Prospero in his Milanese study, while Frye is trying to catch up with him at the end of the play. That, in any event, is the perfectly plausible slant taken in *Slings & Arrows*.

6

The Local and the Typical

As we have begun to see, Susan Coyne's three-tiered description of the overall narrative conception of *Slings & Arrows* implies some fundamental questions about the relationship between art and life, about the way the stories we tell animate our lives even as our lives animate the stories we tell. Along with its mimetic features, however, the show also displays, as I have noted, distinct elements of an ironized modern-day morality play, in which allegorically named avatars of holy and deadly theatre do battle over the soul of New Burbage. Consequently, the pronounced artificiality of the show's allegorical and satirical qualities coexist with an almost *roman à clef* realism vis-à-vis modern classical theatre, especially the Stratford Festival. This combination of real-world reference with televisual contrivance effectively defines how the show's metanarrative structure operates. In combining mimesis and allegory, the show remains deeply rooted in locality while still effectively communicating the triumphs and tribulations of classical theatre to a general audience. On one hand, then, *Slings & Arrows* remains firmly situated in the oftentimes eccentrically insular world of modern classical theatre in late-century Stratford/New Burbage. But on the other hand, the dialectic of conviction and malaise the characters endure in their pursuit of great theatre has effectively communicated with a wide international audience. So while the appeal of *Slings & Arrows* partly derives from its affectionally satirical depiction of what it is like trying to run a professional Shakespeare festival in turn-of-the-millennium Stratford, its broader pathos cannot be properly explained with reference to such local contexts. On the contrary, the show's power of fascination rests in how it expresses the more enduring problem of rediscovering what significance theatre may have in a world driven by economic and egotistical imperatives in a convincing, but not irreducibly local, way. As such, part of the critic's task should be to explain how the show communicates in a way that would allow a Brazilian director to adapt the series mostly shot-for-shot, reaching eighteen million Portuguese speaking viewers in the process. In my view, the show's narrative and cultural appeal owes much to the way it strives to depict theatre as a vocation in the proper sense of the term, but a vocation that is always under threat of becoming nothing more than a peculiarly demanding way of making a living, or, worse yet, an absurd anachronism.

Viewers of the DVD box set are invited, by the inclusion of a 2006 interview with Susan Coyne, to reflect on the tensions between local and global at work in the series. The urgency of the question of how the show successfully communicated with a wide international audience partly arose from the fact that the CBC, which financed the original development of the series, cancelled production of it just days before the deadline for further grant funding.[1] Left in the lurch, the show's producers then had to go in search of alternative production companies, eventually landing with Rhombus Media. Yet when Coyne was asked how the program eventually succeeded in reaching such a wide international audience, she modestly deflects the question. Citing the Irish playwright Brian Friel, Coyne claims that the aim for the show was to tell a story about "the little milieu that we live in. And if people in other parts of the world want to listen in, then that is wonderful" (*S&A*, 3.2). Such modesty, however, is double-edged. It signals the writers' sensitivity to the show's immediate contexts, the world of late-century Canadian classical theatre, especially the Stratford Festival at which Coyne played the lead in *Romeo and Juliet*, Regan in *King Lear*, and Olivia in *Twelfth Night*. Yet such modesty downplays the show's bold narrative conception, the idea that one can tell a story about theatre in twenty-first-century Canada via Shakespeare's plays in a manner that somehow rings true to insiders and outsiders of the theatre world alike.

Coyne's approach to these challenges comes further into relief in the context of one of Frye's major statements on Canadian culture, his 1977 essay "Culture as Interpenetration." Revealingly, the influence of Frye's essay on the Stratford community is clear from Robert Fulford's "The Flowering of Stratford" in the 1984 *Stratford Festival Souvenir Program*, which develops the Stratford thread in Frye's more multipronged essay. A study in cultural maturation, Frye's essay identifies three phases of development in Canadian settler art up to 1977 on the basis of a specific set of general theoretical principles about the social conditions under which art is produced. The result is one of Frye's most fully realized articulations of the tension between the local and the archetypal, one that relies heavily on a particular, and perhaps somewhat surprising, understanding of Shakespeare. At first, Frye explains, colonial artists imitated the traditional styles and conventions of the imperial centres in London and Paris, producing mostly derivative work as a result. In a second, more quasi-modernist phase, artists tried to reject European traditions in the hope of finding something entirely new that would be more appropriate to the different conditions of Canada as a geopolitical entity. But then in a third, more mature phase, artists worked from their local experience while, at the same time, continuing to draw on the resources of European and other traditions in new and surprising ways. In poetry, he identifies Leonard Cohen's *Let Us Compare Mythologies* (1956), Jay Macpherson's *The Boatman* (1957), and Margaret Avison's *Winter Sun* (1960) as examples of this mature phase. Crucially, it is in the context of this third phase of Canadian culture that Frye then also addresses the origins of the Stratford Festival, effectively outlining, in turn, the values and principles animating *Slings & Arrows*. In 1952, Frye wryly explains,

> some people in a small town in Ontario, simply because it was called Stratford, decided to put on some Shakespeare, and a Shakespeare festival began there the next year. The director was Tyrone Guthrie and the leading actors were Alec Guinness and Irene Worth – not precisely what the CRTC would call Canadian content. Those who think in pigeonholes could hardly point to anything more obviously parochial and colonial. Yet there are three factors to be considered. First, the beginning of the Shakespeare festival at Stratford turned out to be a very important event in the history of *Canadian* drama: it helped to foster a school of Canadian actors, and the lift in morale it represented fostered Canadian playwriting as well. Second, it represented an extraordinary recreation of the power and freshness of Shakespeare himself: one almost felt sorry for the British, who, having no Stratford except the one that had actually produced Shakespeare, would find it harder to make this kind of rediscovery of him. And third, Shakespeare at Stratford does not stand alone, because Moliere played a very similar role in the development of French Canadian drama, at roughly the same time.[2]

By this account, the 1950s saw Canadian artists shaking off their sense of colonial dependency even as they rediscovered the ongoing resources of pre-existing traditions. The growing success of Canadian artists thus involved a certain paradox. On one hand, artists at the time began creating directly out of their own particular locales in ways that earlier generations of artists were unable or unwilling to do. But on the other hand, this growing confidence in locality led to a fresh rediscovery of older traditions, thereby appealing to an international audience in the process. As Frye explains, this "is where the principle of interpenetration operates: the more intensely Faulkner concentrates on his unpronounceable county in Mississippi, the more intelligible he becomes to readers all over the world" (DG, 24). Crucially, there is no sense here that Frye advocates disavowing historical or geographical particularity so as to become like those at the Royal Shakespeare Company in England.[3] On the contrary, he understands Shakespeare's communicability in a way that necessarily counters the sort of false universalizing that would underwrite such practices.

One major purveyor of such falsely universalizing views is the eighteenth-century Shakespearean Samuel Johnson. In his 1765 "Preface to Shakespeare," Johnson claims that Shakespeare's characters have such broad appeal precisely because they "are not modified by the customs of particular places ... or by the accidents of transient fashions."[4] Instead, they embody generalized types or social classes. To be fair, Johnson's admittedly brilliant account of Shakespearean characterization is an attempt to justify the plays to eighteenth-century prejudices. As a result, he remains somewhat inconsistent in his description of the characters as he struggles with the limits of his own neoclassical preference for general ideals rather than cultural particulars, thereby pushing at the boundaries of neoclassical theory much as he does in his groundbreaking but negative evaluation of metaphysical poetry in "The Life of Cowley." That said, Frye effectively reverses Johnson's general stress on decontextualized abstraction when formulating his own general principles about the ongoing communicability of older narrative and artistic traditions. In doing so, Frye suggests that Canadians' new-found confidence in their local lives and stories helps explain how the Stratford Festival "represented an extraordinary recreation of the power and freshness of Shakespeare" (DG, 23–4). In other words, the growing confidence Canadian artists and audiences had in locality created the conditions for a fresh perspective on both themselves and

Shakespeare's works simultaneously. Through such confidence, they found themselves in a better position to see their lives reflected in Shakespeare and Shakespeare reflected back in their lives, hence the possibility of a festival in which sixty-four of the sixty-eight actors were Canadian in the opening season.[5]

Given Frye's influence on Stratford, it is perhaps not altogether surprising that his very Shakespearean sense of how the local and the general can fuse in narrative art informs the story in *Slings & Arrows*. We see this in Coyne's insistence that in telling a story about classical theatre in Ontario, she focused intently on the particular quirks of this little world, such as Canadian arts funding and regional Chinese cuisine, while nevertheless operating within the story and character patterns of several Shakespeare plays. Of course, casting attractive actors like Paul Gross and Rachel McAdams helps draw viewers, but it explains nothing of the show's poignancy or cultural translatability. What does explain this is that *Slings & Arrows* is built on the foundations of the Stratford Festival as Frye perceived it in 1977, a cultural space where, at its best, present local conditions interpenetrate with stories of the past to open up the possibility of a more imaginatively capacious world in the future. The appeal of this vision is that it's consonant with Frye's recognition that no meaningful cultural change of any sort takes place without some reference to the creativity of the past, be it "progressive, revolutionary, reactionary, or whatever."[6] At some point, all such changes "have to establish continuity with what has gone before."[7] Or as Robin Phillips noted, how are actors and directors to determine the future of theatre if they have "no idea where theatre has been" (*SFSP*, 1975)? Part of the strength of *Slings & Arrows* lies in how it communicates this increasingly challenging principle.

One storyline in the series that most explicitly engages with the colonial anxieties articulated in Frye's "Culture as Interpenetration" occurs in "Divided Kingdom," the first episode of season 3. At the opening of the season, New Burbage finds itself enjoying the critical and financial successes of its past season's production of *Macbeth*. And yet instead of being happy or fulfilled, the company's artistic and executive directors are both anxious and depressed. While a newly spruced up Tennant sobs uncontrollably in front of audiences, Smith-Jones frets that everything will come crashing down around him as he has lost whatever sense of self he previously possessed. The episode thus begins by having its viewers ask: What accounts for this crisis of confidence at a time of apparent triumph? The primary answer that

The Local and the Typical

unfolds is both distinctly local and yet, at a certain level, broadly common. At the national level, the structure of the episode comically exposes Canada's long-standing historical anxiety that it remains parasitical upon and subordinate to America and Britain. As historian Peter C. Newman explained in his 1985 Stratford lecture, "The Importance of Failure in the Canadian Psyche," "failure, to the Canadian psyche, is what yeast is to bread-making: without its levitating alchemy, we would be nothing but a doughy mush." According to this familiar paradoxical anxiety, Canadians "really do worship failure" and are "rabbit-scared of success."[8] From this perspective, the storyline at the opening of season 3 could not be more topical to Canadian theatre, where such ideas were literally the stuff of Stratford's celebrity lecture series. The plot plays into long-standing Canadian anxieties about success, and such fears are widely shared enough that the basic dramatic dynamics would resonate with a wide audience. In this sense, the lack of confidence haunting the festival in season 3 also suggests that there is something more artistically fundamental behind the shared sense of anxiety.

Appropriately enough, the explanation for Tennant's weeping before a large audience at New Burbage in the season's opening scene begins to unfold in New York, after a successful Broadway run of *Macbeth*. Celebrating the final performance, Tennant's girlfriend and colleague Ellen Fanshaw is visiting her close friend, high-powered African American television star Barbara Gordon (Janet Bailey), who plays Goneril in the season's production of *King Lear*. Revealingly, Gordon's apartment is decorated with stylish black and white images of her wielding a gun in the viewer's face, a decor choice that signals the large cultural gap between small-town Canadian theatre and big-time American television. During the party, Fanshaw is introduced to a flashy agent who flirts with her in the presumptive hope of drumming up some business, thereby presenting a major opportunity for an actress based in a small provincial Canadian town to become better known. No wilting flower, Fanshaw nevertheless remains awkward and self-effacing in the encounter, leading her confident American friend to chide her for not being self-assertive enough. This exchange is scaled up later in the series when Barbara, whose glamorous star power monopolizes all the press attention, berates Fanshaw for not sticking up for herself in the wake of a disastrous opening night. Making matters worse, Barbara, true to the role of evil (American) sister, is trying to lure Fanshaw out of the theatre and into the world of television (one of the show's self-reflexive jokes). The dynamics of this relationship recall the national allegory that plays out in season 1. First, there is the sociopathic American business woman Holly Day, who wants to turn the festival into a theme park, overcoming an insecure Smith-Jones with a sexualized force of will in the process. And second, there is the Hollywood star Jack Crew (Luke Kirby), who refuses to say his lines during most of the *Hamlet* rehearsals on the basis that he uses the method system of acting. In doing so, he throws Fanshaw's Gertrude off-kilter while causing problems within the cast more generally. Here again Cyril plays the role of chorus, noting of Crew's method acting, "that's how they do it in America" (1.5). Throughout the series, then, the festival's struggle for social cohesion and artistic success are repeatedly threatened by powerful Americans, including two strong-willed, aggressive women who are not especially interested in community. The plot parallels between seasons 1 and 3 indicate that across the series as a whole, the show's concern with artistic and professional pusillanimity is as much a function of self-perceived Canadian insecurity as it is of overcoming parochial views of Shakespearean theatre as a predominantly white male domain.[9] And yet, the threat posed by ostensible outsiders in the series ultimately pales in comparison to the one posed by the ultimate insider, Charles Kingman (William Hutt), whose overbearing patriarchal attitude and rather reckless desire to play Lear while terminally ill threatens to wholly undermine the festival's artistic integrity. Typical of Shakespeare's plays, the greatest threats to social cohesion and long-term sustainability come from within, not from without.

The post-colonial themes introduced at the opening of season 3 are reinforced in the scene that is interspersed with the New York party. Back in New Burbage, Smith-Jones is trying to prepare Tennant for an interview with the British Broadcasting Company (BBC). Worried, Smith-Jones warns Tennant to take the interview seriously, asking him: "Are you up to this Geoffrey? It's the BBC and the Queen might be listening" (3.1). Yet just as this colonial anxiety is explicitly evoked, it's immediately exorcized to the extent that Tennant walks away from the interview thinking it more insipid than illuminating. Thanking the BBC interviewer and the Queen "for being on my money," Tennant abruptly ends the conversation, thereby diminishing the colonial anxiety espoused by both Smith-Jones and the scene in New York. So if the writers of the show do not overplay colonial anxieties, they nevertheless allow them to partly explain the shared

The Local and the Typical   123

feeling of anxiety and depression at an apparent high point in the festival's history.

But only partly. After all, what more fully explains Tennant's anxiety and depression is not post-colonial inferiority so much as the vulnerabilities of classical theatre in a postmodern age. As I noted, season 3 opens with a barrage of onstage TV screens blasting sound and light over the New Burbage stage, signalling that Tennant is on the verge of becoming victim to his own success as his new-found money brings with it the temptations of new technology and media, like the Sierra System that can generate excessively realistic storms on stage. This source of anxiety is reinforced by Fanshaw's momentary decision to leave New Burbage for a rather ridiculous American sci-fi program. All to say that the depression and anxiety felt by Tennant and Smith-Jones that opens season 3 is overdetermined, having at least three interrelated causes. First, it arises from a long-standing anxiety that any success Canadians have in the theatre must be a fluke. Second, it arises from racialized anxieties about growing cultural diversity exemplified by the very figure of Shakespeare, who is often seen as a cipher of an exclusively white Anglo-American culture rather than a genuinely global figure.[10] Here we might recall that it's a South Asian man who forecloses on Tennant's Théâtre Sans Argent for unpaid rent in season 1, just as it's an African American woman who doesn't fit particularly well into the mostly white Canadian cast in season 3. But third, and primarily, the anxiety over success arises from a generalized fear about the vulnerability of theatre in an age of new media. If these dynamics are highly localized concerns about the world of Shakespearean theatre, they have nevertheless proven highly communicable to a global audience. And if such communicability is remarkable, it nevertheless should not be altogether surprising. After all, stories about how the desire for a purposeful life is threatened by changing cultural circumstances are as old as classical literature itself. In this respect, *Slings & Arrows* exemplifies Frye's sense that good storytelling works by fusing the local and the typical.

This returns us to Frye's view of Shakespearean character. In stressing the value of cultural locality and historical continuity in Shakespeare and other effective forms of storytelling, Frye endorses the romantic privileging of concrete individualities over idealized generalities sometimes thought to be characteristic of neoclassical aesthetics. While these principles can be found in Blake and Coleridge, it is perhaps William Hazlitt among romantic critics who was most sensitive to Shakespeare's fusion of the concrete and the general. Also setting his sights on Johnson, Hazlitt complained that the Dr "found the general species or *didactic* form in Shakespeare's characters, which was all he sought or cared for; he did not find the individual traits, or the *dramatic* distinctions which Shakespeare has engrafted on this general nature."[11] The necessity of Frye's post-romantic insights about the fusing of the local and the typical for explaining a literary work's longevity helps explain why Hazlitt has undergone something of a recovery in recent years among Shakespeare scholars, including Kiernan Ryan's provocatively titled *Shakespeare's Universality* (2015). Reversing Johnson's view of Shakespeare along pointedly political lines, Ryan asserts that

> Shakespeare's characters are so vivid and unforgettable precisely because they *are* modified by the customs of particular places and by the accidents of transient fashions and temporary opinions; but they are dramatized *from the perspective* of "common humanity" – from the anticipated future perspective of a genuinely universal human community no longer crippled by division and domination. (11)

Ryan's aim in the book is "to reclaim the idea of Shakespeare's timeless universality from reactionary and radical critics alike" (back cover). In his view, Shakespeare's plays function as concrete universals framed within a vision of utopian realism. In other words, they are vitally rooted in history and locality but their specific details are seen from the perspective of a future free of domination and division. From this ostensibly paradoxical perspective, Shakespeare's universality "is the product of the specific historical situation they transcend ... [arising] from the depth and detail in which they dramatize life in Shakespeare's time" (24). In keeping with Hamlet's complexly moralizing conception of dramatic art as a means of showing the age its time and pressure, Ryan's Shakespeare is both rich in local colour and transcendent in ethical perspective. The basic result is a more viscerally partisan but less fully theorized replay of Frye's earlier view that Shakespeare's overall dramatic vision is classless in nature.[12]

In pursuing these themes, Ryan picks up a thread that the Nigerian playwright and poet Wole Soyinka developed in his 1983 essay "Shakespeare and the Living Dramatist." Laced with irony, Soyinka's essay is premised on the wry assumption that Shakespeare's popular-

The Local and the Typical

ity in the Arab world is so widespread, and that his depiction of *Antony and Cleopatra* is so rich with "local colour," that Shakespeare is commonly believed in the region to have been an Arab whose real name was Shayk al-Subair, which, Soyinka demurs, "everyone knows … is as dune-bred an Arabic name as any English poet."[13] One of the targets of the essay is the post-colonial tendency to reduce Shakespeare to narrow frameworks of subversion and containment and to question the common assumption that a colonial literature is primarily repressive.[14] Resisting the materialist idea that social forces determine the scope of human possibility, Soyinka even goes so far as to suggest that in some instances, including with Shakespeare, English and French literature served the revolutionary purpose of freeing Arabic literature from some of its Islamic constraints. But his main purpose in the essay is to stress the convincing particularity of *Antony and Cleopatra*. As he writes, "Much of course is correctly made of the universality of Shakespeare's plays; here, I find myself more concerned with a somewhat less usual particularity, one which, I am convinced, the Arabic, and most especially the North African, poet simply could not fail to identify."[15] In doing so, he comes to the startling conclusion that *Antony and Cleopatra* constitutes the very essence of an African tragedy, thus suggesting that Shakespeare's cross-cultural appeal cannot be reduced to racialized concepts such as "systematic whiteness" or "white humanism," however useful such concepts may be in explaining his performance and reception history.[16]

Given this ongoing rediscovery of Shakespeare's double vision among geographically and ethnically disparate writers, it is perhaps not altogether surprising that such ideas orient the story in *Slings & Arrows*. After all, Coyne follows the principle that being true to one's local conditions is the best way to interest foreign audiences in one's story, hence the echoes and parallels to Stratford, right down to silly swan boats and tacky tourist shops. At the same time, she uses Shakespeare's plays as a way of providing the perspective of common humanity, starting with the show's focus on three basic phases of life: youth, middle age, and old age. Coupled with the show's exploration of extreme states of mind, this narrative structure reminds us of how Shakespeare's work, in Jonathan Bates's words,

> takes us not only through the cycles of birth and copulation and death that we all know, but also on journeys to places such as battlefields and broken minds where we hope that we will never have

126 Shakespeare and the World of *Slings & Arrows*

to go. So that if we do have to confront the worst, we can learn his lesson that people come out on the other side of it.[17]

As far as *Slings & Arrows* is concerned, what makes such learning possible is the way the show communicates its dialectic of conviction and malaise in a manner that is broadly recognizable even as it is discernibly unique to post-millennial, small-town Ontario. Viewed in these intellectual contexts, *Slings & Arrows* invites literary scholars to reconsider how well-crafted stories generally fuse the local with the typical. It is indeed somewhat strange that this important insight remains crucial to non-academic reviewers, while it is generally avoided in academic criticism. Instead of dismissing the fusion of the local and the typical as an empty cliché, or an ideological mystification, academic critics might now rediscover the sense of exigency inherent in critical practices that acknowledge cultural particularity but without fetishizing it to such a degree that its very communicability gets lost in the process. Remarkably, Howard Felperin foresaw the impasses of our current critical situation back in 1995 when he noted, in the context of a defence of radical humanism vis-à-vis *The Tempest*, the outer limits of such cultural pluralism. According to Felperin, "the current logic of cultural pluralism ... will, if carried far enough, lead forward to the reconstitution of a new historical metanarrative and a universal and 'utopian' Shakespeare always already at the end of it."[18] What I am suggesting is that this is precisely what we are now beginning to witness. And in witnessing this inevitable rejection of thoroughgoing cultural relativism what we are watching is a vindication of Frye's attempts to forge strong theoretical links between the culturally particular and the commonly human. Part of the appeal of *Slings & Arrows* as a cultural event is that it reflects the ongoing necessity of such a vision.

7

Mimesis and Emotional Realism

As we've seen, *Slings & Arrows* is committed to the idea that Shakespeare's plays hold a mirror up to nature, thereby giving perspective on human experience that translates across a wide berth of time and space. But as we have also observed, this mimetic process often involves not a direct relationship of life to art, but the more subtle interplay of illusions placed in relation to one another. As such, it is perhaps worth recalling here that Oscar Wilde anticipated much postmodern theory when he suggested that Hamlet described theatre as a mirror of life "in order to convince the bystanders of his absolute insanity in all art-matters."[1] To understand the full consequences of Wilde's witticism is to understand why the three writers of *Slings & Arrows* found it useful to parody postmodern anti-realism to tell a story about the loss and recovery of conviction in classical theatre as a vocation. Like all parodies, this satire is polemical and reductive, and it is not my aim to uncritically reproduce it here. But to dismiss the show's parody of Nichols's anti-realism as indiscriminately anti-intellectual is to seriously misrepresent both the contemporary Shakespeare world and the broader conversation about critical theory of which it forms an influential part. More importantly, it is to lose sight of why literature and theatre matter in the first place.

Implicit in Wilde's remark about Hamlet is a thoroughgoing distrust of mimesis, the idea that literature and drama can mirror social realities in ways that do not simply reproduce the ideological distortions already operative in these realities. As *Slings & Arrows* reminds us, one of the major proponents of Wilde's anti-mimetic views is the brilliantly innovative French critic Roland Barthes, who holds a place of pride in a number of influential studies of Shakespearean performance and criticism from the '80s and '90s. While this Barthes-inflected criticism is too challenging and diverse to reduce to shorthand summary, and while I don't wish to deny his brilliance as a critic, or his own great love of the pleasures of literature, several interrelated ideas are relevant here. The first is that the concept of "the author" is generally construed as a heuristic fiction that unnecessarily delimits the horizons of possible meanings, thus serving a stabilizing, conservative ideological function. But once literary works are freed of the providential author function, they reveal their nature as a space of self-reflexive *free play*. From this standpoint, literature is most itself when it resists the allure of hegemony-affirming mimetic or imitative strategies, allowing itself to become more strictly expressive, all lamp and no mirror as it were. Liberated from psychological verisimilitude and other politically delimiting mimetic strategies, literature communicates the joy of language freed from the tyranny of reference. It follows from this that the very idea of character appears as a retrograde concept resting on the idea that human experience remains legibly continuous across time and that ideas of personal agency and individual personality are essentially anachronistic prior to the modern era. Working from such anti-humanist assumptions, some performance critics conclude that adaptations of Shakespeare's plays cannot, by definition, disclose meanings, patterns, or values intrinsic to the plays as such. Instead, modern productions necessarily generate entirely new modes of significance by imposing unprecedented contexts and pressures onto the plays. The result is a critical practice that stresses the incommensurability between play texts and performance, even going so far as to suggest that "all we can ever do is use Shakespeare as a powerful element in specific ideological strategies" (MS, 3).[2]

For some critics and theatre practitioners, the idea that Shakespeare's works are void of positive content amounts to a liberating release from the order of mimesis and the imperializing dominance of a Eurocentric author function. The roots of this interpretive theory can be found in a liberationist reading of Nietzsche, one in which, as Gilles Deleuze asserts, "We will never find the sense of something (of a human, a biological or even a physical phenomenon) if we do not know the force which appropriates the thing, which exploits it, which takes possession of it or is expressed in it."[3] On this model, sense and value are expressions of creativity and will rather than a consequence of inherent properties or the complex dynamics of part-whole relations. For other theatre critics, however, this "Nietzschean" approach signals waning belief in the entire enterprise of Shakespeare study and performance, constituting nothing less than a counsel of despair, as it substitutes utility for discovery, ideological use for dialectical engagement. Either way, such a bifurcation of interpretive positions suggests that the relative balance between open-ended but structurally contained meaning that Frye articulated as characteristic of Shakespeare in 1964 broke asunder in the 1980s. And in the wake of this breakdown, Shakespeare has been laid bare for becoming an important site in the culture wars of recent decades, as witnessed in the eighteen-month Bardbiz debate over his legacy that took place in the *London Review of Books* in 1990–91.[4]

But what exactly is wrong with such anti-mimetic views? Why take Barthes as the subject of parody? And what implications does all of this have for critical and performance practices? One answer can be found in A.D. Nuttall's *A New Mimesis: Shakespeare and the Representation of Reality* (1983, repr. 2007). A sustained critique of Barthes's influence on Shakespeare criticism, Nuttall's book was an early warning about the long-term consequences of disavowing the idea that narrative art can be a mirror as well as a lamp. In it, Nuttall concludes that "If we fully admit the mimetic dimension, literary criticism becomes harder. We are transformed from cartographers to explorers, exposed to dangers, difficulties and even actual pains unknown to the formalist."[5] According to Nuttall, who is writing here in 1983,

Our literary culture is at present much more alive, much more active than it was twenty years ago. But there is in this activity something febrile. The very energy, as it accelerates, exhibits more and more the character of a malaise. The ordinary appetite for truth is replaced by a competitive cynicism, which stimulates but does not feed the mind. If we wish to produce by education people who are intellectually just, truth-loving, responsive to evidence and curious, now is the time to pause and take stock. (192)

In stressing the extent to which literature provides context for life, Nuttall stands to the postmodern formalists much as Tennant stands to Nichols. Rather than emphasizing how a text's significance changes in new contexts, he advocates the importance of subjecting oneself to the experience on offer in a play. Moreover, he does so on the basis that there is a difference between nourishment and stimulation, edification and entertainment. Revealingly, this pattern repeats what Brook already discerned in 1968 when he also warned about the limits of anti-realism, remarking: "It is foolish to allow a revulsion from bourgeois forms to turn into a revulsion from needs that are common to all men" (ES, 48).

Notably, Nuttall's defence of Shakespearean mimesis involves a subtle approach to the question of archetype. In deploying archetypes and stereotypes, Shakespeare routinely subjects them to critique, modification, and transformation while nevertheless still maintaining their presence and legibility (124). So while stereotypes and archetypes are generally discernible in Shakespeare, Nuttall maintains, they are simultaneously subjected to rigorous critique and reframing, leaving behind irreducibly strange singularities rather than comfortingly familiar types or generalities. This approach to social types is a key feature of Shakespearean mimesis, the way Shakespeare creates characters that are highly individualized even as they are recognizable enough to be legible and compelling. On this basis, Nuttall endorses an essentially romantic mode of character criticism. Correlatively, the satirizing of anti-realism in *Slings & Arrows* is part and parcel of its stress on the way art intersects with life, both mirroring and interpenetrating it. In both cases, a pusillanimous anti-realism is identified with a loss of purpose while a more dangerous, more existentially and aesthetically engaged, response to the plays is presented as the means of recovery. Such ideas form the intellectual background to the contrast between Tennant and Nichols, particularly Nuttall's distinction between two forms of criticism: opaque and transparent.

In the first instance, the opaque critic operates "outside the mechanisms of the art," taking those mechanisms as an object of analysis (80). As we saw, Heather K. Love takes this mode of analysis to its logical end in calling for a purely sociological reading practice, one that is "close" but not "deep." In the second instance, the transparent critic operates within the "'world' presented in the work" (80), experiencing, exploring, and explaining that world to others. In the first instance, Nuttall explains,

> The critic knows how the conjuror does the tricks, or how the tricks fool the audience, and is thereby excluded, by his very knowingness, from the innocent delight of those who marvel and applaud. Such criticism can never submit to mimetic enchantment because to do so would be to forfeit critical understanding of the means employed. (81)

Mimesis and Emotional Realism

In the second mode, however, the critic

> is less afraid of submission, feeling that enchantment need involve no submersion of critical faculties, but that on the contrary without such a willingness to enter the proffered dream a great many factors essential to a just appreciation may be artificially excluded from discussion. After all, [such a critic is not] in any fundamental sense fooled by the conjuror. They know perfectly well that all is done by artificial means. But at the same time they can perceive the magic as magic ... They note that Shakespeare implicitly asks them to do this, but they do more than note the request; they comply with it. (81)

Though the sense of deep engagement with something genuinely consequential that emerges from Nuttall's practice of criticism as impassioned redescription provides the intellectual background to the contrast between Tennant and Nichols, this background comes to the show partly mediated by Brook, who very much shares Nuttall's sense of Shakespearean realism.

Brook outlines his basic take on Shakespearean mimesis in an essay called "What is Shakespeare," which begins:

> *So long as one thinks* that Shakespeare is just Ioneso but better, Beckett but richer, Brecht but more human, Chekhov with crowds, and so on, one is not touching what it's all about ... If one takes those thirty-seven plays with all the radar lines of the different viewpoints of the different characters, one comes out with a field of incredible density and complexity ... A sign of this is that any single word, line, character or event has not only a large number of interpretations, but an unlimited number. Which is the characteristic of reality.[6]

On this score, to lose sight of Shakespearean realism is indeed to lose something of the world itself. For Brook, part of the reason for this is that Shakespeare's realism provides a model towards which to strive in the modern theatre, one that could only be achieved by synthesizing "the Theatre of the Absurd, the epic theatre and the naturalistic."[7] Hence his lifelong fascination with *King Lear*. Taken together, these contexts form the backdrop against which the Tennant/Nichols

132 Shakespeare and the World of *Slings & Arrows*

opposition finds its specific cultural exigency and that thus helps explain its ongoing poignancy.

EMOTIONAL REALISM

Against this cultural and intellectual background, it becomes clear that it is not emotional realism – or the actorly practice of identifying with a character – that best explains the show's narrative power.[8] While such a view is not wrong per se, it's nonetheless too narrow. In truth, it's the series' underlying conviction in Shakespearean realism and its concomitant stress on the importance of fusing interpretive and cultural horizons with the text that do it. After all, a conviction in Shakespearean realism is logically prior to and thus more conceptually fundamental than the secondary practice of emotional realism. Recognizing the logical priority of mimesis to the series allows us to see that the ongoing vitality of emotional realism in contemporary Shakespeare festivals and in popular depictions of modern rehearsal practice, including *Slings & Arrows*, poses no practical or theoretical problem. On the contrary, the practice is a natural consequence of the principle that art matters to the extent that it provides equipment for living.

According to the principles of emotional realism, actors should connect their own affective experience with that of their character, working, as it were, from the inside out. The thrill of such a psychologically focused approach is that life and art interpenetrate so deeply that one rarely loses sight of why the whole enterprise matters in the first place. The danger for an actor, however, is that the process can become too painfully immersive, such as when Daniel Day-Lewis felt the presence of his own dead father while playing *Hamlet*, or when Geoffrey Tennant failed to come out of Ophelia's grave. But for some performance critics, the ongoing existence of emotional realism in contemporary theatre and popular culture is puzzling, much as the afterlife of Shakespearean romance is for others. Expressing surprise at the ongoing use of emotional realism in popular depictions of Shakespeare such as in *Slings & Arrows*, Cary M. Mazer argues that such a practice flies

> in the face of most of the more advanced historicist scholarship on Shakespeare, theoretical writing on performance, and actual performance practice, which has, since the 1980s, either problematized or systematically rejected the entire notion of an "emotional

journey," as well as of much of what had been the fundamental assumptions of theatrical mimesis. Literary and cultural scholars of early modern Britain have challenged as anachronistic such concepts as subjectivity, interiority, and even the term "character," which they claim date from much later in the seventeenth-century, and have dismissed our tendency to read psychology into a dramatis persona as the "character effect."[9]

On this score, emotional realism is outdated for several reasons. First, it is historically anachronistic vis-à-vis early modern drama. Second, it is socially retrograde in the way it tends to endorse repressive ideas of individual autonomy and gendered normativity. Third, and by extension, its reliance on psychological verisimilitude tends to encourage passive responses to characters, stressing self-indulgent spectatorship rather than politically engaged critical distance. Taken together, it is thought, this is an elitist recipe for politically and culturally conservative art.

If this is how things looked in 2009, they look quite different more than ten years later. In hindsight, earlier defences of Shakespearean realism and character now have much greater authority thanks in part to works such as Lorna Hutson's *The Invention of Suspicion* (2007). In this book, Hutson convincingly shows that early modern English legal practices informed the development of psychological modes of characterization in which audiences were expected to interpret individual motivation and probabilities of cause and action according to mimetic principles of character. Vastly different than the French legal practices influentially studied by Michel Foucault (and then misapplied to Britain), the jury-based English system developed in tandem with a dramatic culture sensitive to psychologically inflected questions of character and mimetic accuracy. Moreover, recent work on renaissance grammar schools has stressed the importance of rhetorical practices of *imitatio*, the ventriloquizing of characters from classical literature. As with other rhetorical and oratorical traditions, such schoolroom practices encourage imaginative identification with literary figures, placing oneself within the emotional orbit of figures such as Dido, Aeneas, or, as in *Hamlet*, Hecuba. According to Lynn Enterline, such practices of imitatio do not produce predictably conservative modes of gender identification, but instead allow for a wide range of non-normative expressions of desire and identity. So while such practices of imitatio are distinct from emotional realism in many respects, the forms of identification at work in them recreate similar kinds of affective experience within clearly delineated situations. *Pace* Wilde, there is no necessary correlation between queer theory and anti-realism.[10]

Perhaps most important here, however, is Tiffany Stern's work. In a number of important studies, Stern has effectively reinvented the field of performance criticism by carefully examining early modern rehearsal practices, essentially reversing the consensus to which Mazer refers. According to Stern, "Ideas of 'emotional truth' and 'spontaneity' in the performance of a character, 'how the actor generates passion … what constitutes 'character' – consciousness, subjectivity, interiority, biography, etc.' can indeed be relegated to the 'perennial' rather than purely … the 'specific.'"[11] It is hard to overstate the stakes of this intellectual shift, not least because its consequences have yet to fully register in the academy. For one thing, this shift reasserts a greater sense of historical continuity between Shakespeare's theatre and the theatre of today, while still acknowledging, within the framework of a subtly historical methodology, some distinct differences. By redefining the pattern of continuity and difference between Shakespeare's sense of character and our own, this shift helps explains how the metanarrative structure of *Slings & Arrows* remains possible and convincing today. Because Shakespeare conceived of character in many of the same ways we do now, it makes perfect sense that one could use his plays to tell a story about the loss and recovery of faith in the power of theatre, while still being true to the local conditions on the ground in a manner that nevertheless has wide appeal. In short, emotional realism is a natural by-product of the show's underlying conviction in Shakespearean mimesis, not a symptom of its supposedly retrograde social views.

A related development in Shakespeare studies to the ongoing use of emotional realism in the theatre is so-called vernacular Shakespeare.[12] This phrase identifies the long-standing, but often contested, idea that when viewing the plays we intuitively interpret the motivations, intentions, and ethical dispositions of characters. As with emotional realism, such responses necessarily involve interpreting unobservable states of mind and semi-articulated background information. Crucially, such practices parallel real life insofar as the construction of the social sphere inevitably involves telling stories about one another, as we link people's motivations (ethos) to the their actions (themes) within the context of an evolving plot (mythos). From this point of view, emotional realism and vernacular Shakespeare share one consequential but controversial presupposition: they both assume that for all their particularized singularity the human dispositions depicted in Shakespeare's plays are broadly continuous with human personalities today and that these dispositions remain, at some level, irreducible to changing social circumstances. On the basis of these assumptions, Michael Bristol sees a potentially revitalizing value in naive, or unschooled, responses to Shakespeare. As he explains,

> Naïve readers have to rely on two forms of attention when they read any kind of difficult text. They focus on what happens in the story, and they try to work out how the fictional world is arranged, why the various agents acted as they did, and whether things worked out as intended.[13]

In outlining why this naive approach to Shakespeare is now needed in professional literary studies, Bristol might very well be describing a major theme of "Fallow Time," in season 2 of *Slings & Arrows*. This episode stresses both the import and the danger of what Bristol calls "putting yourself back in the picture" (649), putting the reader or viewer into the frame of the play so as to undergo the challenging experience it has to offer rather than standing outside it at an aloof, "critical" distance. In this respect, "Fallow Time" becomes something of a case study in the sort of "pre-critical" participatory responses to Shakespeare advocated by Bristol and Nuttall.

For instance, Bristol's explanation of vernacular criticism recalls the empirically unlikely but narratively probable elementary school production of *Macbeth* that Tennant and Fanshaw attend as a courtesy to New Burbage Elementary School. While the production looks very low-stakes at first, two minor details suggest the downward direction things will take. First, Fanshaw has a semi-hostile encounter with her brother-in-law, confirming the depth of her workaholism, and second, the crone Moira glares knowingly at Tennant, as though to suggest the play *Macbeth* is starting to take on a life of its own within his world. As these intimations suggest, things soon become dark. In the midst of the performance, Welles reappears to Tennant in a partly comic, yet increasingly unnerving, mirroring of Banquo appearing to Macbeth in the banquet scene. Replete with charming crayon-drawn backdrops, the initially quaint play now becomes increasingly alarming as Tennant struggles to repress his fear and frustration with his

136   Shakespeare and the World of *Slings & Arrows*

reappearing frenemy. The point is conveyed visually through a series of exaggerated close-ups of his face that recall the eulogy scene in which such shots suggest that he may not ultimately fit within the constraints of festival theatre. Revealingly, Welles makes his ghostly reappearance right after the child actor paraphrases Macbeth's "Tomorrow, and Tomorrow, and Tomorrow" soliloquy: "I don't understand life. It just keeps going on and on with no purpose. I'm so sad" (2.2). Genuinely impressed by such compression, Welles turns to Geoffrey and with a touch of smugness and revenge in his voice says to his younger nemesis and friend: "Isn't that poignant. This little boy captured the essence of Macbeth's despair with those few lines. '*I don't understand life. It just goes on and on with no purpose*'" (2.2). Welles then recognizes the relevance of Macbeth's malaise to his own condition, seeing his own experience of the theatre in the tragedy: "Talk about going on and on. That's my burden" (2.2). While there is no small degree of irony in Welles's application of the play to his own life, the irony does not fully undermine his sense that the play illuminates his own lack of direction and commitment. In particular, Welles's response to the comically young Macbeth confirms his general sense of malaise, his feeling, as he later says in season 3, that he is disappearing out of a loss of purpose. The childhood production of *Macbeth* provides Welles with the context by which he clarifies and even in a certain sense accesses his own emotional and spiritual condition. As such, the scene mirrors the show's larger metanarrative structure, not least because Welles's Banquo-like appearance mid-play destroys Tennant's capacity as an audience member to engage the poetic faith necessary for aesthetic experience, turning the quaint childhood play into a living nightmare. In this way, the childhood production illuminates Welles's experience, while, at the same time, threatening to endanger Tennant's fraying sanity.

Revealingly, the childhood production of *Macbeth* follows two previous scenes in "Fallow Time" in which the values and the dangers of implicating oneself within the aesthetic experience of the plays are discussed. Early in the episode, Ellen Fanshaw, speaking over dinner with Tennant, tries to make sense of her character Lady Macbeth according to the principles of emotional realism. She thus asks,

> Exactly how is she weak? I mean I know she has some weakness because she goes mad. But for the first half of the play, she is so overpowering. "Bring forth men children only" ... So when does

Mimesis and Emotional Realism

she crack? And why? And is it evil that has given her, her strength? Is it an unnatural cruelty? Or is she just a horrible bitch? (2.2)

As Fanshaw notes, understanding Lady Macbeth necessarily involves filling in the blanks of her character, wondering, for example, what happened to the child (or was it children?) whom she suckled? As she speaks, Fanshaw becomes emotionally invested in Lady Macbeth, expressing power and confusion in sympathy with her searching questions about a character who is now coming to life through Fanshaw's imaginative investment in her. And then in a subsequent scene, we learn that Tennant wants to honour Welles's desire to have the proscenium stage altered to a thrust, so as to make the audience members more complicit in the action of *Macbeth*, drawing them into the story as it were. Like the show as a whole, these three scenes from "Fallow Time" stress the importance of "putting yourself back in the picture" as a necessary precondition for understanding the play from the inside. Only then will the New Burbage Festival be able to overcome soporific productions like Welles's *A Midsummer Night's Dream* for a sustained period of time.

In making a case for vernacular Shakespeare, Bristol rediscovered the principle that an aesthetically engaged "transparent criticism" is necessary to any proper understanding of a Shakespeare play. Without first having put oneself in the picture, so to speak, a critic is far less likely to be capable of genuine criticism of any kind whatsoever. From this standpoint, even critics who practise the hermeneutics of suspicion must first submit themselves to the dynamics of the play. Otherwise, they are likely to remain too obtuse to be of any real use to other readers. Viewed in this general hermeneutic context, the experience of becoming implicated in the story means that the play begins to read oneself even as one reads the play. Frye succinctly explains this dynamic in *Words With Power* when he notes that the literary work

> does not stop with being an object of study, something confronting us: sooner or later, we have to study as well our own experience in reading it, the results of the merging of the work with ourselves. We are not observers but participants, and have to guard against not only the illusion of detached objectivity but its opposite, the counsel of despair that suggests that all reading is narcissism, seeing every text only as a mirror reflecting our own psyches. (75)

The basic point here provides the main focus of C.S. Lewis's lyrical diatribe against the over-professionalization of literary studies in *An Experiment of Criticism* (1961). According to Lewis, for certain kinds of literary people a first reading of a work can be "an experience so momentous that only experiences of love, religion, or bereavement can furnish a standard of comparison. Their whole consciousness is changed. They have become what they were not before."[14] This stands in contrast to those for whom no such change occurs: "When they have finished the story or the novel, nothing much, or nothing at all, seems to have happened to them."[15] Appearing at the very moment when the possibility of the first kind of reading could no longer be taken for granted, *Slings & Arrows* rediscovers what Harold Goddard meant when he said, with respect to Shakespeare, "We read a poem as we live – at our own risk."[16] As I have been suggesting, it is precisely the dimension of risk that makes such works of art a potential resource for living.

THE CRITICAL SCENE NOW

If Nuttall was a relatively lone voice in 1983, more recent critics have picked up the tune. Along with Pechter's *Shakespeare Studies Today* (2011), there is Richard McCoy's *Faith in Shakespeare* (2013). McCoy notes how peculiar it is that the anti-theatrical and anti-mimetic philosophy of Jacques Derrida has come to have such an influence on Shakespearean performance studies. As McCoy explains,

> In *Of Grammatology*, Derrida invokes Rousseau and Artaud, two notorious enemies of the theatre, to suggest that "the theater is shaped and undermined by the profound evil of representation," adding that "the actor is born out of the rift between the representer and the represented. Like the alphabetic signifier, like the letter, the actor himself is not inspired or animated by any particular language. He signifies nothing."[17]

On Derrida's account, then, the theatre is defined as a site that divides the living voice from itself, as though tensions between actor and role (or representer and represented) are always an embarrassing handicap rather than a productively vivifying feature of the theatrical arts.[18] Put in the blunter terms of Jean Baudrillard, this effectively means that in today's world "All dramaturgy ... has disappeared. Simulation is the master, and we only have a right to the retro, to the phantom, parodic rehabilitation of all lost referentials" (*ss*, 39). With such anti-realist assumptions in mind, McCoy concludes, it is "hard to see how any show can ever go on."[19] In light of such scholarly reassessments of recent performance theory, the diagnosis of postmodern malaise in *Slings & Arrows* appears neither anti-intellectual nor a sign of its nostalgically pastoral insulation from radical critique. Instead, this diagnosis is part and parcel of a growing body of criticism, some of which appeared in the 1980s and '90s in defence of Shakespearean realism, but much of which has emerged subsequent to the series itself.

Among other things, this intellectual context has implications for how we ought to think about the theoretical models we bring to bear on the series. After all, if the show plausibly identifies postmodern anti-realism as one of the causes for malaise in Shakespearean performance, then any attempt to read the show's intermedial aspects in light of such a theory is necessarily working against the grain of its own cultural diagnosis. So when Don Moore adopts a Derridean view of the show without identifying the broader cultural and intellectual contexts in which its anti-realist parodies are working, he relies on theoretical principles that are being satirized in the series without evidently realizing he is doing so.[20] Clearly, then, the moral and aesthetic commitments at work in *Slings & Arrows* can only be properly assessed when they are seen in this evolving intellectual and cultural context. Absent of such contexts, the show's response to the contemporary Shakespeare world and the broader cultural conversation of which it forms an important part will not become properly visible.

8

Sold Out

One of the real-life analogues to the show's depiction of the dialectic of conviction and malaise in festival theatre can be found in Urjo Kareda's article about Richard Monette in *Toronto Life*, "Sold Out" (2000). A dramaturge and critic, Kareda commissioned the stage version of Coyne's *Kingfisher Days*, even commenting on the manuscript in earlier drafts despite being seriously ill at the time.[1] The shared mythopoeic sensibilities of these two Stratford alums are not hard to discern. Indeed, if the thematic preoccupations and mythopoetic allegories of *Kingfisher Days* enrich our understanding of the world presented in *Slings & Arrows*, so too does Kareda's magazine commentary. Reflecting on the career and personality of the Stratford Festival's then current artistic director, Kareda tells a story that suggestively parallels the depiction of theatre as a vocation in *Slings & Arrows*. But it's not the raw information Kareda conveys about Monette that is ultimately valuable for an understanding of the show. Instead, it's the mythopoetic structure in which he formulates his story. By spinning a yarn about Stratford that follows a paradise/fall pattern, Kareda helps us understand the role such recurring patterns play in expressing the dynamics of conviction and malaise that necessarily attend any attempt to sustain one's artistic vocation over time.

Describing his article as a "personal album of snapshots," Kareda presents a modest but effective example of Northrop Frye's claim that the best histories are often visionary or archetypal rather than documentary or journalistic. Disclosing the enormous Blakean intensity of his thought, Frye claims that

> we all find that it is not only, perhaps not even primarily, the balanced and judicious people that we turn to for insight. It is also

Sold Out

people ... whose lives got smashed up in various ways, but [managed to] rescue fragments from the smash of an intensity that the steady-state people seldom get to hear about. Their vision is penetrating because it is partial and distorted: it is truthful because it is falsified.[2]

Working along these lines, Kareda presents his story in a simplifying, but thereby clarifying, paradise/fall pattern. The result of this value-laden temporal structure is an article that resembles fiction more than journalism. Yet it is a type of fiction designed to communicate the real-life potential of modern classical theatre to remain a vocation for those who produce it. As such, one might reasonably describe the article as a "Monette myth," where the term "myth" denotes not "lie" but a metaphorical means of distinguishing, in narrative terms, between a calling and a lifestyle, a vocation and a profession. As I have been arguing with reference to *Slings & Arrows*, for such distinctions to remain meaningful, one must still believe that the theatre can be based on something more significant than careerism, profit, or superfluous entertainment. Hence Kareda's turn to mythopoetic patterns to keep such a promise alive. Absent such recurring archetypes, these dynamics of faith and doubt, of conviction and malaise, would not be widely or effectively communicable.

Kareda begins his article with an anecdote from 1980 in which an indignant Monette, a fifteen-year veteran as an actor at Stratford, rages at the festival's president for his role in the institution's most infamous scandal: the sudden firing of the so-called "Gang of Four."[3] To cut a well-known story short, the festival administration fired four Canadian directors who were going to share the role of artistic director in order to hire the British John Dexter. Indignant at the treatment of his Canadian colleagues, Monette stood up at the festival's annual board meeting and railed: "We have all spent our lives in this theatre, we have given of our time and art. You talk about money all the time. You have no morals. I don't know how you can sleep. I care deeply and passionately about this place, and you must address yourselves to your consciences and to your hearts" (so, 2). In the ensuing months after the tirade, Kareda wryly reports, Monette's "heartfelt and reckless" outburst was "retold and relived, enhanced into a mythic moment, most vividly by Monette himself" (2). Echoes of it can even be heard in Oliver Welles's desire to give free tickets to festival alumni rather than corporate sponsors in the show's first

142 Shakespeare and the World of *Slings & Arrows*

episode. Kareda's story then moves forward fourteen years to 1994, when Monette is the festival's artistic director. By this point, however, Monette is a different person. A subtle villain as well as a gregarious hero, Monette now looks like what Milton, in *Paradise Lost*, calls a "complicated monster":

> Looked at in one light, his nature seems easy to grasp. Certainly, the basic impulse couldn't be simpler: Richard loves the world of the theatre, loves being part of that world. The consequent complementary characteristics are what you might expect. He is, at heart, generous, passionate, candid, gregarious, open, hungry for attention. Yet there are those who feel that Richard has changed, who now find him to be detached, defensive, cynical and secretive. It seems a revealing, even disturbing demonstration of how one's impulses can over time be tempered and altered by experience and the wrong kind of knowledge. The original instincts are compromised, the straightforward characteristic thrust become diffuse and complex. (so, 2–3)

Applying Satan's seduction of Eve to Monette's temptation by administrative responsibilities and financial exigencies, Kareda accuses his ex-colleague of being warped by the wrong kind of experience and knowledge. This neatly mythic view of Monette's career then frames a series of before/after vignettes, which become more subtly complicated as each unfolds.

When looking back with affection on Monette's earlier career, Kareda humanizes the young and impassioned thespian, warmly recommending his sense of artistic calling:

> As an actor, Richard always believed fervently that working in the classical repertoire was a sacred path, the theatre a temple ... Since he became Artistic Director, he has considered it one of his most urgent priorities to translate that sermon into action, into training. He wants to awaken in a new generation of young actors his own spiritual impulses toward the classical theatre ... He is particularly keen to convert actors who might have been too easily seduced by the gloss and financial rewards of film or television. (4)

In retrospect, however, this simple picture coexisted with something that was always-already a little more complicated. Looking back on a

Sold Out   143

balmy Stratford evening in the late 1970s, Kareda recalls something subtly vulgar about Monette's flair for an "old-style world of lovely, antiquated, gauche wannabe luxe" (5). If these features of Monette's aesthetic tastes remained harmlessly out of focus in the 1970s, they nevertheless emerged front and centre in his productions during the 1990s. According to Kareda, these productions no longer kept vulgarity "at whispering distance." Instead, they were "visually overripe, gaudy, [and] overdecorated" (5). The result was an object-lesson in how "familiarity breeds security" (5).

Kareda then relates one other then/now pattern, but this time the focus is on Richard the actor rather than Monette the director. Wistfully recalling Monette's brilliant performance as the self-inventing eponymous hero Hossana in Michel Tremblay's play, Kareda observes: "As a metaphor for the allure and danger of self-invention, Hossana remains tremendously potent. Much of the astonishing power of Richard's performance as Hosanna came from his own identification with that metaphor" (6). Yet a decade after his triumph as Hossana, Monette "began to notice that the giddy exhilaration of acting was being replaced by a paralyzing anxiety. The actor's nightmare: acute stage fright. Richard said that some nights as he waited for his cue to go on, he thought he would have a heart attack and die" (7). As a result, he gave up acting to focus on directing.

This returns us to the year 2000, when Monette was in control of the Stratford Festival. Like others at the time, Kareda saw Monette's "instincts for programming" as amounting to "middlebrow predictability and unadventurous execution" all for the sake of financial profiteering (8). So much so that Monette has "refashioned the famous Festival Theatre so that the audience must now run a gauntlet of greedy boutiques selling theme-park inventory before they can even catch a glimpse of the doors" (8). The result is a profanation of the festival's celebrated origins:

In this tragedy, what was once, within living memory, a visionary artistic enterprise has now been remade as a show palace, with leadership that has greater affinities with P.T. Barnum than Tyrone Guthrie, himself no mean showman. The Stratford that now just Manufactures shows must surely be a tragedy for Richard as well, who began as a passionate, searching artist and has now willed himself to serve as a huckster. But to rescue Stratford in terms of the artistry, rather than just the balance sheet, he will need to reconnect

144   Shakespeare and the World of *Slings & Arrows*

with his old sense of kamikaze fearlessness. That is well within the range of this master of self-transformation. Richard Monette is nobody's fool. (8)

If Kareda's mythopoetic retelling of Monette's career is more capacious and humane than the neo-Marxist critiques of the festival that it parallels, it is nevertheless a simplification. But its simplifications serve a humanizing and clarifying purpose. They bring a complex, value-laden cultural problematic into enough focus for readers to become emotionally engaged in the article's real purpose: it's proselytizing call to faith to recommit to theatre as a vocation.

As a call to conversion, the article's value for understanding *Slings & Arrows* is more literary than historical, more a matter of its form than its content. To be sure, "Sold Out" provides historical information that is clearly of some value in understanding the show's origins and exigencies. As a charismatic actor who succumbs to paralyzing stage fright only to become a struggling director at a major Shakespeare festival, Kareda's Monette broadly parallels Geoffrey Tennant. At the same time, however, Kareda's Monette bears an obvious resemblance to Oliver Welles, the gregarious showman turned bitter cynic who speaks in a suspiciously Monette-like manner. Yet this parallel is further complicated by the fact that Welles re-emerges in the story as a ghost haunting Tennant. In this respect, *Slings & Arrows* begins to look like a show in which the older Monette both hinders and helps the younger as he seeks to redeem himself. At this point, the parallels are no longer between Stratford and New Burbage, history and story. Instead, they become more strictly archetypal in nature, thereby bearing out Frye's claim that the more culturally particular a story becomes the more communicable it will be. Ultimately, it's the proselytizing dimensions of "Sold Out," expressed through its paradise/fall structure, that most deeply links Kareda's account of Monette's festival to the story of *Slings & Arrows*. Thus just as Coyne's memoir rediscovers the value of myth for understanding the modes of belief operative in non-dogmatic modes of aesthetic and spiritual experience, so too does Kareda's article.

Instead of presenting Monette as an historical personage per se, Kareda presents him as a set of symbolic tendencies and possibilities vis-à-vis theatre as a more or less sacred endeavour. That is, he looks more like a character in an allegory about theatre as a sacred vocation than the sort of fully rounded person we might find in a realist novel or autobiography. If such a vision has any authority, it's because the mythic contours of his story map onto the actual conditions of the festival with enough veracity to be something other than a presumptuous insult. After all, his aim is less neutral description than artistic conversion. His proselytizing purpose is to recall a great man of the theatre to the sources and values of his vocation and, in doing so, to have others in his community heed the call as well. As such, the article brings into focus why some young viewers of *Slings & Arrows* identify the show as the source of their own conversion to theatre. For the story told in the series constitutes a successful deployment of the same mythopoetic patterns and modes of characterization organizing Kareda's clever and impassioned article.[4] Viewed this way, the show's popularity is part and parcel with its poignancy, both of which are a function of its deep structures, its underlying narrative patterns and the ethical and artistic commitments voiced through them. Central to these patterns, however, are decisively satirical energies, to which we now turn.

9

Bardbiz

In season 1, the satirical side of *Slings & Arrows* largely pivots around Holly Day and Darren Nichols. Portraits of possessive individualism and deadly theatre respectively, these two characters represent the narrowing of aesthetic and spiritual horizons. In the context of the show, they embody two distinct but related ways in which artistic and spiritual potential get diminished or occluded in advanced capitalism. In sum, they both embody the view that dramatic art can no longer operate as a means of disclosing what James Joyce called an epiphany, an authoritative manifestation of moral or spiritual reality.[1] For Day and Nichols, the sort of anamnesis that Coyne depicts in *Kingfisher Days* and the concomitant view of Shakespirituality attendant upon it simply make no sense.

Presented through the heavy hand of parody, these two characters emerge out of debates over Shakespeare's legacy that occurred in the 1980s and '90s. But rather than passively mirroring such controversies, their portraits constitute an active, if implicit, intervention into them. Surprisingly, however, this intervention is not a polemical replay of the end-of-the-millennium culture wars. Instead, the show registers how the frames of reference that structured those debates have shifted, and that in the wake of these cultural transformations, it has become clear that both Nichols's postmodern left and Day's neo-conservative right bear some responsibility for the corrosive processes of cultural deracination responsible for the loss of faith in the idea of classical theatre as a vocation. Season 1 therefore offers a plausible, if blunt, diagnosis of the contemporary Shakespeare world and the broader social context animating it.

To appreciate the cultural context at work in this aspect of the show's satire, it is helpful to go back to a debate about Shakespeare's legacy that took place in *The London Review of Books* in 1990–2001. Now referred to as the Bardbiz debate, the moniker for this heated exchange is shorthand for the commodification of Shakespeare, the exploitation of his work for financial profit and social cachet bemoaned by Kareda in "Sold Out." Occurring over an eighteen-month period, the Bardbiz debate was occasioned by a witty and irreverent take down of Britain's veneration of Shakespeare as a cornerstone of its national heritage by a prominent Shakespeare scholar. Composed by the late literary critic Terence Hawkes, the immediate occasion of the review was the furor over the recently unearthed foundations of the Rose and Globe theatres. Behind this immediate occasion, however, lurks the broader political subtext of Margaret Thatcher's eleven-year reign as prime minister of Britain, including her military campaign in the Falkland Islands and a sustained program of financial and corporate deregulation that would produce enormous wealth for investors but bring much hardship to unionized workers, the underpaid, and the underemployed, helping to set the stage for the banking crisis of 2007–08 that nearly wiped out the global finance system.

For many in England's culture industry, the discovery of the Rose and Globe theatre ruins inspired a kind of veneration, an almost religious awe at what had been unearthed. Hawkes was not among them. For him, the displays of national piety were all a little perplexing, particularly a shared prayer that took place at one of the sites among a group of actors. Detecting something insidious in such cultural piety, he wryly notes that the very "possibility that one these sites might fall prey to property developers generated more squeaking and gibbering in the London streets than you could shake a severed head at" (MS, 141). The reference here is to the building of Rome, where the discovery of a severed head was interpreted as a sign of the imperial greatness to come. As the politics of the allusion suggest, Hawkes was worried that the religious language being used to describe the theatres as "authentic origins" of modern English culture might be concealing something more nefarious than a love of Shakespearean comedy. In his view, such rhetoric hid the economic and nationalist interests being served in this whole archeological and theatrical enterprise, interests that he thought dovetailed with the neo-conservative agenda dominating British politics over the previous decade. He thus turns the tables on those calling for the preservation of the foundations of both theatres by describing their agenda as an example of nationalist idolatry, one that obscures more mercenary, even imperialist, designs. Recalling Derrida's "Structure, Sign, and Play," Hawkes exposes the dangers inherent in the use of "sacred sites" as sources of national origin and cultural authority, arguing that the

> potential of "origin" as an agent of affirmation, confirmation and limitation makes it a powerful ideological tool. If we can persuade ourselves that in some way origins generate authenticity, determine, establish and reinforce essentials, then we can forget about change and about the history and politics which produce it. A covert, idolatrous agenda backs temptingly into view. The "original" Globe Theatre! That firmest of rocks on which the true unchanging English culture is founded! To bolt the shifting uncertain present firmly to that monument must be a project worth encouraging. Let Europe loom, the pound wilt, Shakespeare's wooden O offers a peculiarly satisfying bulwark against change. (MS, 142)

What most perturbs Hawkes is the way Shakespeare's legacy might be used to reinforce the social and economic status quo. Although imperialistic uses of the Bard's legacy have a long history in the British Empire, they were only just beginning to be critically understood in the '80s. Hence the unprecedented stress on the imperialist side of Shakespeare's reception history among literary scholars working in the Reagan/Thatcher years when market deregulation, post-colonial wars, and possessive individualism were the status quo. In such a context, cultural critique was a meaningful way of doing politics, of redressing the systems of power that generate and perpetuate injustice. In the wake of Brexit and the rise of right-wing nationalisms across Europe, including the Russian invasion of Ukraine and a planned coup in Germany, Hawkes's wariness about the reactionary, xenophobic forces re-energized in Thatcherite Britain is not hard to understand.

And yet, the Bardbiz commentary ends on an anti-American note that implicitly reproduces the cultural snobbery disavowed in the review. Hawkes concludes his piece by claiming that the American presence behind the Globe Theatre project undermines its authenticity as an expression of British culture. He approaches the rather delicate point by noting that the planned theatre was the product of American actor Sam Wanamaker's "transatlantic vigor," one of those arch-English insults disguising itself as praise. Having established the connection, he then asserts that the Globe Theatre is less a natural expression of English cultural tradition than yet another example, going back to Adams and Jefferson, of Americans shaping and defending "our [British] way of life" (157) – a phrase he deploys with withering irony. Calling the project's authenticity into question, Hawkes warns:

> Is Bardbiz in this guise merely the continuation of American foreign policy by other means? The praying actors might ponder that. Meanwhile, a line drawn across the road from the original location of Shakespeare's wooden O, not more than a fret and a strut from its immemorial stage, will all but touch a brand new building which soars indifferently skywards. No less of a monument to our present way of life, it houses the *Financial Times*. (MS, 153)

As one might expect, these links between Shakespeare's legacy, the new Globe project, Anglo-American imperialism, neo-liberal capitalism, and Little Englandism appeared hysterical and inflammatory to less irreverent readers of the *LRB*.

Compounding matters, Hawkes's review gave expression to a postmodern view of Shakespeare that was relatively new to the Anglo-American world at the time. According to Hawkes, Shakespeare's plays are best understood within a social context that is fundamentally defined in terms of competing claims for power among vying groups. If such a hard-nosed theory of the social field accurately describes most historical moments in Western history, it is helpful to remember that it came very close to being an official ideology under Thatcher. The result is a view of Shakespeare that stresses how the plays are more or less locked into existing power relations, one that spoke to the relative sense of political helplessness many on the political Left felt in the neo-conservative '80s and early '90s. Given the somewhat reductive view of art and humanity driving such a perspective, it is not surprising that Hawkes's provocations in the Bardbiz review set off an almost two-year debate about the nature of Shakespeare's legacy and the role of literary scholarship in both establishing and critiquing it. On one side are "conservatives" who stress Shakespeare's capacity to transcend parochial interests, while on the other are "radicals" concerned with exposing how the Bard continues to serve the turns of the privileged classes.

The "conservative" side of the debate was led by James Wood, a little-known journalist at the time, but now a celebrated critic and essayist in his own right, known particularly for his graceful and erudite study *How Fiction Works* (2008). His first salvo in the exchange makes the main objection to Hawkes's view of Shakespeare clear. When mishandled, post-structural theory generates too much relativizing imprecision, thereby corroding literary criticism as a critical practice and culture more generally:

> Terence Hawkes, in his sprightly piece on Shakespeare (*LRB*, 22 February), indulges in the post-structuralist's customary tendency to extend a useful insight to a logical extremism which then disables itself. Most of us can agree with Hawkes's caution against searching for a fixity of meaning in Shakespeare. Equally, most of us can see that plays so mediated by hundreds of readings and interpretations through the centuries have in a sense become "unreachable," as he puts it – or at least harder to reach. It can be valuable to study the history of these readings. But it is more difficult to agree with Hawkes that the meanings of Shakespeare's plays have not only been produced by Shakespeare, but also by these very readings. These plays, he writes, are "constituted not only by an author but also by the interpretative strategies of readers and the material political and social pressures of the historical contexts helping to shape those strategies." Naturally, if one believes this, then, as Hawkes writes, these readings may well be "more interesting and more revealing than they" – Shakespeare's plays – "could ever be." ... And if this is the case, then of course Shakespeare comes to seem, as Hawkes put it, "a writer of no necessary distinction, a former star, now reduced to the status of a 'black hole.'"[2]

A relatively isolated voice in the debate, Wood's basic warning was that Hawkes's style of reading had a corrosively levelling effect, one that "puts each reading on the same level as the next."[3]

Wary of these levelling consequences, Wood's letter calls for more careful parsing among hardline purveyors of post-structural theory. While it's clearly true that communities of readers make sense of texts according to specific conventions of interpretation, it does not follow from this that the text has no agency in the process. Of most concern to Wood was the extent to which those practising this new style of interpretation seemed obtuse to its long-term implications. Carried to its own logical conclusions, such a post-truth way of thinking would make it more or less impossible to distinguish between responsible and irresponsible, persuasive and unpersuasive, interpretations outside of very small silos of like-minded people. The result would be a world where distinctions of value and quality cannot be widely defended, only distinctions of power and victimization. Underneath the left-wing radicalism of post-structural theory, then, Wood detected a cynicism worthy of Thomas Hobbes, the political theorist who saw all forms of human authority simply in terms of power and domination. In some respects, he was not wrong to do so. After all, in 1977 Michel Foucault, a leading proponent of post-structural thought, hypothesized that the contemporary social field is a conflict of "all against all ... Who fights against whom? We all fight each other. And there is always within each of us something that fights something else."[4] Wary of where this view leads both politically and academically, Wood wonders aloud what, exactly, is liberating about such Hobbesianism? Responding to Hawkes, he worries that such a view would produce a cultural conversation in which we can't distinguish between better and worse drama, or, as we might say today, true and fake news. In this respect, he was making the same point about Hawkes that Iris Murdoch would make about Derrida two years later. Responding to Derrida's early work, which underwent significant and for many surprising modification in his later career, Murdoch warned that "the severance of meaning from truth, and language from the world can be seen, not only as philosophically baseless and morally intolerable, but as politically suicidal."[5] After all, she averred, a post-truth culture is more likely to embolden right-wing populist authoritarianism than it is to cultivate new forms of enlightened socialism. Or as Richard Strier said of Hawkes's reading of *Hamlet* in a 1995 commentary, "To think that we can be genuinely revolutionary either by subscribing to a particular literary interpretation ... or by asserting that there is no such thing as a definitive interpretation seems to me disturbingly self-promoting and delusive."[6]

Looking back on the Bardbiz debate with about five years distance, Canadian Shakespeare scholar Michael Bristol saw more heat than light. In his view, the eighteen-month exchange was "a major battleground in the deplorable public spectacle known as the culture wars" (xii). His lament over the affair is telling, as his 1990 book *Shakespeare's America/America's Shakespeare* (1990, repr. 2014) stood at the very centre of the Bardbiz furor. On side with Hawkes, Bristol's 1990 book explores how Americans used Shakespeare to legitimate narrow political and national interests. The result is a politically hard-hitting exposé of the ideological uses to which Shakespeare has been put. In his following book, however, *Big-Time Shakespeare* (1996), Bristol adopts a more conciliatory tone as he saw the critical and political impasses that were forming.

Its satires notwithstanding, *Slings & Arrows* is written, as I noted, in the same spirit as Bristol's *Big-Time Shakespeare*. For all of its high-flown idealism about the possibilities of classical theatre, the show openly acknowledges the realities of Bardbiz, the crass commercialization of theatre as yet one more form of self-interested profiteering. After all, it was written at a time when many in the Stratford theatre community were warning about the long-term effects of increased commercialization on artistic integrity. For example, in the 1998 *Globe and Mail* article "Saving Stratford from the Excesses of Success," theatre critic Kate Taylor effectively discloses the basic context for Holly Day's characterization as the sociopathic Texas-based American businesswoman who wants to turn the festival into a theme-park called "Shakespeareville." "This season at the Stratford Festival," she writes, "as administrators boast of record attendance, artistic staff are joking that they're about to be taken over by Disney ... Today at Stratford, lavish musicals and populist dramas are as prominent as the classics, while many of the Shakespearean offerings are outrageously over-produced comedies."[7] While Taylor was the most vociferous newspaper critic of the festival under Monette's direction, she was not entirely alone in her views. Writing a week earlier in the *Globe and Mail*, Ray Conlogue noted that

> behind the busy marquees, classical theatre – and classical culture – are in big trouble. Institutions from Ontario's Stratford to England's Royal Shakespeare Company are adding modern titles to their seasons and quietly dropping the more difficult Shakespeare plays. The ones they still do are flossy and dumbed down, the comedies played for laughs and the tragedies for melodrama.[8]

Such reviews clearly provide the immediate context for the threats posed by Day's neo-liberal agenda. Intriguingly, however, *Slings &*

Arrows combines such right-wing threats with the left-wing anti-Americanism of Hawkes's Bardbiz review, a phenomenon far more characteristic of progressives in Britain and Canada than conservatives. As Canadian viewers of the show do not need to be reminded, Holly Day touches anti-American sentiments that effectively define the national character, especially its more liberal side. Combined with the cultural and spiritual corrosion embodied by the postmodern Nichols, the show's depiction of Day's neo-conservative brand of cultural decline makes for a story that does not easily reduce to the political pigeonholes that made for the culture war in the first place.

DEEP MARKET PENETRATION

In keeping with the season 1's allegory, Day's name is a double bastardization from holy day to holiday to Holly Day. It's a perfect moniker for someone who combines an "aw shucks" Southern informality with a stab-you-in-the-eye neo-liberal sadism. We first meet Day in episode 1 at the headquarters of Cosmopolitan Lenstrex, a major sponsor of the New Burbage Festival. Filmed at City Hall in Toronto, the architectural setting consists of swirling ceilings and bending hallways that echo the vertigo-inducing modernism of Munch's *The Scream*. The visual echo is apropos given that Smith-Jones has been summoned, Kafka-like, to a meeting without knowing why. This anxiety-inducing situation is the show's first example of someone exercising power to keep others off-balance. When he arrives, Smith-Jones finds a mood that mixes funereal sadness with moral outrage, thus echoing the eulogy scene that will follow. While women quietly weep, a man using a wheelchair lashes out at the security guards accosting him with "keep your hands off me," while one of the guards says, "We don't care about your wheelchair." Moments later, a female voice speaking with military precision intones on the intercom, "Security in the right stairwell, exit seven." This general Orwellian mood indicates that Cosmopolitan Lenstrex is "downsizing," a euphemism that became commonplace in the '90s during the era of free-trade agreements and the mass globalization of markets (a process signalled in the recent addition of Cosmopolitan to the name Lenstrex). The dispassionate corporatism structuring the scene is cemented by Day's snide remark about her recently transferred underling David: "He will *just love* Anchorage." Capping off the picture is a boardroom table shaped like an upside-down T, the perfect setting for the later revelation from the same "downsized" employee that Day is "the devil."

In keeping with the symbolism, the conversation that follows pivots entirely around power, first financial and then sexual but with no clear distinction between the two. This toxic blurring of finance and eroticism is signalled by a whiteboard behind Day with the words "Deep market penetration" written on it. Ever in control, Day discombobulates Smith-Jones with the unspoken threat of withdrawing sponsorship only to surprise him with the ostensibly good news that she is going to increase the company's financial support for the festival. She then follows up with a mildly flirtatious request to go as Smith-Jones's date to the production of *A Midsummer Night's Dream*. Covering his surprise with a thin veneer of self-confidence, he reacts like a man only dimly aware that he is caught in someone else's power game. The result is a brilliantly executed portrait of a world in which everything is a matter of domination and submission, even the most minute exchanges between people. It is Hilary Mantel crossed with Mark McKinney.

Sitting at the upside-down T-shaped table, Day sneers in good neo-liberal fashion that "all change is opportunity." As this defining moment indicates, what is offensive about Day is not that she likes musicals, but that she embodies a view of change in which the only potential is profit or, at best, the momentary distractions of entertainment. As the show sees it, such withering of potential, such narrowing of the horizons of possibility, happens when people lose conviction in culture as an ethical and imaginative resource, seeing it as nothing more than a reflection of narrow interests or passing pleasures. Crucially, the program's power as a work of art lies in the way it diagnoses how this loss of faith, and the processes of cultural deracination concomitant with it, are happening in advanced capitalism on both the postmodern left (Nichols) and the neo-conservative right (Day). From this perspective, Day embodies the ruthlessly modernizing forces that the actors praying at the foundations of the Globe sought to keep at bay. In short, she is deracination incarnate.

In its fuller narrative context, Holly Day's characterization suggests an alternative to Hawkes's view of Shakespeare's legacy in its critique of the effects of advanced capitalism on the world of high art. From the perspective offered in the show, Hawkes takes insufficient notice of how the modern forms of Anglo-American imperialism with which he is concerned do not reinforce the cultural status quo so much as they erode all forms of tradition and community. Put simply, he does not distinguish between the two styles of conservatism that came to loggerheads under Thatcher, even within her own cabinet. On one hand, there is a Burkean conservatism in which past, present, and future are held together as a kind of sacred bond, a view in which responsibility to and gratitude for tradition and community exist in tandem with the pursuit of progress and respect for individual freedoms.[9] On the other hand, there is the more libertarian free market theory in which present and future profits take priority over everything else and where egotistical individualism is elevated to the status of dogma. In both theory and practice, these political styles have differed starkly at times, especially in Canada, where they helped split the Progressive Conservative Party of Canada in 2003. But for Hawkes such differences are negligible because "tradition" is ultimately an inauthentic construction serving the interests of an undifferentiated "elite." Consequently, any act of ancestor veneration must necessarily conceal a hidden agenda.

What Hawkes's postmodernism fails to take on board is the spiritual and cultural need to form living relationships with the past. Sensitive to this need, the writers of *Slings & Arrows* depict Holly Day as an incarnation of the neo-liberal tendency to adopt a hedonistic view of the present while focusing wholly on the future. In this sense, she represents a world in which there is no possibility of fusing Shakespeare's otherness with the world of today, no meeting of horizons between past and present. Tellingly, Day's brand of sociopathy is the reverse of the sort that is more typical of post-millennial television. As Adam Kotsko argues in *Why We Love Sociopaths: A Guide to Late Capitalist Television* (2012), contemporary television is awash in sociopathy, from the womanizing Don Draper of *Madmen* (2007–15) to the misanthropic doctor of *House, M.D.* (2004–12). But in these instances, the sociopath's lack of empathy and relative amoralism become attractive, a way for the character to succeed in the world. Through such characters, Kotsko argues, viewers are allowed to indulge in fantasies of successfully exploiting the broken social contract of the post-millennial moment, not least because such televisual sociopathy bears only a vague relation to the clinical variety which has little to envy about it.[10] In contrast, Day is an embodiment of that very broken contract, a walking allegory of neo-liberal sadism. At no point in the show does she become an attractive figure with whom we identify. One reason for this is that she poses a threat of cultural amnesia, a loss of the past as a resource for the present so valued in the series. In this respect, the series demonstrates a level of cultural sensitivity to which the radical side of the LRB debate in 1990–2001 remained somewhat obtuse.

By 1996, however, the issues at stake for Shakespeareans would be clearly delineated in Bristol's *Big-Time Shakespeare*. In his effort to reconcile conservative intuitions about the importance of cultural memory with politically progressive insights into the operations of power and oppression, Bristol writes:

> The contemporary culture wars are a deplorably vulgarized and increasingly vitiated contest, not over what should be read, but over what reading is for. The stark alternatives of affirmation and resistance leave no room for mature and realistic assessment of traditions or for the achievement of a "deep subjectivity" that would enable the inheritors of Western modernity to understand their complex situatedness as fully as possible. Shakespeare's works remain as conspicuous landmarks in the modern cultural terrain. In order to discovery how we can best be oriented to these remarkable features of our cultural landscape, it is imperative to consider how we regard our historical past. The possibility for "deep subjectivity" and for a well-oriented social position depends on how intelligently we interpret the cultural traditions that define us as members of a particular community. (140)

Bristol then goes on to argue that "Shakespeare's plays represent the pathos of tradition with extraordinary force and clarity" (145). Importantly, however, he defines the term "tradition" in dialectical terms. In other words, he sees the relation between Shakespeare's plays and future readers as involving a complex historical process of negotiation and redefinition in which neither our perception of the past nor our experience of the present remain identical over time. Such a view differs from concepts of tradition as consisting of direct continuity or pure identity across time, but it is also a view of tradition that does not view the past simply as an occasion for political critique in the form of demystification.[11] To this extent, Bristol construes tradition as an ongoing conversation, coupled with habits, practices, and institutionalized forms, in which those who identify with the tradition engage in debate about precisely what the tradition is. From this standpoint, tradition becomes a living thing that necessarily changes over time, much as a language does. In thinking of Shakespeare's plays and their reception as a self-reflexive example of such a tradition, Bristol pursues in analytical terms what *Slings & Arrows* undertakes in narrative form. That is, they are both using Shakespeare to ask: Why is it worth being a member of this tradition at a time when it can so easily be exploited for narrow material interests? Can the horizons of past and present fuse at such a moment? Or are we just looking at ourselves in the mirror when we read Shakespeare? In narrativizing such issues, the opening episode of season 1 sets into motion the conflict between artistic integrity and commercial enterprise besetting performers and scholars of Shakespeare at the century's end.

The problem of artistic integrity is neatly conveyed in the juxtaposition between two conversations that take place following the final production of *A Midsummer Night's Dream* at the opening of season 1. First, there is the exchange between Day and Smith-Jones in front of the gift shop, in which they commiserate about the artists' general lack of business savvy with snide remarks as the plush sheep and the Munch blow-up doll stare back at us, reminders that New Burbage is indeed the "arts-skewed commercial enterprise," as Day's soon-to-be-fired Lenstrex colleague unselfconsciously calls it. But immediately following their banter, the pompous, faux-British theatre critic Basil rings the death knell of all past greatness as he smugly whispers to Ellen Fanshaw, "You see, Oliver isn't saying anything. He's just putting on the show. I've seen the show, many, many times. When I say that, I don't mean *The Dream*. I mean, *this show*" (1.1). Then pointing at a Lenstrex representative, he prophesies: "That's the future of this festival right there, a sweaty middle manager, soiling the works of Shakespeare." Given Basil's evident oleaginousness, we inevitably sympathize with Fanshaw's "shut up, Basil." Making Basil an object lesson in how not to communicate faith in holy theatre, the show deflects easy accusations of elitism. In doing so, it leaves an audience willing to believe that Shakespeare offers something that *Mamma Mia!* doesn't. Yet Basil's underlying criticism echoes a widely shared concern about Shakespeare festivals, namely the inevitable problem of exigency vis-à-vis Shakespeare. After all, why perform *A Midsummer Night's Dream* for the umpteenth time? When the same plays are recycled, there comes a sense that the whole enterprise is relatively arbitrary except when it's financially profitable. For theatre to be alive, there needs to be a sense that the plays are responsive to current forms and pressures. In the absence of such urgency, two major dangers emerge: the danger of comforting and familiar productions like Welles's *A Midsummer Night's Dream* and the danger of experiment and change for their own sake, as evinced in Nichols's productions. In registering the intertwined pressures of mercenary neo-conservativism with Hobbesian postmodernism, *Slings & Arrows* reminds us that "the real 'avant-garde' is advanced capitalism, with its built-in need to destroy all vestiges of tradition, all orthodox ideologies, all continuous and stable forms of reality."[12] In turn, it reminds that there is now little to be gained, and much to be lost, by demystifying the Shakespeare myth.

While *Slings & Arrows* has been seen as a polemical intervention into the culture wars on the so-called "conservative" side, such a reading fixes the show at a political and cultural moment that has undergone subtle but significant changes. As such, this kind of interpretation obscures more than it explains. The series is better seen as exposing the unnecessary polarities that gave rise to the Shakespeare wars in the first place, something that is much easier to do today than in 1990. Neither reductively materialist nor blandly idealist, the show recognizes a deep human need to connect with the living traditions of the past while, at the same time, acknowledging how those traditions are corroding under the pressures of the market. However deep such corrosion goes, though, the need to experience epiphanic moments through art shows no sign of disappearing. And in that specific sense, we still do live in the same basic cosmos underwriting Brook's *The Empty Space*, as the show insists.

10

Being Darren Nichols

In 1990, Alasdair MacIntyre published a book that describes in historical and conceptual terms the three traditions of moral enquiry available to modern Western intellectuals, one of which is being parodied in the person of Darren Nichols. These three types of intellectual inquiry are signalled in the subtitle of *Three Rival Versions of Moral Enquiry: Encyclopaedia, Genealogy, and Tradition*. As its title suggests, modern Western intellectuals exist in a world where there are three basic ways of thinking about ethical problems: the Enlightenment model as enshrined in the 9th edition of the *Encyclopaedia Britannica*, the genealogical model embodied in Nietzsche's mature philosophy, and the dialectical view initiated by Thomas Aquinas. In exploring these three traditions, MacIntyre's book attempts to move beyond the impasse of methodological incommensurability besetting the humanities and social sciences in the early '90s, a situation that has arguably deepened in subsequent years as interpretive methods with competing theoretical underpinnings continue to proliferate without, at the same time, any overarching attempt at synthesis. In doing so, he not only distinguishes the ideas of each rival tradition but also identifies the forms in which these ideas are communicated and, most importantly for our purposes, the interpretive disposition characteristic of the interpreter within each rival tradition. In short, he locates three different interpretive stances or existential dispositions at work across the three modes of inquiry. In the Enlightenment model, the interpreter adopts a stance of impersonal neutrality analogous to that of the natural scientist. In the genealogical model, the interpreter adopts the critical, but morally invested, stance of the demystifier, or hermeneut of suspicion. While in the dialectical model, the interpreter engages in morally invested

160 Shakespeare and the World of *Slings & Arrows*

critique of opposing positions while overtly subjecting themselves to such critique in turn.

Operating at the highest levels of philosophical professionalism, MacIntyre avoids polemic and caricature throughout. But in his account of the interpretive stance of the genealogical or deconstructive method of analysis, he might appear to indulge in a degree of satire in his own right. In doing so, he provides the proper philosophical context for what, precisely, is being parodied in the figure of Darren Nichols. Characteristically, MacIntyre explains,

> The genealogist not only explores the unacknowledged oppositions and tensions within the texts which he or she aspires to discredit but continually explains to him or herself and to others what he or she is doing by drawing a set of contrasts between how disastrously Socrates or Plato or Augustine or whoever thinks and how insightfully by contrast the genealogist thinks. Behind the genealogical narrative there is always a shadow of self-congratulatory narrative. This shadow narrative is characteristic of some familiar but unacknowledged genre. Sometimes it is recognizable as the story of a wandering knight who reads the riddle or discovers the hidden name, so rescuing the imprisoned captive; sometimes it is the story of a magic ring which has to be safely transmitted in order to avert some monstrous fate; sometimes it is the story of a journey into a labyrinth guided by a thread. These are all stories of avowed achievement, achievements not of the masks but of their wearer. All such genealogical utterance contains a strain of what is not quite boastfulness because it rests upon a rejection of any table of the virtues in which humility is accounted a virtue. But the achievement of the narrator behind the masks in the continuity of this rejection requires a stable and continuing referent for the "I" – the "I," for example, of the section headings of Nietzsche's *Ecce Homo*: "Why I am so wise. Why I am so intelligent. Why I write such good books. Why I am a destiny." (*TRV*, 209)

The self-protecting overconfidence characteristic of the postmodern genealogist finds comic expression when Nichols introduces himself at a cast reading of *Hamlet* by declaring, "I am Darren Nichols. Deal with *that.*" Notably, Nichols here conspicuously parallels the self-help tapes that Holly Day listens to while driving two episodes later, the creepily intoned mantra: "I am the centre of my universe. All things revolve around me. My power is beyond measure. I am God" (1.5). Among other things, this parallel links Day's neo-liberal egotism to Nichols's self-styled postmodernism. To this extent, Nichols verifies Terry Eagleton's observation that for "all its vaunted openness to the Other, postmodernism can be quite as exclusive and censorious as the orthodoxies it opposes," knowing, for instance, "that authority is repressive ... with all the certainty ... of an archbishop."[1]

MacIntyre's aim is to identify the internal contradiction characteristic of deconstruction as a style of interpretation, the way it exempts itself from its own underlying premises. In terms of theory, deconstruction insists that the "I" or subject is a set of masks or performances that has no underlying continuity over time, no metaphysical or ontological grounding as it were. Instead, it is construed as an epiphenomenon of language, history, and power rather than as an effect of the limits of the imagination as in Frye. But at the level of practice, deconstructive analysis empowers the critic with a moral authority that finds its formal narrative instantiation in a set of familiar archetypal patterns involving heroes who pursue and thereby exemplify authentic identity. What is fundamentally at issue here, then, is a concept that Nichols dismisses in his final conversation with Tennant before leaving New Burbage in season 1: "Always the hero Geoffrey, the defender of *integrity*" (1.4). As this exchange reminds us, the concept of integrity is crucial to the show's moral and aesthetic vision but in a way that requires some patient thought to properly assess. Easy charges of "essentialism" or naively humanist "authenticity" simply obscure the issue, answering the questions before they have been properly formulated.

According to MacIntyre, one of the peculiar features of literary applications of deconstruction involves its practical reliance on a notion of moral integrity for which it has no corresponding theory. This tension arises, he argues, in the work of Paul de Man, a leading exponent of deconstruction in literary studies in the '70s and an ongoing influence after his death in 1983. On one hand, MacIntyre observes, "The concept of having to be a certain sort of person, morally or theologically, in order to read a book aright ... is alien to the assumption of liberal modernity that every rational adult should be free to and is able to read every book" (*TRV*, 133). On the other hand, however, "this liberal assumption consorts uneasily with the idiom of recent literary interpretation. Consider, for example, the role played in Paul de Man's writings by such words as 'blindness,' 'insight,' 'asceticism,' 'irony,' and 'bad faith,' words that signal to us moral relationships between author and text and between text and reader which can have the power to disrupt and undermine academic *explication de texte*" (*TRV*, 133). MacIntyre thus accuses de Man of smuggling in a set of moral concepts whose full meaning cannot be explicated within the Nietzschean framework orienting his overall analysis. After all, these terms derive from moral traditions that are antithetical to the project of genealogy that Nietzsche instituted, a project that valorizes the will to power over the will to truth. But rather than arguing that de Man has not sufficiently demystified his own claims to self-presence, he argues that his critique of the subject as a moral agent is taking place from a position where that decon-struction has not, and cannot, properly occur. Which is to say, de Man is writing from a practical standpoint that presupposes a form of identity that recurs over time and thus has durable integrity even as he deconstructs such an idea. According to MacIntyre, this is because there is an irresolvable tension between theory and practice in deconstruction, one that goes back to *The Genealogy of Morals*. Hence MacIntyre's prediction that Nietzschean genealogy as a mode of moral inquiry is doomed to fail, eventually bringing down post-structuralism with it. But from his standpoint, this doesn't mean such practices will disappear or lose authority altogether. Instead, it means that they will be modified and contained within some kind of larger philosophical structure and accompanying set of social prac-tices, a process that could happen so slowly that many practitioners may not even notice it's happening.[2]

Viewed in this philosophical context, the parody of Nichols is not indiscriminately anti-intellectual or anti-academic. On the contrary, it is a historically and even institutionally specific parody of a particular set of attitudes that became prominent in the '80s and '90s in some literary and theatrical circles. The immediate context here are the "excesses or irresponsibilities of much depoliticized North American postmodernism" that Richard Knowles identified in his 1993 review of the Stratford Festival.[3] No less importantly, however, there is also something discernibly perennial at play in Nichols, namely the self-protecting habits traditionally called pride. As an embodiment of interpretive and directorial pride, Nichols stands in contrast to Ten-nant's interpretive and directorial humility. This widely recognizable and morally consequential contrast emerges from their respective approaches to direction, both in terms of how they treat their plays and how they are disposed towards their casts.

As a character, Nichols is an extreme example of a style of interpretation that presupposes the critic or director's dominance over the text rather than the text's influence over them. To use Nuttall's terminology, he is an example of an "opaque" rather than "transparent" reader. Moving our sympathies against such an approach, the show systematically undermines Nichols's authority.[4] First off, he speaks in a Toronto accent with the whiff of something absurdly Oxbridge about it, a further attempt on the part of the show's writers to deflect accusations of arbitrary elitism. Second, when we first meet him he is set beside a table topped with some depressing looking fruit juices and last year's blue towel rag. Making matters worse, the camera shoots him from below, recalling the lifelessness of Welles's black and white photo in the eulogy scene. Behind him sits a lame mock-up propped up on a chair, looking like it had been pulled out of storage. But what is perhaps most telling is the way he holds his copy of *Hamlet* as though it were filled with cockroaches. All of this contextualizes his very peculiar self-denomination, one that suggests a dramatically ironic allusion to God's declaration in Exodus: "I am that I am." Once the *mise en scène* is in place, Nichols shares his views of the play with the cast:

> Alright, re: *Hamlet ... Hamlet ...* This play is dead. It has been dead for over three hundred years. It has been strip-mined for quotations, and propped up like Lenin in his ice cave. I don't worship dead texts, but that doesn't mean I don't find interest in them. (1.3)

Nichols's defensive attitude and presumed superiority over the Shakespearean text are made clear in the main concept governing his proposed production of *Hamlet*. "Now as to my vision," he says, "I am taking the word 'rotten,' as in 'something's rotten in the State of Denmark,' *very seriously*. I want a rank and foul looking, foul acted, and if possible, foul smelling *Hamlet*. A decomposed vessel, somewhere between the swamp and the sewer" (1.3). How Nichols intones his words is very telling. He expresses the Shakespeare lines with bemused indifference while emphasizing everything after "I want," as though the production were to be the fulfillment of a desire he brings to the process from the outset. He thus gives the distinct sense that what he takes seriously is his own vision and not the play itself.

Helping to convey the hostility at work in his approach to Shakespeare, the camera lights on the beautiful Kate McNab (Rachel McAdams) when Nichols says "foul looking." The implication is that his vision stands at odds with his cast, and thus has not been fully thought through in terms of the specific community he will be working with. The camera then shoots almost straight up his nose, the angle ironically confirming the philosophical presuppositions of his aesthetic: that he is imposing himself on the play rather than forming a relationship with it in the context of his specific cast, which, as the crone Moira says after the final show, is "a bit too pretty" for the theatre. What is at stake here is something far more fundamental to a theatrical production than whether a director should have an organizing "concept" in mind or not. What is at issue is whether readers and performers should submit themselves to the otherness of the text, whether they should fuse horizons with the play, or simply use it for a set of ideological or aesthetic programs that existed prior to any encounter with the work as a source of energy in its own right. The contrast here is between a postmodern *overstanding* of the text and a dialectical *understanding* of it.

One likely source for this postmodern kind of approach to the plays can be found in Terence Hawkes's witty and entertaining 1992 work *Meaning by Shakespeare*. According to the book's blurb, "these essays put the case that Shakespeare's plays have no essential meaning, but function as resources by which we use to generate meaning for our own purposes." From this standpoint, "Shakespeare doesn't mean: *we* mean *by* Shakespeare." As reviewers pointed out, however, the problem with such an interpretive approach is that it is only persuasive if the book is exempted from its own interpretive premises.[5] More importantly, such a style of interpretation remains willfully indifferent to the edifying dimension of literature and theatrical performance as modes of experience, to the idea that readers and audience goers might be different at the end of the experience than they were going in. Frye refers to this style of interpretation as "the counsel of despair that suggests that all reading is narcissism, seeing every text only as a mirror reflecting our own psyches" (WWP, 75).

If such styles of interpretation get parodied in *Slings & Arrows*, it's not because the show is anti-intellectual. On the contrary, it's because the show is centred in a rival interpretive tradition rather than the tradition of Nietzschean genealogy on which such books are based. Centred in a more dialectically moral and interpretive tradition, the show is about the process by which readers and viewers are transformed in and through aesthetic experience, rendered subject to the power and authority of Shakespeare's stories. In this respect, the show is about "putting ourselves back in the picture." If the show is an example of humanistic approaches to Shakespeare, it is in this very broad sense of being about why Shakespeare matters in the first place.

Here again, Peter Brook's approach to directing helps explain the contrast between Nichols and Tennant. In his reflections on a lifetime of directing Shakespeare, Brook defends an organic approach to the plays, one that is sensitive to the interplay between cast and text. Crucially, his point is not that directorial concepts or interpretive visions are irrelevant, but that they should evolve through the rehearsal process rather than serving as a framework from the get go. Otherwise, it will be very difficult to form a living relationship with the text within the specific context and situation in which one encounters it. Today, more than ever, Brook claims,

> I am left with a respect for the formless hunch which was our guide, and it has left me with a profound suspicion of the now much-used word "concept." Of course, even a cook has a concept, but it becomes real during the cooking, and a meal is not made to last. Unfortunately, in the visual arts, "concept" now replaces all the qualities of hard-earned skills of execution and development. In their place, ideas are developed as ideas, as theoretical statements that lead to equally intellectual statements and discussions in their place. The loss is not in words but in the draining away of what only comes from direct experience, which can challenge the mind and feeling by the quality it brings.[6]

Exquisitely sensitive to the elements of risk and vulnerability inherent in producing plays, Brook errs on the side of discovery over preconceived concept. As he says,

> Any scene in Shakespeare can be vulgarised almost out of recognition with the wish to have a modern concept ... Fortunately there is another way. Always, an ever-finer form is waiting to be found through patient and sensitive trial and error ... A concept is the result and comes at the end. Every form is possible if it is

discovered by probing deeper and deeper into the story, into the words and into the human beings that we call the characters. If the concept is imposed in advance by a dominating mind, it closes all the doors.[7]

Particularly significant here is Brook's wariness of the "dominating mind," a mind more imperialist than receptive. Viewed in this context, the contrast between Nichols's and Tennant's respective directorial styles is not a contrast between the conceptual and the non-conceptual approach. More subtly, it is a contrast between those who begin with a concept and those who find it during the rehearsal process in conjunction with the cast, as Tennant does in his production of *Hamlet*. Indeed, the parallel with Brook becomes clear when, at a key turning point in the rehearsal process, Tennant tells his cast that he wants the production "to be about us," leaving the discovery of what that might mean exactly to be part of the process. In one final reflexive turn, it may be worth noting here that Lewis Baumander, who directed the Keanu Reeves 1995 Manitoba Theatre Centre version of *Hamlet* that is wryly echoed in season 1, remarked that his approach to the play, like his approach to life, was based on the assumption that "Bullshit is made up. Truth is discovered."[8] So like Tennant, Baumander built his version of the play around what Reeves brought to the lead role rather than on a prefabricated concept imposed on the play from the outset.

To be sure, however, Tennant's open-ended approach brings its own problems. These are treated at the opening of season 2 when he uses this approach as an excuse for his overall lack of vision for the new production of *Macbeth*. Moreover, if Nichols's approach to the plays is characterized by a lack of identification, Tennant's sometimes tends towards overidentification with them. The result is a self-sabotaging tendency to overexpose himself to both art and people. This point comes through in his confession at the bar in episode 2 that he misses the intense intimacy of acting with Fanshaw: "I never felt so close to someone," he says of being onstage with her. The issue of intimacy is vital here, a further expression of the show's awareness of the pitfalls inherent in any interpenetration of life with art. Reminiscing about his past as an actor, Tennant complains that life cannot compete with art anymore. In doing so, he articulates a morally dangerous view of theatre as a substitute for life. Hence his rash decision moments later to try to turn life into art by attacking Nichols with a sword at Fan-

Being Darren Nichols

shaw's cast party. Prior to this juvenile stunt, Tennant imagines theatre as a substitute for life rather than as a dialectical means of exploring and transforming it. From this perspective, theatre is no longer holy, but an opiate, or perhaps in this case, a stimulant. Theatre at this nostalgic moment, then, is not envisioned as a way of seeking truth but a way of avoiding it. As with any good moral allegory, the struggle between what is holy and what is deadly happens within the hero as well as in the larger community to which he belongs. Yet behind the basic contrast between Tennant's and Nichols's directorial styles lies a more fundamental interpretive distinction, one that emerges in stark relief in the '90s, between those who see interpretation as an imposition on a radically indeterminate text and those who see it in terms of a dialectical relationship with an open but nevertheless delimited text. Reframed in archetypal terms, this can be simplified as a distinction between pride and humility.

As I noted, the contrast between Tennant's and Nichols's directorial approaches is established through two key scenes in the aptly named episode "Mirror Up to Nature." In the first instance, Tennant, with a little help from Oliver, has a dream in which he appears naked on a stage with flames suddenly bursting out in front of him. The imagery suggests a contrast between Nichols's visually spectacular approach and a much more stripped-down style, one broadly similar to Brook's 2000 production of the play at the Theatre des Bouffes du Nord in Paris with Adrian Lester in the lead role, or some of Phillips's and Hirsch's productions during their tenures at Stratford. In Brook's production, large parts of the text were cut, creating a strongly streamlined version. In turn, the stage pulsed with an orange-red ambiance, used to create a slightly tense atmosphere appropriate for Hamlet's reflections and the play's political drama. This was accomplished with something as simple as a single carpet setting off the space's scuffed stone walls. Apart from that, however, the stage consisted simply of two stools, two skulls, and a few brightly coloured cushions. Arriving at a similarly minimalist vision, Tennant decides to throw out his previous concept and simplify the whole play in a way that he hopes will be appropriate for the cast. With the camera looking up at him in a manner that places the viewer in the position of a cast member, Tennant finds a quote appropriate to his directorial style on the first rehearsal in which his new Ophelia, Kate McNab, will be acting by saying: "Lord. We know what we are, but not what we might be. Who said that? Ophelia. Welcome

Kate?" Then describing the opening of the play as extended knock-knock joke, he asks his cast, "Who is there indeed? Who are these people? Who is Hamlet ... and Ophelia? The answer: whoever is playing them. I want this production to be about us" (1.5). In context, Tennant makes Brook's general point that the rehearsal space should be one of discovery, one that respects both the text and the situation in which the production takes place. Hence the contrast between Tennant's welcoming attitude towards McNab and Nichols's aloof indifference to her and the rest of the cast. In order to allow the process of discovery to happen, Tennant invites his cast to find their own way into the characters, to find a way to fuse their horizon of expectation with their characters. Hence his redeployment of Ophelia's lines about discovery in an interpretive and performative context.

At this point in the rehearsal, the process of discovering the character takes the simple form of selecting costumes. Two rehearsals later, however, the deeper challenge posed by Nichols about the weight of past performances and interpretations reappears. Worried that his cast is losing confidence in the Hollywood star cast as Hamlet, Tennant asks Jack Crew to perform the most famous soliloquy in the Western tradition to reassure everyone, including himself, that he is up to the task. Alone onstage, Crew confesses to Tennant that the speech terrifies him because it has been performed so many times that the audience will not hear Hamlet the character speaking, but Jack the Hollywood star. Tennant reassures Crew by reminding him that he can use this anxiety about acting versus sincerity in his performance. After all, Hamlet is a character who is always acting for others, including the antic disposition of madness. The most important advice Tennant gives Crew, however, is that he has to be specific with his intention. Most significantly, he has to decide whether Hamlet knows Claudius and Polonius are spying on him. For Hamlet's intention in delivering the lines differs depending on who he believes his audience is. This is basic interpretive advice that surely applies to virtually any style of modern production, advice that shows Crew thinking himself into Hamlet's concrete situation as a character at this particular moment in time and space. That he succeeds in fusing with his character in a believable manner is signalled a number of ways in the scene: as lights are dimmed, Crew is suddenly in costume, candles appear, and, most tellingly, the harp arpeggios are cued.

No less importantly, Oliver appears onstage gently summoning Tennant to join him, which Tennant does, but presumably only in his mind rather than in reality. Revealingly, this summons contrasts Hamlet Senior's violent summoning of Hamlet, which is echoed earlier in the season with Oliver appearing as the Ghost and Tennant as his bewildered son. In this instance, Oliver no longer appears as a haunting threat, or dark father, but a helping figure. Perhaps most importantly, the copresence of the three men onstage suggests that past, present, and future become momentarily fused through the work of the theatrical imagination. Crucially, though, this fusion is delicately dissolved as Oliver leaves the stage when Jack refers to the "dread of something after death / (The undiscovered country from whose bourn / No traveller returns)" (1.5). In its fuller narrative context, the scene works to dispel Nichols's cynical view that the literature of the past is too radically ruptured from persons in the present for such a fusion of horizons to occur.

If viewers of this scene have found it moving, it's partly because it answers to our need for a sense of continuity with the past, a need that Simone Weil famously articulated when she warned that

> It would be useless to turn one's back on the past in order simply to concentrate on the future. It is a dangerous illusion to even think that such a thing is possible. The opposition of future to past or past to future is absurd. The future brings us nothing, gives us nothing; it is we who in order to build it have to give it everything. But to be able to give, one has to possess. And we possess no other life, no other living sap, than the treasures stored up from the past and digested, assimilated and created afresh by us. Of all the human soul's needs, none is more vital than this one of the past.[9]

Given this need to connect with the past, the parallels between Tennant and Brook remind us that the directorial approach outlined in *The Empty Space* bears only a superficial resemblance to minimalism as a movement within artistic modernism. In minimalism proper, the aim is to liberate the work of art from its traditional frames, opening the aesthetic experience to materials and objects normally excluded from artistic perception so as to produce an oceanic feeling of limitlessness.[10] With Brook, however, the exact opposite is the case. In his practice, the stripping down of the play constitutes a submission to greater limitation for the sake of making clear, dramatically effective choices. If the scene in which Crew performs Hamlet's soliloquy with

Oliver and Tennant onstage with him is poignant for many people, it's because the avowal of such limits can still produce a sense of clarity and connection with the text.

In achieving such pathos, the scene with Crew parallels the general feeling that Brook articulated around the time of his 2000 production of *Hamlet*, the view that

> We're in a very low moment of history for artistic creation ... People in the past have done what we're trying to do infinitely better. That's why, for one's own sanity, to keep one's own sense of proportion, one must regularly go back to them. The same goes for painters, sculptors, musicians and architects. One loses all sense of quality and meaning if one gets caught up in what one is trying to do oneself.[11]

The recurring theme that links Brook, Tennant, and Coyne is less a matter of theatrical styles than an underlying sense of humility and gratitude for the classics of the past coupled with an outsized ambition about what is still possible in the theatre as a form. The return to basics advocated by each figure is not an end in itself but a substitutable strategy for rediscovering this tense combination of, on one hand, humility in the face of what has been accomplished, and ambition about how to recreate such achievement anew.

11

The Promised End

Having discussed two mythopoetic narratives that are broadly analogous to *Slings & Arrows* in *Kingfisher Days* and "Sold Out," and having analyzed the show's satirical dimensions, we are now in a position to describe its overall structure with greater precision. Among other things, such formal analysis will bring the operation of the show's narrative modes, generic conventions, and story structures into sharper focus. Broadly understood, the series combines an ethically coherent, if morally shifting, mythopoetic pattern of fall and redemption with a simultaneous movement from youth to middle age to old age. In this way, the show traces a double movement of life in time, one linear and chronological and one mythic or archetypal. In the first instance, the show's storyline follows the chronological movement of life lived in an alienating experience of time as the source of decay and loss, most poignantly figured in the person of Charles Kingman (William Hutt). While in the second, it traces a mythic movement of life as lived in an experience of communal revelation, most clearly expressed in Tennant and Welles's chastened recovery of lost idealism in the show's final episode, "The Promised End." This latter temporal movement is the hinge on which the story's investment in theatre as a vocation rests. After all, without a conception of time as fulfillment the very idea of vocation would not be properly communicable.

The temporal distinction at stake here involves two attitudes towards time, one called *chronos* (or clock time) and one called *kairos* (or time as the source of revealed meaning). From the standpoint of chronos, the story traces a disheartening movement from youth to old age and death. But from the standpoint of kairos, the narrative traces a fall and recovery story as the beautiful idea of holy theatre is lost and then momentarily found again. In one respect, then, the story of New Burbage is so relentlessly linear as to become viciously circular, since deadly theatre wins out with the hiring of Darren Nichols as artistic director at the end. From this standpoint, New Burbage ends up more or less where it began in episode 1 with the bleating sheep. This ironic movement partially justifies the view that the show depicts the impossibility of sustaining holy theatre within the prescribed institutional limits of festival theatre in an age of advanced capitalism. But only partially. After all, the story of *Slings & Arrows* is meaningfully, if melancholically, comic, as the final not-for-profit production of *King Lear* marks the show's fullest realization of holy theatre. So if deadly theatre wins out in New Burbage, holy theatre wins out in *Slings & Arrows*. By maintaining such tension between social reality and imaginative hope in its conclusion, the series sustains a degree of narrative contradiction, thus avoiding the tendency to offer formally contrived resolutions to ideological conflicts so often visible in televisual storytelling.

The show's double movement across time as chronos and kairos frames the overall journey undertaken by Geoffrey Tennant. Revealingly, his journey conforms to the three-part pattern Frye defines as characteristic of romance generally, including a) the *agon* or perilous journey and preliminary minor adventure b) the *pathos* or critical struggle with one's enemy or mimetic rival, and c) the *anagnorisis* or recognition and exaltation of the hero, his apotheosis. This three-part pattern covers Tennant's descent into madness during a performance of Hamlet; his struggle against various avatars of deadly theatre, most notably his mimetic rivals Nichols and Sanjay; and finally his recognition of holy theatre in the final performance of *King Lear* in which he appears as actor, director, friend, colleague, and partner. Bob Martin, one of the show's co-writers, confirms the quasi-allegorical nature of Tennant's characterization when he indicates in multiple places that a number of minor characters were designed to clarify the dynamics of his particular story. As is often the case with allegorical quest romances, secondary characters reflect the central hero's struggles to mature or individuate. In extreme instances, such as in the case of Sanjay, secondary characters effectively mirror the dangers and threats the hero undergoes; in this case, the threat of becoming wholly immersed in a destructive world of make-believe where dangerous risks are the self-destructive norm, not the performance-enhancing exception. In this way, the show deploys a double-plot pattern typical of Shakespearean tragedies such as *King Lear* but within the context of what is ultimately a comic romance. Part of the show's success thus lies in the way it infuses the formulaic storylines and patterns of film and television with some of the richness of Shakespearean tragicomedy from which some of those formulas descend.

Like many quest romances, *Slings & Arrows* is threatened by the possibility that the hero of the story may turn out to be more failure than triumph, perhaps even more villain than hero. Such moral ambivalence is certainly characteristic of Tennant, who has been described as "the show's anti-hero, a character so paralyzed by self-importance as to become sympathetic and charming."[1] One way Tennant's moral ambivalence is signalled early in the show is through his allusions to Shakespeare. During his eulogy of Oliver Welles, for example, he not only sets out the terms by which New Burbage might be revitalized, but he also insinuates the extent to which he might destroy the very thing he will be hired to regenerate, as though he were more regicidal Macbeth than reconciling Prospero. Importantly, the promise of regeneration articulated verbally in the speech is redoubled by the scene's camera movements, as this scene sets the visual cues for instances of holy theatre later in the series. During his eulogy, the camera oscillates between extreme close-ups of Tennant, shots of the general audience, close-ups of faces in the audience, shots of Ellen Fanshaw in the wings, and balancing shots of the whole stage with Welles's picture visible. This general pattern will become familiar over the series as a whole because it constitutes the formal means by which the series communicates the possibility that in holy theatre the diverse individuals witnessing and participating in the show can momentarily approximate a true community. After all, at such moments young and old viewers, television watchers and theatre goers, as well as offstage actors and stagehands, all share one compelling focus.[2] Yet several details distinguish the camera movement of this early scene from genuine instances of holy theatre later in the season, most importantly those extreme close-ups of Tennant's face shot from below. Initially, the proximity of the camera is emotionally affecting, if still slightly jarring. But as Tennant develops his eulogy, the close-ups become more unsettling, thereby alienating us somewhat from Tennant. Our impatience with him conforms to the funeral audience's growing impatience too. In this way, the extreme close-up communicates the extent to which Tennant doesn't quite fit within the institutional limits of New Burbage, that he may destroy it and it he. Hence Fanshaw's disgusted turn away from the stage during

Tennant's critique of Welles along with the audience's deadpan response to Tennant's inappropriate and dramatically ironic allusion to *Macbeth*. In a state of self-indulgent exasperation, Tennant rages: "When I look around at the wreck this theatre has become under Oliver's reign, I am reminded of those words from *Macbeth*: 'If thou couldst doctor, cast the water of my land, find her disease. And purge it to a sound and pristine health, I would applaud thee to the very echo'" (1.2). In its original context in act 5 of the play, Macbeth's plea is inadvertently self-refuting, as he is the cause of the land's disease from which he seeks to escape. Inadvertently self-annihilating in its logic, Macbeth's allusion is thus a highly fraught, if not outright inappropriate, text for the occasion. After all, it bespeaks Tennant's self-destructive inclinations more than any genuine desire to be the source of communal regeneration.

This ironic use of allusion is itself a very Shakespearean trick. As we saw with Theseus from *A Midsummer Night's Dream*, proverbial language in Shakespeare often paradoxically signals some kind of moral erring or confusion. A related adaptation of this strategy occurs in episode 1 when a festival sponsor accepting a token of thanks from Oliver Welles quotes Macbeth's "Life is a tale, told by an idiot, full of sound and fury, signifying nothing" before intoning a set of moral platitudes designed to have precisely the opposite effect (1.1). Despite the sponsor's intentions, the effect is to inadvertently make Macbeth's point that the tale is indeed being told by an idiot, thereby recalling commercial misuses of Shakespeare such as a 1968 Bank of Montreal advertisement from the Stratford program that cited Iago's "Put money in thy purse" as prudential advice. Similarly, if less ludicrously, Tennant's allusion to Macbeth shows him blurring his own anger, pain, and contempt with the good faith efforts of New Burbage to create meaningful theatre. Ultimately, then, the eulogy scene oscillates between despair and hope, a tension communicated formally in the movement from uncomfortable close-ups to balanced stage shots. Coupled with the competing allusions to Peter Brook on one hand and Macbeth on the other, this formal pattern moves us from Tennant's soul-destroying pain to the promise of his reintegration into a revitalized theatre community. The result is a morally complex characterization built out of verbal and narrative Shakespearean strategies effectively redeployed in televisual terms.

Yet this uncomfortable tension between hope and despair is broken with the thunderous shock of homophobic anti-theatricalism. Some-

The Promised End   175

what paradoxically, however, this comically absurd scene momentarily re-humanizes Tennant, who responds with childlike delight to the chaos that ultimately ensues. Due to poor last-minute organization, coupled with the general unease about death in a desacralized age, the choice of minister for Welles's funeral turns out to be a wholesale disaster. Rather than finding someone appropriate, the festival administration inadvertently invites an outspoken homophobe who rages, as I noted, in a manner that recalls the seventeenth-century puritan William Prynne, author of the anti-theatrical diatribe *Histriomastix: The Player's Scourge, Or Actor's Tragedy* (1633). Comically ridiculous, the unhinged minister resuscitates a long Puritan tradition of anti-theatrical hectoring that is rooted in fear of same-sex desire, the sort of desire Shakespeare takes delight in expressing in gender-bending plays such as *Twelfth Night* and *As You Like It*. Unsurprisingly, the raging homophobe succeeds only in reaffirming the deep-rooted associations of the Shakespearean stage with sexual liberation. Keeping with the demystifying intent of absurdism as a theatrical mode, the hilariously goofy scene effectively defangs homophobia as anything other than outdated bigotry. If not Brechtian, the campy effect is sufficiently demystifying while still being funny. Intriguingly, it is the scene's absurdity rather than its potential for moral outrage that serves to momentarily re-humanize Tennant. As the over-the-top ridiculousness of the situation unfolds, we see Tennant offstage with a warmly bemused, even somewhat childlike, expression on his face. The effect is to reintroduce a degree of humanity into him, allowing him to regain some of the warmth that he lost seconds earlier, while still communicating the release of dangerous electric energy into the staid atmosphere of New Burbage. The opposition between Welles and Tennant is further reinforced in the scene's final shot. As we leave the tackily decorated stage among blaring fire alarms and shuffling bodies, we see an oversized black and white photo of Oliver Welles staring back at us, his deadened expression countering Tennant's childlike grin. The result is a dim but discernible sense that the ground is being laid for a reconnection with what Kareda called the "old sense of kamikaze fearlessness" that is needed to rescue a theatre artistically rather than just financially (so, 8).

The overall arc of Tennant's journey in *Slings & Arrows* is completed by a fortuitous association with Kent, a figure of loyalty and service who can be read as the moral center of the play alongside Cordelia, in the final production of *King Lear*. The trajectory of

Tennant's character is thus capped in the season's final episode, "The Promised End," in which the actors of New Burbage put on a one-time, not-for-profit performance of *King Lear* in a multi-purpose room of a church, not heeding warnings that they would be fired from the festival if they did so. Adding to the power of the performance, Charles Kingman, the appropriately named overbearing Lear-like actor who is playing the title role, is dying, something Tennant conceals from the rest of the cast so as to protect the veteran actor. Rather remarkably, William Hutt, the legendary thespian referred to in 1962 as the King of the Canadian Stage,[3] was himself dying of cancer while performing the role, succumbing to the disease in 2007. The result is the show's most effective layering of life, the story of New Burbage, and Shakespeare. This is especially so given that the scenes from *King Lear* in the show constitute the only available footage of Hutt's celebrated performance of the role, which he also took on at Stratford in four separate productions. To be sure, Kingman's impending death makes the play a gift that the other actors are bequeathing to him, even as his world-class performance is a grace that he gives in return. The result of this rich interlacing of life and art is the purest expression of holy theatre realized in the series, including an extraordinary sense of its exquisite fragility.[4]

The series reaches its compromised apotheosis, its final recognition scene, by setting two apocalypses or moments of revelation against one another. On one hand, there is the cry of agony in *King Lear* in which "tragedy assumes the figurations of apocalypse, of death and judgment, heaven and hell; but the world goes forward in the hands of exhausted survivors."[5] And on the other hand, there is the "soft apocalypse" of the story itself in which a chastened version of holy theatre is reawakened through an amateur production of *King Lear*. This layering of *King Lear* with the story of *Slings & Arrows* creates the effect that we are seeing the play from the reconciling perspective of the late romances. The show's overall structure thus implies a view of Shakespeare's career as culminating in the great romances, as though their promise of reconciliation were the final and most mature vision Shakespeare offers.

The fragility of holy theatre achieved at the end is partially signalled in the final episode by the fact that the actor playing Kent, a figure of loyalty and service, is unable to perform, forcing Tennant to step into the role at the last minute. This shows Tennant returning to the stage for the first time in ten years, not altogether unlike Richard

The Promised End

Monette's surprise return to the Stratford stage after a ten-year hiatus for similar reasons. However, Kent is badly treated by Lear in precisely the same way Tennant is abused by Kingman, thus signalling the need for reconciliation at the level of both art and life. The symbolic significance of Tennant's performance as Kent becomes clear in a culminating exchange between Tennant and the ghost of his friend and nemesis Oliver Welles. Having just watched Lear and Cordelia reunite from the wings of the stage, Tennant asks Welles: "What are we doing here, you and I?" to which Welles pauses and then matter-of-factly replies: "Putting on a play" (3.6). Seeing the justice of the answer, Tennant concurs in a moment that constitutes his *anagnorisis* or recognition scene: "Putting on a play. This isn't about us, is it?" In a defining moment in the series, both men convey the distinct sense that their shared epiphany and sense of reconciliation has mysteriously descended upon them from outside themselves. Touched by the fragile grace of the whole situation, Welles avers: "Nope, it never was." This poignant exchange constitutes the show's culminating moment, the point at which its hero undergoes the sort of anamnesis or "spiritual memory" that drives Coyne's *Kingfisher Days*, the feeling of having discovered something one has "always known, but somehow forgotten" (*KD*, 1). What Tennant recalls at this defining moment is a deep intuition about why holy theatre has the peculiar effect that it often does, the sort of moralizing effect that Iris Murdoch describes, with *King Lear* in mind, when she writes:

> The pointlessness of art is not the pointlessness of a game; it is the pointlessness of human life itself, and form in art is properly the simulation of the self-contained aimlessness of the universe ... Art transcends selfish and obsessive limitations of personality and can enlarge the sensibility of its consumer. It is a kind goodness by proxy. Most of all it exhibits to us the connection, in *human* beings, of clear realistic vision with compassion ... The death of Patroclus, the death of Cordelia, the death of Petya Rostov. All is vanity. The only thing which is of real importance is the ability to see it all clearly and respond to it justly which is inseparable from virtue. Perhaps one of the greatest achievements of all is to join this sense of absolute mortality not to the tragic but to the comic.[6]

The ending of *Slings & Arrows* has perhaps proven affective for many viewers because it dramatizes the way art is both disinterested and transformative at once, pointless yet consequential simultaneously. Even more, the show's ending reframes the tragic vision of *King Lear* into a melancholically comic vision, gesturing, in its own modest way, to the union of compassionate virtue and aesthetic beauty avowed by Murdoch. Admittedly, however, the show's intimations of immortality, along with its solidarity with the late romances, means that it does not demand the sense of "absolute mortality" that Murdoch, speaking in a rather existential mood, identifies with the greatest possible art. So despite its Canadian fatalism, the show is perhaps not as cosmically bleak as Murdoch's vision of artistic authenticity would demand.[7] What does further link the ending of *Slings & Arrows* to Murdoch, however, is their shared stress on the role of imagination in art. Writing in 1967, Murdoch also responded to the growing emphasis on anti-realism in modern art. In doing so, she stressed how

> in intellectual disciplines and in the enjoyment of art and nature
> we discover value in our ability to forget self, to be realistic, to
> perceive justly. We use our imagination not to escape the world
> but to join it, and this exhilarates us because of the distance
> between our ordinary dulled consciousness and an apprehension
> of the real.[8]

For Murdoch, as for *Slings & Arrows*, *King Lear* is one of the fullest realizations of these principles.

As his performance of Kent suggests, Tennant began the series embodying the troubled masculinity of Prospero at the beginning of *The Tempest* but ends it by embodying the sense of service and self-sacrifice Prospero demonstrates at the play's end. What is thus disclosed at the end of the series is not the theatrical optimism of Hippolyta's speech but something more like the chastened view expressed by Prospero's "We are such stuff / As dreams are made on" (4.156–7) or Puck's thinking "this weak and idle theme, / No more yielding but a dream" (5.1.12–13). The result is a vision in which the dream of holy theatre as expounded in Tennant's eulogy for Welles both is and is not fulfilled. While the production of *King Lear* achieves genuine greatness, it is a one-off production that occurs outside the institution that has the authority to grant social legitimacy to this artistic achievement. The show thus ends with the sense that the promise of holy theatre remains, as it were, in the wilderness rather than in the church. But if the ending of the show is an elegy for holy theatre, it is so not

The Promised End 179

in the fully literal sense that capitalism will soon kill off the human desire for great art. On the contrary, it is elegiac only in Coyne's sense that "there's something very melancholy about doing something you love, because it will never be good enough, it will always break your heart."[9] If hope in holy theatre remains alive at the end of the show, it's in the restricted sense with which we began in Théâtre Sans Argent in season 1. Hence Tennant and Fanshaw's return to low-budget theatre at the end.

Importantly, the final episode's title, "The Promised End," comes from the devastating final scene in *King Lear*. Spoken by Kent when Lear enters howling with the dead Cordelia in his arms, the line is posed as a question: "Is this the promised end?" Complicating matters further, Edgar adds to Kent's question the haunting "Or image of that horror?" (5.3.262–3). Despite the play's pagan setting, these questions place Lear's response to Cordelia's death in an apocalyptic context, as a sign that judgement day must be upon them. Such allusions to the Book of Revelation thus deepen the apocalyptic energy of the play, the way its drama is repeatedly heightened by an end-of-days discourse that gives the story an almost unbearable weight and magnitude. Such apocalyptic language is an example of the way Shakespeare exploits his religious inheritance. From one perspective, it creates an almost unbearable sense of spiritual claustrophobia as the traditional forms of transcendence through faith no longer seem to bear weight. From the opposite point of view, however, Kent's question suggests the possibility that Cordelia's loving forgiveness of her father's trespasses redeems her and her father's death at the end of the play, though even he remains unsure such optimism is warranted. Viewed this way, the story's ending places an audience in a position analogous to those standing at the crucifixion before knowledge of the resurrection comes. As such, the play has been plausibly described as broadly Christian in nature. But not everyone agrees, as the final episode can be seen in more fully fatalistic terms. So on the other hand, then, the play's ending can be seen as presenting a world apparently evacuated of moral transcendence, a world just as purposeless and arbitrary as Beckett's. Neither the faithful nor the pessimistic reading is wrong, as the play contains both possibilities. Yet it seems clear that the choices Kent, Edgar, and Cordelia make are more justifiable than the actions Edmund, Goneril, and Regan take. So in that limited sense, the moral vision of the play stands much closer to the Gospel tradition than to Nietzsche's *The Genealogy of*

Morals. If this observation does not take us very far in understanding *King Lear*, it nevertheless helps account for the very different form of poignancy achieved at the end of *Slings & Arrows*.

After all, the final performance of *King Lear* is the show's fullest, and yet most melancholic, articulation of the idea that theatre makes visible the dream of a diverse community united as an audience in a shared story. This vision is given further, but very subtle, expression in the show's post-Lear ending with a conspicuous guest appearance by Ann-Marie MacDonald, author of a celebrated feminist revisioning of *Othello*, *Goodnight Desdemona (Good Morning Juliet)*.[10] This cameo by MacDonald, in which she interviews for the job of artistic director at New Burbage, intimates the fragile and fading hope that the future of the festival will be less dominated by fathers and sons and more welcoming to mothers and daughters.[11] In many respects, MacDonald is a perfect figure to introduce in this capacity, as her major Shakespeare-inflected play expresses a humanist feminism inspired by Jung's exploration of spiritual alchemy rather than the post-structural sort that was so popular in the academy of the 1990s.

A similar trajectory is traced across the show vis-à-vis race. In the first season, the only major character of colour is Nahum (Rothaford Gray), a Nigerian-born theatre director exiled for his politically revolutionary theatre now working as New Burbage's janitor. In the final episode, however, Nahum finally takes his place among the artists, working the sound booth. Similarly, season 2 includes a mild-mannered, Shakespeare-loving Black female tax auditor with significant power over Ellen Fanshaw, while season 3 includes the high-powered, self-asserting African American actress Barbara Gordon (Janet Bailey). The trajectory here is of increasing, but still unrealized, inclusivity and equality. On one hand, this pattern echoes the promise of equality intimated in *A Midsummer Night's Dream*, its prefiguring of true community as "ruling-class lovers are elbowed aside and forced to give equal room … to 'rude mechanicals / That work for bread upon Athenian stalls."[12] But closer to home, it parallels the belated but substantial changes made at the Stratford Festival at the turn of the twenty-first century when concerted efforts were made to diversify the festival.[13] In a happy development, Paul Gross performed the lead role in *King Lear* at the 2023 Stratford Festival alongside Qualipu Mi'kmaq First Nation actor Gordon Patrick White in a production directed by Kimberley Rampersad, a woman of colour. One hallmark of Gross's performance was its acute attention to the play's dark comedy, an element enhanced by White's wry yet cutting humour as Lear's wise fool. Indeed, the presence of a First Nations actor as Lear's fool added a subtle sense of post-colonial irony to the production, as the fool's critique of Lear's overbearingness and obtuseness resonated, however obliquely, in the context of the ongoing process of truth and reconciliation in Canada.

In the show's final episode, the soft utopian vision of a diverse community united in a shared project for the right reasons is fleetingly realized. To convey this orienting vision, camera angles include not only close-ups of the stage but also shots of the audience, sound booth, dressing rooms, and wings. In doing so, the show communicates the unifying intersection of life and art made possible through theatre. The result is a generous vision in which "we are invited to see the performances through multiple viewpoints," thereby encouraging the show's viewers to become part of one diverse audience.[14] This observation confirms the view that *Slings & Arrows* "ultimately unites different types of spectators, including business- and art-minded viewers, the youth and the elderly, and television and theatre audiences."[15] Such a vision runs explicitly counter to criticisms of the 1993 Stratford Festival's construction of a homogeneously white, male, and affluent audience.[16] Importantly, however, this hopeful vision of unity in diversity is rooted in the show's mythopoetic pursuit of a holy theatre, a theatre in which aesthetic experience remains distinct from and irreducible to market and ideological forces even as it inevitably remains mediated by them.

But what are we to make of the final production's amateurism at the end of *Slings & Arrows*? How does its non-professional status resonate in the broader Shakespeare world? As far as literary studies go, it's helpful to remember that English as a discipline has long oscillated between bouts of professionalism and amateurism, with each call for rigour and method being met with a counter-affirmation of loving literature for its own sake.[17] In this sense, the professional/amateur binary exists within the institution of Shakespeare scholarship, just as it often does within the context of classical theatre.[18] Ever since professional literary studies emerged out of the shadow of belles lettres criticism, it has had to rediscover the source of its own cultural and spiritual exigency from time to time.[19] So if the amateur half of this binary is now taking precedence over the professional half in some quarters, it is in order to recalibrate the needs of the profession in the post-millennial moment, as those insisting they are amateurs are often expert professionals. Given that the sequel to the series will be titled *Amateurs*, it's clear that the writers of the show recognize the value of affirming first principles at this particular historical moment. In many respects, the argument I am making in this book is simply one more tipping of the scales towards first principles vis-à-vis Shakespeare studies and performance.

Conclusion

After the debacle of Charles Kingman's *King Lear*, Darren Nichols is hired as the next artistic director of New Burbage, his final words in the series being, "Let's talk box office." As this ending suggests, Nichols is an essential part of the program's sustained critique of corporatized art, exposing, as critics have noticed, "the curious alliance between postmodern cultural practices and capitalism."[1] In this sense, his character embodies the way that "critiques of logocentrism, foundations, and the hierarchies of value dependent on them can have a leveling effect, reducing all cultural objects to the status of commodities circulating, and competing for attention, within a global marketplace."[2] It is testimony to the show's intelligence that these tensions have already played out in Shakespeare scholarship, appearing in Michael Bristol's response to Terence Hawkes's *Meaning by Shakespeare* (1992). Responding to Hawkes, Bristol explains how the

> notion that signification is perpetually mobile, changing, and incommensurable actually describes the increasingly absolute sovereignty of the free market in contemporary society, where the fading away of reliable meaning in discursive practices such as advertising has become a familiar feature of everyday life. (BTS, 27)

So when Nichols makes imperious allusions to Roland Barthes – telling his actors that he is interested in a play's signifiers not its characters – he exemplifies how structuralism colludes "with the strategies of modern capitalism ... by ... treating individuals as the mere empty locus of impersonal codes."[3] Presenting Shakespeare's characters in precisely this abstracted manner, Nichols's pseudo-absurdist *Romeo and Juliet* reminds us that capitalism is the ultimate form of

184   Shakespeare and the World of *Slings & Arrows*

the avant-garde, with its relentless need to dissolve every tie between past and present.

The dialectical relationship between Tennant and the avatars of anti-mimesis such as Nichols echo the more strictly metafictional relation between the playwright Lionel Train and Susan Coyne, whose character Anna Conroy has an emotionally and ethically complicated relationship with the playwright. In several respects, this relationship provides a way for the writers of the series to address the risks involved in their boldly conceived narrative structure, particularly their intertwining of the New Burbage Festival with the Stratford (Ontario) Festival. While it's one thing to mistreat the work of a firmly established playwright who has been dead for four hundred years,[4] satirizing one's colleagues, however affectionately, is another thing entirely. Clearly aware of these risks, the writers of the series integrate the problem into their story. They do this in season 2 through the symbolically composite figure of Lionel Train, a pusillanimous playwright who is work-shopping a new play at the festival. While at New Burbage, Train begins dating Anna Conroy, the festival's sweet-tempered, hyper-competent associate director, who is played by Coyne herself. After a couple of comic intimate encounters, Train selfishly exploits the private experiences Anna shares with him. As the prefix of his name may intimate, Lionel retells Conroy's most intimate experiences in a self-aggrandizing rather than truthful way.

By exploiting Anna's experiences in a self-aggrandizing manner, Lionel foregrounds the ethical risks that Coyne has taken on in writing a story which self-consciously interlaces life and art. Calling attention to these interrelations, Conroy's last name is a close anagram of the woman who created and played her. The close yet far relation between Coyne and Conroy cements Anna's role as the moral centre of the series, just as Kent is arguably the moral center of *King Lear*. In this respect, Train embodies the threat that the show as a whole seeks to avoid, that peculiar mix of cowardice and cruelty that often characterizes the worst of human behaviour. Such narrative strategies disclose Coyne's tendency to write in subtly allegorical ways, giving rise to the kind of cultural and aesthetic commentary I have argued *Slings & Arrows* offers.

It's important to acknowledge, however, that semi-allegorical modes of writing tend to run the risk of reinscribing normative conceptions of human subjectivity that may be oppressive in some instances. Perhaps this is one reason why *Slings & Arrows* has been

Conclusion 185

charged with fostering a heteronormative view of sexuality. The critique turns on the subplot involving the two young actors who play Romeo (the gay and slightly retiring Patrick) and Juliet (the headstrong but unselfconsciously feminine Sarah). The basic claim is that Patrick is "straightened" by his performance as Romeo because he sleeps with his Juliet, thus reinforcing an oppressively normative reading the play. Yet this against-the-grain critique overlooks a number of important features of the subplot, thereby misrepresenting the story as a whole. Following a comic plot pattern, the two young leads (played by David Alpay and Joanne Kelly) resist the patriarchal tyranny of Nichols's rather deadening direction by seeking help from Tennant. Overcome during rehearsal by the sensuality of the aubade scene, the two actors sleep together, though it remains unclear whether the sexual act involved Patrick and Sarah or Romeo and Juliet or some mysterious combination therein. Crucially, this confusion is remarked on at a pivotal moment in the subplot by the show's gay chorus figure, Cyril. Dispirited by the laughable rigidity of Nichols's production, Patrick publicly kisses Sarah during rehearsal despite her reticent worry that "everyone will laugh at us" (2.6). Importantly, this kiss coincides with and thus helps trigger Nichols's realization that his design for the play has been hampered by his need for mastery and self-control, his fear, as it were, of the text's agency over him. Witnessing the kiss, Cyril, who opens and closes every episode with a musical number, and who is always shown in intimate affection with his partner Frank (whom he calls "Ducky"), wryly remarks: "There's something you don't see every day of the week" (2.6). The intergenerational context of the aside is as telling as the further insinuation that there is something queer about heterosexuality in the theatre. What we are witnessing in this kiss is not Patrick's heterosexual coming out but, more simply, the rejuvenation of the older generation by the younger (the opposite of what happens in *Romeo and Juliet*).

There is no suggestion in season 2 that Patrick has changed his sexual orientation or that he is having any sort of identity crisis. Sexuality is not the primary issue here. On the contrary, Patrick's journey aligns with the show's broader concern of immersing oneself in the Shakespearean story, something Patrick, a professional actor, is trying his best to do despite hostile direction and comically absurd costuming. Moreover, Patrick is not the only gay man to sleep with a woman for complex reasons in the story. As we might recall, the original sin behind Tennant's breakdown in season 1 is that his gay director Oliver

Wells slept with his girlfriend Fanshaw out of a complex brew of envy, power, and attraction to Tennant. Consequently, the issue of heteronormativity that critics have raised is not so much beside the point as it is actively exorcised by the show. Taken as a whole, *Slings & Arrows* is self-consciously queer-friendly, something that will presumably become clearer in the prequel's exploration of Cyril and Frank's early years.

But what is more important to Patrick's kissing of Sarah than sexual orientation per se is the public release of youthful libido, a release that momentarily renews Nichols's love of theatre, bringing him closer to his art and cast. This emphasis is one of many indications that the series is much more interested in general dynamics of intimacy and vulnerability requisite to aesthetic and theatrical experience than it is in the now more familiar questions of gender and sexuality. So rather than being an attempt "to cure the gays and the academics," *Slings & Arrows* is cleverly imbricated in ongoing debates about Shakespearean mimesis that inevitably touch on basic questions of artistic exigency and purpose. If the show succeeds in communicating to a large audience why Shakespeare matters, it's partly because of the way it translates Brook's updated Coleridgean views on Shakespearean theatre to televisual terms. In the process, the series is a suggestive reminder that *The Empty Space* presciently foresaw the limits of demystification and anti-realism as critical and aesthetic practices. While Brook advocates relentless demystifying of dated conventions, he nevertheless remains more focused on the underlying needs to which those conventions once answered. Partly as a result of his intellectual and spiritual capaciousness, Brook continues to have important things to say to Shakespeareans. In turn, the show provides further evidence that Frye's concept of the popular as imaginatively resonant yet easily accessible still has untold purchase for our understanding of contemporary culture and Shakespeare's late romances. As such, both Frye and Brook remain of particular value to those who think that the potentialities characteristic of post-Romanticism and high modernism have not been systematically eclipsed by the dialectical operations of capital, but remain with us today as ongoing, if oftentimes dormant, possibilities for re-enchantment. So too, in its own modest way, does *Slings & Arrows*.

CODA

John Hirsch's *Tempest* (1982)

With more than forty years of hindsight, it should now be evident that John Hirsch's 1982 Stratford production of *The Tempest* constitutes a major moment in Canadian cultural history and is certainly a milestone in the history of Shakespeare in Canada. It is perhaps no surprise that this production powerfully articulates the tensions between created and revealed meanings so crucial to *Kingfisher Days*, *Slings & Arrows*, and Coyne's work more generally. [1]

Hirsch's production is significant precisely insofar as it is exquisitely personal, the product of his lifelong meditation on the play's themes of exile, freedom, and illusion in the context of his own experience being orphaned during World War II, when his entire immediate family was killed in the Holocaust. As he says in his notes "On Directing *The Tempest*," "You might say that I've spent my lifetime preparing to meet the challenge, or rather, accept the challenge of the romance plays of Shakespeare."[2] Hirsch's adopted sister Sybil Shack clarifies the meaning of this statement when she explains how his attitude towards Germans changed over the course of his life. In an interview that is now part of the John Hirsch oral history at Library and Archives Canada, Shack notes that the first time Hirsch drove through Germany while travelling from Switzerland to Austria he felt very uncomfortable, but afterwards

> he got over that ... [and was] able to forgive and understand and I remember him saying one time ... that hatred is the worst thing that we can have and as long as we perpetuate hatred in one form or another we are contributing to it. So along with his [avowed] Jewishness is this ability to forgive.[3]

From this perspective, the most relevant context for understanding Hirsch's critically celebrated production is his own sustained identification with Prospero as an exiled and spiritually embattled theatre director, one capable of great imagination but also, as Hirsch's actors will testify, enormous terror. Not in the least sentimental, Hirsch's fascination with Prospero comes through in a harrowing and to the best of my knowledge unpublished account he gave in 1988 of his return to his family home in Siófok, Hungary, just as the Russians were pushing the German army out of Eastern Europe. Holding to what he describes as the hallucinatory hope that his family would still be alive, Hirsch discovered that the Nazis had used his relatively large family home as a kind of warehouse, with furniture and books piled throughout. In the process of telling the story of how he was emotionally overcome at the sight of his family's books piled up in his parents' abandoned bedroom, he reflects on how difficult it is to narrate such traumatic events in a way that is not exploitative or self-pitying. In doing so, he stresses the importance of emotional and temporal distance to the processing of one's past, much as he does in his discussion of *The Tempest* six years earlier. So in 1988, he said,

> You know distance is very important – an emotional distance is essential, if one is to describe what one went through and who one was, at the time. I was fourteen years old, going on fifteen. So you know, how do you talk about these things, without beginning to realize that you are sort of playing on other people's emotions, or whatnot. I don't know how you do that.[4]

Similarly, in 1982, Hirsch claims that in *The Tempest*

> Shakespeare says that if you want to regain your sanity, you have to run away from society. It's essential for our spiritual well-being. But it's a paradoxical self-exile and flight because it is also the duty of the ruler to stick with it, and you cannot co-opt your responsibility. What is good for your soul, finally, must be of benefit to the society in which you live.[5]

If Hirsch's personal connections with Prospero's healing in exile, along with the coincident concern with over-theatricalized exploitation, remain tacit in this late account of his wartime experience, the identification becomes fully thematized when he reflects on his expe-

Coda 189

rience in Winnipeg, the fourth of the four "mafias" to which he famously said he belonged: Hungarian, Jewish, Homosexual, and Winnipeg. In a 1988 special issue of the arts magazine *Border Crossings* on the exiled imagination, Hirsch confessed that "I was healed here [in Winnipeg], I was reborn here. It was a most marvellous sea voyage that I undertook and the seas, as Shakespeare said in *The Tempest*, were indeed merciful" (*BC*, 83). Part of the reason for this personal renewal had to do with Hirsch's sense that in Winnipeg

> there was [simply] culture … It was only in Toronto that I began to hear this business about ethnics and multiculturalism. It was a terrible shock when I got to Upper Canada, which was like Deathsville. All these people with lemons stuck up their arses kept responding to me by saying, "Oh my God, here's a person who actually is yelling and crying and feeling." You don't do that. It's impolite. (*BC*, 84)

Coming from a well-to-do, upper-middle-class culturally German family, Hirsch admits to having had no experience or even understanding of the rich mixture of Judaism and socialism he encountered in the North End, especially among the Ukrainian Jews such as the Shack family he was adopted into as one of the five hundred war orphans sponsored by the Canadian Jewish Congress. Perhaps most importantly, though, his experience in North End Winnipeg allowed him to "suddenly recognize that Ukrainians and Germans and Russians and Jews were living together and not killing one another. That was something very new. I couldn't believe it" (*BC*, 83). So just as Hirsch brought his experience of war and exile to his celebrated production of Brecht's *Mother Courage* (1964), so too did this experience inform his Stratford production of *The Tempest* (1982). Such experience was certainly on the mind of at least one cast member, as Richard Monette wondered if Hirsch's distinction between Antonio's aggressive evil and Sebastian's passive evil paralleled "those who actually ran the … camps and those who just stood by and let it happen."[6]

However, a more general intellectual context animating Hirsch's production of *The Tempest* also makes it of critical and historical interest and may bring its poignant personal dimensions into further relief. In this production, Hirsch continues his decades-long negotiation of two critical polarities, the two extremes represented by, on one side, the moral and aesthetic idealism of Northrop Frye and, on the other, the moral and aesthetic pessimism of the post-war Polish critic Jan Kott. While Frye and Kott embody sharply opposing sensibilities, they nevertheless both took it for granted that *The Tempest* is not one play among others in the Shakespearean or even the Western canon. For both critics, as we have seen, *The Tempest* is paradigmatic of larger aesthetic and social dynamics, even serving as a cipher for the power of drama as such. Consequently, the stakes involved in how we make sense of its depiction of the relationship between life and art, between moral and theatrical illusions, could not be higher. Given the play's importance to these two critics, it came to form a distinct leitmotif in their work, just as it did in Hirsch's life and art. Little surprise, then, that both Frye and Kott are conspicuous presences in the literary materials associated with Hirsch's production, showing that the director was consciously responding to them here much as he was in earlier productions, going back at least as far as his 1965 *Hamlet* and 1968 *A Midsummer Night's Dream* productions, both of which are especially affiliated with Kott.

As we saw, Kott views *The Tempest* not as a story of forgiveness and reconciliation, but as an elegy for Renaissance humanism, an expression of civilizational exhaustion. On his grandly Schopenhauerian view, Prospero's "great globe" "is a theatre ... in which everything is repeated but nothing is purified," making the play a striking expression of the social impotence of drama, a lament for "the very end of Elizabethan tragedy."[7] From this anti-apocalyptic and in its Polish context anti-Stalinist perspective, *The Tempest* becomes "a drama of lost illusions, of bitter wisdom, and of fragile – though stubborn – hope."[8] One of the primary things I believe Hirsch was working through in his own response to *The Tempest* was whether Kott's stress on the value of dispelling illusions, on achieving a state of bitter lucidity, can in fact sustain even the most stubborn forms of hope. In other words, is demystification a sufficient rather than simply necessary means of arriving at truth? To be sure, we can still hear echoes of Kott's "hope beyond hope" in Hirsch's 1985 comments on *King Lear*, when he said "we live in a time when people must be reminded over and over in the most disturbing way, perhaps, that things may not last forever, that we all have some degree of responsibility to hold up the shapes and structures and values we hold dear and make sure they go on ... We are living, after all, just one minute before midnight ... But this must not be cause for despair" (SFSP, 1985). And yet, something quite different emerges from his *The Tempest* three years earlier.

This difference partly arises from the fact that in addressing the questions of hope and illusion in his production of *The Tempest*, Hirsch also had simultaneous recourse to Frye's various commentaries on the play, including his 1982 Stratford lecture on the romances. Yet here it's helpful to go back a little further in time. For as we also saw, in the very same year a seventeen-year-old Hirsch was resettling in North End Winnipeg, a thirty-five-year-old Frye was finally seeing his long-awaited study of William Blake into print. Crucially, *Fearful Symmetry* identifies Blake not so much as a Romantic poet but as a revivification of Renaissance humanism, particularly the more radical strains of visionary Christianity that emerged out of its left flank, as it were.[9] In situating Blake this way, Frye was consciously responding to midcentury totalitarianism and global war, producing an anti-fascist statement quite distinct from Kott's anti-Stalinist one. As we also saw, Frye's Blake book opens with an epigraph from *The Tempest* disclosing how on Prospero's magical island, "the quality of one's dreaming is an index of character," making imagination revelatory of both existing as well as possible ethical realities (*NFWS*, 48). Implicit here is Frye's view of *The Tempest* as paradigmatic of how imaginative hypotheses can renew collectively shared visions, the idea that "no other work of literature … illustrates more clearly the interchange of illusion and reality which is what literature is all about" (*NFWS*, 7). On this account, *The Tempest* does not operate according to an opposition between appearance and reality, but between two contrasting forms of aesthetic illusion. On one hand, there are aesthetic illusions that engender solipsism and false idealization (like Caliban's misconstruing Stefano as a god). But on the other, there are the kind that lead towards something much more like the sort of disposition Kierkegaard identifies when he says that while "love believes everything and yet is never to be deceived," cynicism mistrusts everything and is nevertheless thoroughly duped.[10] For what the cynic overlooks is that the ultimate horizon of truth does not emerge once all our illusions are dispelled. Moving beyond the horizon of cynicism and brute realism, *The Tempest*, according to Frye, discloses "for an instant [that] there has been an epiphany, when how things should be has appeared in the middle of how things are" (*WWP*, 86). On this account of the play, what emerges is not a triumphalist romantic vision, but a fleeting glimpse of transcendence that is very much in keeping with Hirsch's 1982 production. Indeed, to understand Hirsch's achievement in 1982 is to see it in the context of Frye's view of the play's metaleptic dynamics and his sense that its dramatic structures disclose a form of repetition in which long-standing myths of regeneration momentarily disclose their self-exteriorizing authority rather than betraying their hollowness and exhaustion. At the same time, though, Hirsch's production modifies Frye's more optimistic formulations by introducing a certain clear-eyed Kottian realism, giving the dispelling of illusions their due but without mistaking the hermeneutics of suspicion as the ultimate horizon of interpretive action. In this respect, we might say that Hirsch used Frye's stress on the relationship between illusion and revelation to modify Kott's pessimism, while also using Kott's stress on the dispelling of false illusions to modify Frye's sometimes overstated idealism. But to see all this we need to consider some of the details of the production and how these details were perceived by some early reviewers.

If Frye's influence on Hirsch's production went unremarked among its initial reviewers, his general effect on it most certainly did not. Writing for *Shakespeare Survey*, veteran British critic Roger Warren enthused that Hirsch's production was "the first coherent version of the play I have seen, the only one to weld the disparate elements of the play into a unity."[11] To substantiate the point, Warren adduces the interpolated song Hirsch composed for Ariel prior to the wedding masque. Clarifying the relation among the various parts of the play, the song includes allusions to Aeneas's descent into hell and Tamino's trials of fire and water in *The Magic Flute*, thus making it clear that the masque is a celebration of Ferdinand's enduring of Prospero's trial by magic. Writing for the *Times London*, Irving Wardle also praised the production's striking unity of vision. In this case, however, Wardle stresses the emphasis given to Stephano's role as aspiring tyrant in the play. "Instead of a poetic drama with a comic sub-plot," he notes, "the play emerges as a unitary action, translating the same cycle of events into the terms of magic, politics, and simple human greed."[12] The crucial decision here was a matter of casting, as Hirsch had his most experienced classical actor, Nicholas Pennell, play Stefano, making him a terrifying if still pathetic aspiring tyrant. The result is a clear sense of how Stefano's cruelty mirrors Antonio's cynicism, and how both Stefano and Antonio embody energies threatening Prospero's moral and spiritual integrity. What neither critic observes, however, is how much the production's unitary vision owes to Frye's sense of the play's dramatic structures. After all, it's Frye who stresses how *The Tempest*'s Aeneas-like descent patterns animate Prospero's journey throughout the play. Moreover, it was Frye who observed that *The Tempest* "is a spectacular and operatic play, and when we think of other plays like it, we are more apt to think of, say, Mozart's *Magic Flute* than of ordinary stage plays" (*NFWS*, 52). Despite Kott's withering criticisms of this approach to the play, Hirsch did not shy away from its more spectacular features, stressing, for example, Len Cariou's Pavarotti-like grandness. At the same time, though, he played up its depiction of Machiavellian calculation and sniggering cynicism, thus integrating the best of Frye's and Kott's insights while eschewing their respective shortcomings.

This stress on the play's vicious elements within the context of a unified depiction of its moving parts is further enriched by Cariou's portrayal of Prospero's anguished movement from rage to individuation during his renunciation of magic speech. As Warren notes, Cariou's performance had the effect of this renunciation seeming to cost Prospero nothing less than "everything." Wardle came to the same conclusion when he wrote:

> Trembling from head to foot in a gradually intensifying circle of white light, Len Cariou (as Prospero) at last nerves himself to address his Ovidian farewell to the island's spirits. I have heard it better spoken, but never with a stronger sense of what Prospero was giving up.[13]

In context, this speech contributes to Prospero's overall attempt to avoid the two extremes of magic for magic's sake and magic for power's sake – thereby turning the play into a commentary on the ethics of theatrical illusion, on the need for art to interpenetrate with the traumas of life in ways that are morally expansive rather than self-pitying or exploitative. In this respect, Hirsch's *The Tempest* both responds to and rejects Kott's pessimism in ways that parallel Giorgio Strehler's celebrated 1978 Italian adaptation of the play. While Strehler's production began in consultation with Kott, it ultimately went in a different direction as the Italian director also took as authoritative Gonzalo's view of the play as a journey into knowledge for everyone, including Prospero.[14]

In keeping with such a view, the climax of Hirsch's production draws on the symbolism of spiritual alchemy, which is deployed at the moment Prospero renounces revenge. As a memo from the production indicates, during this scene "Prospero stays in the circle [of white light while] the Royal Party are scattered around outside of it. The effect is that the circle protects Prospero from the Royal Party."[15] Prospero's moment of self-realization is then communicated iconographically, as he dons his ducal costume, consisting of a bright gold crown with a golden, green-sleeved robe. In context, the costume symbolizes his integration of opposing psychic energies, reconciling his aggressive (Caliban) side with his compassionate (Ariel-Miranda) tendencies, which, until now, have not been coordinated with one another. This union of passive and active principles is figured through Prospero's carefully ritualized placing of his hand on his heart and then on his sword, denoting his union of love and strength. Both physically imposing yet convincingly sensitive, Cariou performs the renunciation to great effect. The general result is an emerging sense that Kott's "bitter lucidity" very easily devolves into and more often than not expresses itself as Kierkegaard's "superficiality of shrewdness."

Taken as a whole, then, Hirsch's production confirms sentiments he expressed six years after its staging when asked if he remained an optimist about human destiny despite the horrors that he lived through, to which he responded: "You come of out of the furnace and you should be pessimistic? You'd have to really be an idiot. Still, you are not going to become a blithering optimist either … It is just simply that you cannot really live without believing that all this has some meaning. Not meaning that's given to you, but meaning that you have to create for yourself" (BC, 84). But as his own production reminds us, the idea that we create meanings for ourselves nevertheless involves the sort of metaleptic dynamics that Frye stresses are pivotal to *The Tempest*, to the idea that the work of art takes on a self-exteriorizing agency over and against us, even when we are authors or performers of it. On this account, *The Tempest* thematizes the very tension between created and revealed meaning that must be at play in human culture if we are in fact capable of forms of repetition that renew past conventions in adaptative or liberating ways. What links Brook, Frye, Hirsch, and Coyne is a deep fascination with the Shakespearean exploration of these dynamics.

Buttressing Hirsch's production of *The Tempest* is a distinctly European Caliban, part wild man, part green man, who is carefully linked to Prospero through his mossy, Caliban-like magical cloak. This visual echo conveys how Prospero's potential inhumanity finds disavowed embodiment in Caliban until, at the end, he acknowledges Caliban's monstrosity as "his own." In turn, it foregrounds the way that Caliban's half-acknowledged lyricism and suppressed love of beauty finds disavowed expression in his hatred of Prospero, until, at the end, he achieves a discernible sense of dignity by confessing that "I will be wise hereafter and seek for grace" (5.1296). While stressing the play's darker elements, the production refrained, as a third reviewer put it, "from pushing in the direction of Kott's view of the play as a spectacular enactment ... of history as a madness we are condemned to repeat."[16] Thus if Kott's vision of a hope beyond hope remained part of Hirsch's theatrical vocabulary when discussing *King Lear* in 1985, Frye's vision of momentary transcendence became part of his aesthetic repertoire when tackling *The Tempest* for the final time in his career. After all, if *The Tempest* simply repeats the traumas of human history then it does not provide the aesthetic distance that Hirsch sees as essential to drama as such, a dimension he thought so crucial that he invited psychiatrist Vivian Rakoff to discuss it in the 1983 celebrity lecture "Play and the Theatre of Fantasy."

With its unlikely mixture of semi-Brechtian strategies and spiritual alchemy, of taut realism with fairy-tale fantasy, Hirsch's *The Tempest* is a striking example of how Shakespeare's play can be made to express this problematic of created and revealed meaning – the very tension that plays out between Alonso and Prospero at the end of the action. So if there is any truth to the complaint that suspicion too often overrides identification in literary criticism, or that Shakespeare studies has become dangerously deracinated from its origins in Romantic aesthetics, then this 1982 production remains as much an ongoing provocation as it does an institutional memory. Viewed this way, Hirsch's *The Tempest* remains a striking example of the tension between realism and idealism, between created and revealed meaning, animating *Slings & Arrows* – one real-life source of its deepest convictions.

Notes

EPIGRAPHS

1 Italo Calvino, *Six Memos for the Next Millennium*, trans. Patrick Creagh (Cambridge, MA: Harvard University Press, 1998), 112.
2 Robert Lloyd, "'Slings & Arrows' Made Shakespeare Must-See TV," *Los Angeles Times*, 5 November 2019.

INTRODUCTION

1 Cited in Halliwell, *Aesthetics of Mimesis*, 297.
2 Cited in Gebaur and Wulf, *Mimesis*, 100–1. For Coleridge, see *Coleridge: Lectures on Shakespeare*, 28.
3 Nuttall, *Two Concepts of Allegory*, 102. See also Righter, *Shakespeare and the Idea of the Play*.
4 Thomas Heywood, *The Dramatic Works of Thomas Heywood*, vol. 1 (London: John Pearson, 1874), xlviii. See Nuttall, *Two Concepts of Allegory*, 102.
5 Brook, *Empty Space*, 75. Subsequent references given in text as ES. Phillips cited in Cushman, *Fifty Years at Stratford*, 94. For full interview, see https://www.cbc.ca/player/play/1464491829.
6 Baudrillard, *Simulacra and Simulation*, 53. Subsequent references given in text as SS.
7 Baudrillard, *Screened Out*, 176–7. See also McLuhan, *Understanding Media*, 116–17.
8 Baudrillard, *Screened Out*, 177.
9 Ibid.
10 Frye, *Writings on the Eighteenth and Nineteenth Centuries*, 106. Subsequent references given in text as NFWE.

198 Notes to pages 5–9

11 Fiske, *Television Culture*, 115.

12 For a succinct formulation of the links between neo-liberalism and postmodern relativism, see During, "The Historical Status of Postmodernism." For a more sustained articulation, see Taylor, *A Secular Age*.

13 Baudrillard, *Consumer Society*, 10.

14 Cited in McGrath, *The Intellectual World of C.S. Lewis*, 56.

15 While I am obviously sympathetic with Pechter's diagnosis, I do not think his recuperation of Coleridge is well served by his simultaneous commitment to the philosophical pragmatism of Richard Rorty. As will become clear in the course of my argument, I think Rorty's great philosophical opponents Alasdair MacIntyre and Charles Taylor provide greater purchase on central questions pertaining to interpretation, understanding, and ethics in a postmodern age and are thus better guides out of the malaise Pechter persuasively identifies than Rorty. Unsurprisingly, perhaps, the ethos of *Slings & Arrows* more closely aligns with Taylor's rather Canadian championing of *culture* and *authenticity* than MacIntyre's neo-Thomist defence of *virtue* and *tradition*, though there is a palpable degree of overlap between the two thinkers. For the similarities and differences between Taylor and MacIntyre, see Perreau-Saussine, *Alasdair MacIntyre*, 131–7.

16 For other examples of this recovery of romantic Shakespeare, see Bate, *Shakespeare and the English Romantic Imagination*; McCoy, *Faith in Shakespeare*; Ryan, *Shakespeare's Universality*; and Mousley, *Re-Humanizing Shakespeare*.

17 Love, "Close but Not Deep," 381. One of the telling weaknesses of Love's proposal is its misreading of Bruno Latour as a post-metaphysical anti-humanist when he is, in fact, a professed Roman Catholic, whose major aim was, as Barbara Hernstein Smith says, to tie "together a theoretically sophisticated account of scientific knowledge with a rhetorically deft Christian apologetics to forge a singular quasi-symmetrical anthropotheology." In short, he was nothing less than a "missionary to the Moderns." See Hernstein Smith, "Anthropotheology: Latour Speaking Religiously," 340, 334.

18 For this critique of Goffman's role-playing theory, see MacIntyre, *After Virtue*, 115.

19 Love, "Close but Not Deep," 387.

20 Guillory, *Professing Criticism*, 99–100.

21 Produced by Rhombus Media, the show aired on Showcase, Movie Central, and Movie Network. At the time of writing, the show is available at CBC Gem, iTunes, Acorn Media, and YouTube.

Notes to pages 10–22 199

22 Cochrane, *Small Screen Shakespeare*, 462; Emily Nussbaum, "'Smash': It Had Me at Hello," Culture Desk, *New Yorker*, 6 February 2012, https://www.newyorker.com/culture/culture-desk/smash-it-had-me-at-hello.

23 Lloyd, "Slings & Arrows."

24 Martin Chilton, "*Slings & Arrows*: So Good It Gave David Simon Writer Envy," *The Telegraph*, 13 July 2013.

25 Frey, "Slings & Arrows."

26 Kostihova, "Myth of Shakespearean Authenticity," 48. See also Klett, "Shakespearean Authority"; Mazer, *Double Shakespeares*, 95–110; Pittman, *Authorizing Shakespeare*, chap. 6; Moore, "Race, National Identity, and the Hauntological Ethics"; and Fischlin, *Canadian Adaptations*.

27 Bristol, "Macbeth the Philosopher," 650.

28 Knowles, "Shakespeare, 1993, and the Discourses," 213, 225.

29 For a parallel critique of the festival from within its own general ranks, see Kareda, "Sold Out," 76, the focus of chap. 11. Subsequent references given in text as so. For a balanced academic view of the festival in this period, see Parolin, "'What Revels Are in Hand.'"

30 Parolin, "'What Revels Are in Hand,'" 205.

31 Ibid., 201.

32 Bristol, *Big-Time Shakespeare*, xiii. Subsequent references given in text as *BTS*.

33 Levin, "Bloom, Bardolatry, and Characterolatry," 77.

34 Dobson, "Afterword," 263–4.

35 Bate, *Genius of Shakespeare*, 325.

36 For expositions on the limits of ideological critique, see Sedgwick, "Paranoid Reading and Reparative Reading," and Felski, *Limits of Critique*. For Guillory's critical response to this movement, see *Professing Criticism*, part 1, chap. 3. For an earlier warning of debunking as a counterproductive strategy for literary education, see Lewis, *An Experiment in Criticism* (1961).

37 Durkheim, "Durkheim's Individualism," 25. See also Dupuy, *Mark of the Sacred*, 122.

38 Hirsch, "Interview with John Hirsch," 41.

CHAPTER ONE

1 Brook, Preface to Kott, x.

2 Wellington, dir., *Slings & Arrows*, 3.2. Subsequent references given in text as *S&A*, cited by season and episode.

200   Notes to pages 23–35

3 John Gaspard, "Actress/Writer Susan Coyne on 'Slings & Arrows.'" LinkedIn, 3 August 2018, https://www.linkedin.com/pulse/actresswriter-susan-coyne-slings-arrows-john-gaspard. Coyne identifies Brook as an influence on the series in her lecture at Western University, "The Antidote to Loneliness."

4 Coleridge, *Coleridge on Shakespeare*, 157.

5 The following discussion of ships as metaphors for playhouses and the evidence adduced derive from Bruster, "Local Tempest."

6 Ibid.

7 William Shakespeare, *Shakespeare's Sonnets*, ed. Stephen Booth (New Haven: Yale University Press, 1977), 39. This theme found expression in Robin Phillips's 1975 Stratford production of *The Two Gentlemen of Verona*. See *Stratford Festival Souvenir Programme*, 1975. Subsequent references to Stratford programmes given in text as SFSP with year and page when paginated.

8 The idea that the tempest-music opposition constitutes an organizing principle across Shakespeare's plays was famously expounded in Knight, *The Shakespearean Tempest*. Northrop Frye adapts the idea in more precisely structural terms in *A Natural Perspective*. For a discussion of Knight's influence on Frye, see *Northrop Frye's Writings on Shakespeare and the Renaissance*, xliv. Subsequent references given in text as NFWS. For a critique of Knight's place within modern Shakespeare criticism, see Grady, *Modernist Shakespeare*, chap. 2.

9 Coleridge, *Coleridge on Shakespeare*, 166.

10 "London 'Hamlet' Loses Star to Illness," *New York Times*, 16 September 1989; Emily Nussbaum, "*Slings & Arrows* Reunion Panel Presented by Acorn Media," ATX TV, 19 October 2020, https://www.youtube.com/watch?v=odlEJ7Ni2jA; Monette, *This Rough Magic*, 247–8.

11 On this point, see also Brook, *Tip of the Tongue*, 84–6.

12 Brook, *The Quality of Mercy*, 2.

CHAPTER TWO

1 The following discussion of Coleridge is indebted to, among others, McCoy, *Faith in Shakespeare*, 4–5, 16–18; Bate, *Shakespeare and the English Romantic Imagination*, chap. 3; and Tomko, *Willing Suspension of Disbelief*.

2 For more on this dimension of Coleridge's poetic faith, see Tomko, *Willing Suspension of Disbelief*.

Notes to pages 35–50

3 See "John Hirsch Discusses His Production of 'Hamlet,'" Studs Terkel Radio Archive, 1 January 1969, https://studsterkel.wfmt.com/programs /john-hirsch-discusses-his-production-hamlet.

4 Coleridge, *Biographia Literaria*, 168–9.

5 Cited in Bate, *Shakespeare and English Romantic Imagination*, 58.

6 Coleridge, *Coleridge on Shakespeare*, 36.

7 Ibid. See also McCoy, *Faith in Shakespeare*, 23.

8 Jameson, *Postmodernism, or, The Cultural Logic of Late Capitalism*, 309. Subsequent references given in text as PM.

9 Berkowitz, *Nietzsche: The Ethics of an Immoralist*, 4–5.

10 Brook, *Threads of Time*, 134. See also Brook, *Quality of Mercy*, 22–7.

11 For an overview of pop culture references to *The Scream*, see Dery, "The Scream Meme."

12 For a related discussion of Jameson, see Devaney, 'Since at least Plato ...,' 136–8, 144, 154.

13 Jameson, "Postmodernism," 62–3.

14 Prideux, *Edvard Munch*, 167. Subsequent references given in text as EM.

15 James Howell, *Epistolae Ho-Elianae*, cited in Earl Miner, "The Cavalier Ideal of the Good Life," in *Seventeenth-Century British Poetry, 1603–1660*, eds. John P. Rumrich and Gregory Chaplin (New York: W.W. Norton 2006), 807.

16 Beck, *Risk Society*.

17 Weil, *Need for Roots*, 33.

18 Knausgaard, *So Much Longing*, 50.

19 Ibid., 11.

20 Brook, *Open Door*, 15.

21 I am grateful to Nola Accili for sharing her insights about this visual trope with me.

22 Kate Taylor, "Saving Stratford from the Excesses of Success," *Globe and Mail*, 18 July 1998; Ray Conlogue, "Troubled Times for Classic Theatre," *Toronto Sun*, 2 June 1998; John Coulbourne, "Hail, Caesar, and Farewell," *Toronto Sun*, 2 June 1998; John Coulbourne, "Stratford Needs to Take New Direction," *Toronto Sun*, 26 July 1998.

23 For the challenges experienced by the RSC in the '90s, see Adler, *Rough Magic*.

24 Clive Barnes cited in David Selbourne, *Making of "A Midsummer Night's Dream,"* xxxvi.

25 Ibid., 15.

26 Mousley, *Re-Humanising Shakespeare*, 8. For broadly similar arguments,

see also Headlam Wells, *Shakespeare's Humanism* and Parvini, *Shakespeare's Moral Compass*.

27 See Noble, *Dance to the Tune of Life*.

CHAPTER THREE

1 Baudrillard, *Gulf War*, 28.
2 Ibid.
3 For this general thesis, see Halpern, *Shakespeare among the Moderns*.
4 Ross, "*Slings & Arrows*: The Best TV Show to Stream," *Front Mezz Junkies* (blog), 20 May 2020, https://frontmezzjunkies.com/2020/05/20/slings-and-arrows/.
5 Trussler, Introduction to *Making of "A Midsummer Night's Dream,"* xxv.
6 Sinfield, "Royal Shakespeare," 187. See also McCullough, "Cambridge Connection," and Knowles, *Shakespeare in Canada*.
7 Pickstock, *After Writing*, 101–2.
8 Ibid., 102.
9 See *Macbeth*, 4.1.14–15, 235.
10 For this controversial but broadly persuasive view of Baudrillard, see Norris, *What's Wrong with Postmodernism*, 165–6.
11 Frye, *Northrop Frye on Modern Culture*, 20. Subsequent references given as NFMC.
12 Shookman, "Barthes's Semiological Myth," 460.

CHAPTER FOUR

1 Hawkes, *Meaning by Shakespeare*, 141. Subsequent references given in text as MS.
2 Ryan, *Shakespeare's Universality*, 96.
3 Adorno, *Aesthetic Theory*, 11.
4 See Tolkien, *Tree and Leaf*, 22.
5 For a sustained articulation of the view of aesthetic consciousness as an outgrowth of childhood make-believe, see Walton, *Mimesis as Make-Believe*.
6 For the role of the blue flower in Lewis, see McGrath, *Intellectual Life of C.S. Lewis*, 22.
7 See Burns and Coyne, *Robin, Mark, and Richard III*, 2016.
8 Cayley, *Northrop Frye in Conversation*, 41, and Ayre, *Northrop Frye*, 25.
9 Lamb and Lamb, *Tales of Shakespeare*, 7.
10 Hamilton, "Northrop Frye as a Cultural Theorist," 118.

Notes to pages 72–89

11 Holland, *Dynamics of Literary Response*, 247.
12 For a succinct explanation of myth and its readerly effects, see Lewis, *An Experiment in Criticism*, chap. 5.
13 Bettelheim, *Uses of Enchantment*, 73.
14 For a description of this scene as a restoration rather than a resurrection, see Coghill, "Six Points of Stage Craft."
15 Cited in Coyne, *Kingfisher Days*, 1. Subsequent references given in text as KD.
16 T.S. Eliot, *Collected Poems 1909–1962* (London: Faber and Faber, 1963), 179.
17 Richard Eyre cited in Thomson, *Why Acting Matters*, epigraph.
18 Brook, *Threads of Time*, 5.
19 Ricoeur, *Figuring the Sacred*, 42–3.
20 Ibid., 45–6.
21 Frye, *Words with Power*, 105. Subsequent references given in text as WWP.
22 Frye, *Myth and Metaphor*, 26. Subsequent references given in text as MM.
23 Broadly similar critiques of Derrida have been articulated in different methodological and philosophical contexts. See, for example, Fiske, *Television Culture*, 117, and, in a very different register, Pickstock, *After Writing*, chap. 6.
24 Derrida, *Writing and Difference*, 292.
25 Taylor, *Malaise of Modernity*, 60–1.
26 For parallel assessments of Derrida's early work, see Taylor, *Sources of the Self*, 488–9. See also my discussion of Alasdair MacIntyre in chap. 14.
27 Frye, *Anatomy of Criticism*, 345.
28 Frye, "Auguries of Experience," 6–7.
29 Burns and Coyne, *Robin, Mark, Richard III*.
30 Bennett, "Oh Canada!: *Slings and Arrows*."

CHAPTER FIVE

1 Frye notes the Latin meaning of *tempestas* in NFWS, 49. For his general structural approach to Shakespearean comedy, see *A Natural Perspective*. For a critique of *A Natural Perspective*'s over-generalizations, see Berry, "Shakespearean Comedy and Northrop Frye."
2 On the loss of temporality in postmodernity, see Jameson, "End of Temporality."
3 For the popularity of Frye's Shakespeare writings, see the editorial introduction to NFWS, xxiii and xxvii. For Frye's influence on Shakespeare studies, see Merrill, "Generic Approach in Recent Criticism," Rebhorn, "After Frye," and Denham, "Frye's Shakespeare Criticism."

204   Notes to pages 89–93

4 The lectures were subsequently published in the *Stratford Papers on Shakespeare* series. See *NFWS*, xxxii–iii.

5 According to Warren, *Staging Shakespeare's Late Plays*, 5, Hirsch's plan to perform all four romances in one season was deterred by financial considerations.

6 For an account of this period in Hirsch's career, see Martz and Wilson, *A Fiery Soul*, 265–310. Subsequent references given in text as *AFS*. For an account of Hirsch's *The Tempest*, see Warren, *Staging Shakespeare's Late Plays*, 177–8, 185–6, and the coda to the present book.

7 Gaspard, "Actress/Writer Susan Coyne."

8 Hirsch, "Father Courage: An Interview with John Hirsch," 84. Subsequent references given in text as *BC*.

9 Frye, *Fearful Symmetry*, xl.

10 Frye, *Correspondence of Northrop Frye and Helen Kemp*, 1:426.

11 Denham, "Northrop Frye and Edmund Blunden."

12 For a summary of critiques of Frye from various methodological standpoints and for a synthesis of responses to those critiques, see Denham, introduction to *Anatomy of Criticism*, lv–lxvi, and introduction to *Reception of Northrop Frye*. See also Hamilton, "Coda," *Northrop Frye*. For early critiques of Frye's thought, see the essays by Krieger and Wimsatt in *Northrop Frye in Modern Criticism*. For elegies of his thought, see Fekete, *The Critical Twilight*, chap. 9; Lentricchia, *After the New Criticism*, chap. 1; and Halpern, *Shakespeare among the Moderns*, chap 3. For defences of major aspects of Frye's overall project, see, along with the editorial apparatus in the *Collected Works of Northrop Frye*, 30 vols., Paul Ricoeur, "*Anatomy of Criticism* or the Order of Paradigms," and Glen Gill, *Northrop Frye and the Phenomenology of Myth*. Among many others, see also the essays in *The Legacy of Northrop Frye* and *Rereading Frye: The Published and Unpublished Works*.

13 For a full summary and a parallel application of Wilde's adage to Frye's reputation, see Denham, introduction to *Reception of Frye*. Denham notes Frye's influence on narrative studies, especially narrative studies in law, historiography, music, religion, and psychotherapy. For a judicious review of Frye's reception history, focusing on *Anatomy of Criticism*, see Warkentin, "The Age of Frye." See also Denham, *Reception of Northrop Frye*.

14 For the influence of myth studies on popular writing, see, for example, Vogler, *The Writer's Journey*.

15 Frye, *Anatomy of Criticism*, 174–5. In *The Writer's Journey*, Vogler calls this dialectical structure *polarity* (315–40).

Notes to pages 93–102

16 For such polarized coding, see Fiske, *Television Culture*, chap. 1.

17 See, for example, Felperin, *Shakespearean Romances*, 16. I deal with counterviews to this argument in the course of the book.

18 M.G. McIntyre, "With *Slings and Arrows* Canadians Prove They Know How to End a Series," *Film School Rejects* (blog), 20 May 2019, https://filmschoolrejects.com/with-slings-and-arrows-canadians-prove-they-know-how-to-finish-a-tv-series/.

19 Jameson, *The Political Unconscious*, 134.

20 Ibid., 148.

21 MacIntyre, *Marxism and Christianity*, 111. Originally composed in 1953, when MacIntyre was twenty-three years old, the book was first published in 1968.

22 MacIntyre, *Secularization and Moral Change*, 75. See especially pages 29–31.

23 For the view that Coleridge's concept of dramatic illusion is inadequate to the religious inflections of Shakespearean theatre, especially *The Winter's Tale*, see Monta, "'It is requir'd you do awake your faith.'" For a defence of Coleridgean aesthetics vis-à-vis Shakespeare, see McCoy, *Faith in Shakespeare*. For a synthesis of these two views in which the religious dimensions of Coleridge's thinking are stressed, see Tomko, *Beyond the Willing Suspension of Disbelief*.

24 Osborne, "Serial Shakespeare."

25 Kierkegaard, *Works of Love*, 23.

26 See Shakespeare, Sonnet 139, *Shakespeare's Sonnets*.

27 Kierkegaard, *Works of Love*, 213–30. See also Žižek, *The Fragile Absolute*, 127.

28 James, *The Portable Henry James*, 464.

29 Frye, "Romance as Masque," 35.

30 Like Frye, Lynn Magnusson, in "Interruption in *The Tempest*," sees *The Tempest* as confessing "the unmaking and the 'being made of' that are the perpetual conditions of making," but she stresses the more sombre aspects of the play, reflected in its dramatic and linguistic patterns of interruption. She thus concludes that Prospero's revels speech "confesses his limited control over the making process," acknowledging a "'being made of' by no personal or specific Agent" (63), which sounds very much like an non- or even anti-Blakean response to Frye's "Romance as Masque."

31 For a Girardian approach to this dynamic, see Dupuy, *Mark of the Sacred*, 2.

32 Cox, "Recovering Something Christian," 44.

206 Notes to pages 103–5

33 Hayes and Schonberg, eds., *Tempest As Directed by John Hirsch*, 7.
34 "In pace, in idipsum dormiam et requiescam. / Si dedero somnum oculis meis, et palpebris meis dormitationem, dormiam et requiescam." For a discussion of Hirsch's fascination with Catholic ritual, see AFS, 24–5.
35 For this reading, which undercuts the reconciliation at the end, see Orgel, introduction to *The Tempest*. For an orthodox Christian response, see Cox, "Recovering Something Christian."
36 Frye, *Natural Perspective*, 165. The idea that theatre was generated out of ritual, including magical rites, is a commonly held but often contested idea in anthropology, history, and theatre studies. For a critique of this thesis from the standpoint of semiotics, see Rozik, *Roots of Theatre*.
37 For a recent articulation of this view, see Lerer, *Shakespeare's Lyric Stage*.
38 Kott, "*The Tempest*, or Repetition," 21.
39 Ibid.
40 Ibid., 36.
41 In his suggestive essay "Two-Voiced, Delicate Monster," Mark Fortier tries to synthesize historically opposing views of the play as romance and as post-colonial. He endeavours to do this by critiquing Frye's idealism while nevertheless expanding on Frye's dialectical reading of romance as a genre, and his recognition of romance as a play of opposing forces (including idealism and realism). The result is a significant step forward from some of the more reductively colonial readings that have dominated criticism for some time. In doing so, however, Fortier does not account for Frye's stress on the metaleptic reversal Prospero undergoes in the play, a feature of his reading that comes through more fully in *A Natural Perspective*, "Romance as a Masque," and the lecture "The Stage Is All the World," none of which appear in Fortier's bibliography. Consequently, Fortier draws on too narrow a sampling of Frye's responses to *The Tempest* to provide a fully accurate view of how he approached the play, relying, for example, on his undergraduate lectures rather than more major statements in which the dialectics of romance with which he is concerned are more fully articulated. For a brilliant application of Jameson's Marxist refiguring of Frye to *The Tempest*, see Felperin, "Political Criticism at the Crossroads." I question, however, if Felperin's endorsing of "radical humanism" is really quite as distinct in practice from Frye's "apocalyptic humanism" as he suggests. For Frye's brand of "apocalyptic humanism," see Gill, *Northrop Frye and the Phenomenology of Myth*.
42 For a major and influential critique of Frye's reading of the play as blandly idealist, see Berger, "Miraculous Harp," 258.

Notes to pages 106–19

43 For this distinction and a subtle critique of skeptical readings of the play's politics, see Norbrook, "'What Cares These Roarers for the Name of King?'"

44 Hazlitt, "On Shakespeare and Milton," 123.

45 Decker, *Anatomy of a Screenplay*.

46 For a competing theory of mimesis from analytical philosophy, see Lamarque and Haugom Olsen, *Truth, Fiction, and Literature*. For alternative perspectives from a more post-structural standpoint, see Holmes and Streete, *Refiguring Mimesis*.

47 For a full philosophical articulation of these principles, see Ricoeur, *Time and Narrative*. For a brilliant attempt to translate Frye's theory of character into broadly Lacanian terms, see Grossman, "The Vicissitudes of the Subject."

48 The quote is Jacques Derrida ventriloquizing (and deconstructing) Antonin Artaud in *Writing and Difference*, 234–5.

49 Powe, *Marshall McLuhan and Northrop Frye*, 12.

50 This point has been widely discussed. See, for example, Compagnon, *Literature, Theory, and Common Sense*, 72.

51 Barthes, "Introduction to the Structural Analysis of Narratives." For discussion, see Compagnon, *Literature, Theory, and Common Sense*, 72; and Wood, *How Fiction Works*, 230.

52 Prendergast, *Order of Mimesis*, 72. Prendergast here draws on A. Giddens, *Central Problems in Social Theory* (London: N.P., 1979), 37.

53 Prendergast, *Order of Mimesis*, 72. See also Devaney, 'Since at least Plato ...,' 136 and Tallis, *In Defence of Realism*.

54 Brook, *Peter Brook's Production of Midsummer Night's Dream*, 24.

55 Ibid., 14. For an opposing account of Frye and Brook, see Knowles, *Shakespeare in Canada*.

CHAPTER SIX

1 Lynn Smith, "Theater of the Absurd to Them Is Just Life," *Los Angeles Times*, 16 February 2007, https://www.latimes.com/archives/la-xpm-2007-feb-16-et-slings16-story.html.

2 Frye, *Divisions on a Ground: Essays on Canadian Culture*, 23–4. Subsequent references given in text as *DG*.

3 For an influential articulation of the view that Canadian Shakespeare has been historically defined by a rejection of historical and cultural particularity, see Salter, "Acting Shakespeare in Postcolonial Space." Richard P. Knowles dismisses Robert Lepage's formulation of Frye's

Notes to pages 119–28

principle about the local and the typical on the basis of prior methodological and ideological assumptions, rather than on the basis of a careful analysis of the phenomenon, in *Shakespeare in Canada*, 113. For a
more sympathetic treatment of Brook's attempt at cross-cultural thinking, see Kustow, *Peter Brook*, chap. 16.

4 Johnson, "Preface to Shakespeare," lx.

5 While this sanguine account of the festival's origins was widespread at
one time, it has undergone multiple post-colonial qualifications in
recent years. For examples, see Knowles, "From Nationalist to Multinational," and Salter, "Acting Shakespeare in Postcolonial Space." For the
festival in the context of cultural tourism, see Kennedy, "Shakespeare
and Cultural Tourism." For a summary of post-colonial critiques of
Frye's Canadian criticism and a sound response to them, see Calin,
Twentieth-Century Humanist Critics, 135–7. A careful reading of Frye's
essay indicates that he recognized the possibility of these sorts of political criticisms and made some effort to head them off at the pass.

6 Frye, *Creation & Recreation*, 15.

7 Ibid.

8 Newman, *The Importance of Failure*, n.p.

9 For a reading of the same plot dynamics in the context of gender and
race, see Royster, "Comic Terror and Masculine Vulnerability."

10 For this view of Shakespeare, see Smith, *Black Shakespeare*.

11 Hazlitt, *Characters of Shakespeare's Plays*, 8.

12 For a discussion of the different theatrical traditions generating this
doubleness, see Felperin, *Shakespearean Representation*.

13 Soyinka, "Shakespeare and the Living Dramatist." My summary is
indebted to Graham, "Soyinka and the Dead Dramatist."

14 Graham, "Soyinka and the Dead Dramatist."

15 Soyinka, "Shakespeare and the Living Dramatist," 3.

16 See Graham, "Soyinka and the Dead Dramatist," 35. For these racialized
categories see Smith, *Black Shakespeare*.

17 Bate, *Mad About Shakespeare*, 26.

18 Felperin, "Political Criticism," 59.

CHAPTER SEVEN

1 Wilde, *Decay of Lying*, 30.

2 Also cited in Worthen, *Shakespeare and the Authority of Performance*, 68.

3 Deleuze, *Nietzsche and Philosophy*, 3. For an opposing view of Nietzsche,
see Berkowitz, *Nietzsche*.

Notes to pages 129–51

4 And yet, some critics worried as far back as 1961 that professional literary criticism was becoming too focused on using texts rather than
receiving them. See, for example, Lewis, *Experiment in Criticism*, chap. 3.
5 Nuttall, *A New Mimesis*, 190. Subsequent references given in text by
page number.
6 Brook, *Shifting Point*, 76.
7 Ibid., 86.
8 For this view, see Mazer, *Double Shakespeares*, 95–110.
9 Mazer, "Sense/Memory/Sense-Memory," 330.
10 Hutson, *Invention of Suspicion*, and Enterline, *Shakespeare's Schoolroom*.
11 Stern, "(Re)historicizing Spontaneity," 109.
12 See Bristol, "Vernacular Criticism."
13 Bristol, "Macbeth the Philosopher," 652.
14 Lewis, *Experiment in Criticism*, 3.
15 Ibid.
16 Goddard, *Meaning of Shakespeare*, 12.
17 McCoy, *Faith in Shakespeare*, 8.
18 See Derrida, *Of Grammatology*, 306–7. For a positive assessment of Derrida's direct responses to Shakespeare, one focused on philosophy rather
than performance, see Alfono, *Derrida Reads Shakespeare*.
19 Ibid., 9.
20 Moore, "Race, National Identity, and the Hauntological Ethics."

CHAPTER EIGHT

1 Coyne, *Kingfisher Days: The Play*, 2.
2 Frye, *Creation & Recreation*, 9.
3 For a full account of the episode, see Knelman, *A Stratford Tempest*.
4 For the observation about young viewers converting to theatre after
watching *Slings & Arrows*, see "*Slings and Arrows* Cast Reunion 2020,"
ET Canada, 7 August 2020, https://www.youtube.com/watch?v=brHOeZk
_5V4.

CHAPTER NINE

1 See Taylor, *Sources of the Self*, 419.
2 Wood, "Letter to the Editor."
3 Ibid.
4 Cited in MacIntyre, *Three Rival Versions of Moral Enquiry*, 53.
5 Murdoch, *Metaphysics as a Guide to Morals*, 214.

210 Notes to pages 151–62

6 Strier, *Resistant Structures*, 56.
7 Kate Taylor, "Saving Stratford from the Excesses of Success," *Globe and Mail*, 18 July 1998.
8 Ray Conlogue, "Troubled Times for Classic Theatre," *Toronto Sun*, 2 June 1998.
9 Broadly speaking, this is the view espoused in Blond, *Red Tory: How the Left and Right Have Broken Britain*, the title of which translates a term native to Canadian political history to a British context. In Canada, however, this general attitude is not a monopoly of the right wing but has historically been characteristic of major leftist traditions, embodied by democratic socialists such as Eugene Forsey and updated in the more liberal, multicultural communitarianism of Charles Taylor. More recently, this tradition even found something of a place in the Green Party, which was most successfully led by Elizabeth May, a faithful Anglican with deep roots in the Red Tory tradition who served in Brian Mulroney's Progressive Conservative government (1984–93). The political complexity in the Canadian context is further evinced by the fact that Red Tories traditionally defected from the Progressive Conservative Party to the socialist Co-operative Commonwealth Federation or New Democratic Party, not the Liberal Party. From this perspective, traditions and norms are respected as resources for progress as well as a context for community, not just a bulwark against change. The difficulty of pigeonholing the show's politics is partly an expression of the Canadian Left's historical openness to old-fashioned ideas of tradition, service, and communitarian values.
10 Kotsko, *Why We Love Sociopaths*, 2.
11 The key source for Bristol's understanding of tradition is Alasdair MacIntyre's *Three Rival Versions of Moral Enquiry*. Subsequent references given in text as TRV.
12 Graff, *Literature Against Itself*, 8.

CHAPTER TEN

1 Eagleton, *Illusions of Postmodernism*, 26.
2 For Judith Butler's response to the charge that genealogists do not engage in the self-critique characteristic of dialectical approaches to tradition, see *Giving an Account of Oneself*, 23. In their view, the practice of putting oneself at risk as a subject is crucial to being ethical. But this, it would seem, bears out MacIntyre's point that post-structuralism tacitly presupposes a notion of authenticity that the theory explicitly rejects.
3 Knowles, "Shakespeare, 1993," 222.

Notes to pages 163–83

4 Pittman, *Authorizing Shakespeare*, chap. 6.
5 See Kermode, "Hawkesbiz," 9–10.
6 Brook, *Quality of Mercy*, 82–3.
7 Ibid., 84–5.
8 "1995 Keanu Reeves / Lewis Baumander about the production of *Hamlet*," Keanu Video Archive, 11 June 2021.
9 Weil, *Need for Roots*, 48.
10 See Michaels, *Shape of the Signifier*, 82–128.
11 Alan Riding, "Peter Brook Prefers His Hamlet Lean," *New York Times*, 10 December 2000.

CHAPTER ELEVEN

1 Southard, "Theatre on the Small Screen."
2 For a fuller articulation of this dynamic, see Wright, "'Who's There.'"
3 Hutt, "William Hutt, King of the Canadian Stage."
4 For more on these connections, see Ormesby, "'This Famous Duke of Milan.'"
5 Kermode, *Sense of an Ending*, 82.
6 Murdoch, *Sovereignty of Good*, 14–15.
7 For the Canadian fatalism of the ending, see McIntyre, "With *Slings and Arrows* Canadians Prove."
8 Murdoch, *Sovereignty of the Good*, 19.
9 Robert Lloyd, "'Slings & Arrows' Made Shakespeare Must-See TV," *Los Angeles Times*, 5 November 2019.
10 Pittman, *Authorizing Shakespeare*, 201.
11 Ibid.
12 Ryan, *Shakespeare's Universality*, 96.
13 Parolin, "'What Revels Are in Hand," 206.
14 Royster, "Comic Terror and Masculine Vulnerability," 348.
15 Wright, "'Who's There," 79.
16 Knowles, "From Nationalist to Multinational."
17 Lynch, *Loving Literature*, 2.
18 Garber, *Academic Instincts*, chap. 1.
19 Guillory, *Professing Criticism*, 172–80.

CONCLUSION

1 Fedderson and Richardson, "*Slings & Arrows*: An Intermedial Adaptation," 225.

212 Notes to pages 183–95

2 Ibid.

3 Eagleton, *Illusions of Postmodernism*, 131.

4 For a reading of the series that balances its reverence of Shakespeare with a sense of its irreverence, see Wareh, "'Base Respects of Thrift.'"

CODA

1 One negative review, perfunctorily describing the production as extravagantly vulgar, can be found in B.A. Young's "Stratford Ontario: Shakespeare – and G & S – in Canada," *Financial Times*, 30 June 1982.

2 Hayes and Schonberg, eds., *Tempest as Directed by John Hirsch*, 1.

3 John Hirsch Oral History, Library and Archives Canada, R15958-263-1-E.

4 Sybil Shack Fonds, University of Manitoba Archives, MSS 152, PC 159, TC 104 A2002–56, A2004–31, box 26.

5 Cited in AFS, 280.

6 Cited in AFS, 281.

7 Kott, *Shakespeare Our Contemporary*, 179.

8 Ibid.

9 Michael Dolzani, preface to Northrop Frye's *Notebooks on Renaissance Literature*, xxi.

10 Kierkegaard, *Works of Love*, 23.

11 Warren, "Shakespeare at Stratford."

12 Irvin Wardle, "Review of Stratford *Tempest*," *Times London*, 1 July 1982.

13 Ibid.

14 Kleber, "Theatrical Continuities," 147.

15 Stage management files, *The Tempest* (1982), Stratford Festival Archives.

16 Garbian, "1982 Stratford Festival," 110.

Bibliography

Adler, Steven. *Rough Magic: Making Theatre at the Royal Shakespeare Company.* Carbondale: Southern Illinois University Press, 2001.

Adorno, Theodor. *Aesthetic Theory.* London: Continuum, 2004.

Alfono, Chiara. *Derrida Reads Shakespeare.* Edinburgh: Edinburgh University Press, 2020.

Ayre, John. *Northrop Frye: A Biography.* Toronto: Random House, 1989.

Barthes, Roland. "Introduction to the Structural Analysis of Narratives." *New Literary History* 6, no. 2 (1975): 237–72.

Bate, Jonathan. *The Genius of Shakespeare.* London: Picador, 2016.

– *Mad about Shakespeare: From Classroom to Theatre to Emergency Room.* London: William Collins, 2022.

– *Shakespeare and the English Romantic Imagination.* Oxford: Clarendon Press, 1986.

– *Shakespearean Constitutions: Politics, Theatre, Criticism 1730–1830.* Oxford: Clarendon Press, 1989.

Baudrillard, Jean. *The Consumer Society: Myths and Structures.* Translated by Chris Turner. London: Sage, 1970.

– *The Gulf War Did Not Take Place.* Translated by Paul Patton. Bloomington: Indiana University Press, 1995.

– *Screened Out.* Translated by Chris Turner. London: Verso, 2002.

– *Simulacra and Simulation.* Translated by Sheila Faria Glaser. Ann Arbor: University of Michigan Press, 1994.

Beck, Ulrich. *Risk Society: Towards a New Modernity.* London: Sage, 1992.

Bennett, Sarah. "Oh Canada! *Slings and Arrows.*" *The Airship* (blog). http://airshipdaily.com/blog/oh-canada-slings-and-arrows.

Berger, Harry. "Miraculous Harp: A Reading of Shakespeare's *The Tempest.*" *Shakespeare Studies* 5 (1969): 253–83.

Bibliography

Berkowitz, Peter. *Nietzsche: The Ethics of an Immoralist*. Cambridge: Harvard University Press, 1995.

Berry, Ralph. "Shakespearean Comedy and Northrop Frye." *Essays in Criticism* 22, no. 1 (1972): 33–40.

Bettelheim, Bruno. *The Uses of Enchantment: The Meaning and Importance of Fairy Tales*. New York: Vintage Books, 1976. Reprint, 2010.

Blond, Philip. *Red Tory: How the Left and Right Have Broken Britain*. London: Faber and Faber, 2010.

Bristol, Michael. *Big-Time Shakespeare*. London: Routledge, 1996.

– "Macbeth the Philosopher: Rethinking Context." *New Literary History* 42, no. 4 (2011): 641–62.

– "Vernacular Criticism and the Scenes Shakespeare Never Wrote." *Shakespeare Survey* 52 (2000): 89–102.

Brook, Peter. *The Empty Space*. London: Nick Hern Books, 1968.

– *The Open Door: Thoughts on Acting and Theatre*. New York: Anchor Books, 2005.

– *Peter Brook's Production of William Shakespeare's A Midsummer Night's Dream for the Royal Shakespeare Company*. Edited by Glen Loney. Chicago: Dramatic Publishing, 1974.

– Preface to *Shakespeare Our Contemporary*, by Jan Kott, ix–xi. London: Metheun, 1964.

– *The Quality of Mercy: Reflections on Shakespeare*. London: Nick Hern, 2013.

– *The Shifting Point: Theatre, Film, Opera 1946–1987*. New York: Theatre Communications Group, 1987.

– *Threads of Time: A Memoir*. London: Metheun, 1998.

– *Tip of the Tongue: Reflections on Language and Meaning*. London: Nick Hern, 2017.

Bruster, Douglas. "Local *Tempest*: Shakespeare and the Work of the Early Modern Playhouse." *Journal of Medieval and Renaissance Studies* 25, no. 1 (1995): 33–53.

Butler, Judith. *Giving An Account of Oneself*. New York: Fordham University Press, 2005.

Calin, William. *Twentieth-Century Humanist Critics: From Spitzer to Frye*. Toronto: University of Toronto Press, 2007.

Cayley, David. *Northrop Frye in Conversation*. Toronto: House of Anansi Press, 1992.

Cochrane, Peter. *Small Screen Shakespeare*. Newcastle: Cambridge Scholars, 2013.

Coghill, Nevill. "Six Points of Stage Craft in *The Winter's Tale*." *Shakespeare Survey* 11 (March 1958): 31–41.

Bibliography

Coleridge, Samuel T. *Biographia Literaria*. Edited by George Watson. London: J.M. Dent & Sons, 1975.

– *Coleridge: Lectures on Shakespeare* (1811–19). Edited by Adam Roberts. Edinburgh: Edinburgh University Press, 2016.

– *Coleridge on Shakespeare*. Edited by R.A. Foakes. London: Athlone, 1989.

Compagnon, Antoine. *Literature, Theory, and Common Sense*. Translated by Carol Cosman. Princeton: Princeton University Press, 2004.

Cox, John D. "Recovering Something Christian about *The Tempest*." *Christianity and Literature* 50, no. 1 (2000): 31–51.

Coyne, Susan. "The Antidote to Loneliness: Stories With Other People." Lecture, Western University, 12 November 2019. https://www.youtube.com /watch?v=41u7zMtrHBc.

– *Kingfisher Days*. Toronto: Vintage Canada, 2001.

– *Kingfisher Days: The Play*. Toronto: Playwrights Canada Press, 2003.

Coyne, Susan, and Martha Burns, dirs. *Robin, Mark, and Richard III*. Devil's Gap Inc., 2016.

Cushman, Robert. *Fifty Years at Stratford*. Toronto: McClelland & Stewart, 2002.

Decker, Dan. J. *Anatomy of a Screenplay*. Self-published, 1998. Reprint, 2020.

Deleuze, Gilles. *Nietzsche and Philosophy*. Translated by Hugh Tomlinson. New York: Columbia University Press, 1962. Reprint, 2006.

Denham, Robert. "Frye's Shakespeare Criticism." In *The Importance of Northrop Frye*, edited by S.K. Aithai Kanpur, 1–18. Kanpur, India: Humanities Research Center, 1993.

– "Northrop Frye and Edmund Blunden." *English Studies in Canada* 41, no. 4 (2015): 69–92.

– *The Reception of Northrop Frye*. Toronto: Toronto University Press, 2021.

Derrida, Jacques. *Of Grammatology*. Translated by Gayatri Chakravorty Spivak. Baltimore: Johns Hopkins Press, 1976. Corrected edition, 1997.

– *Writing and Difference*. Translated by Alan Bass. Chicago: University of Chicago Press, 1978.

Dery, Mark. "The Scream Meme." 20 January 1998. https://archive.the-next.eliterature.org/trace/frame/frame1/no-js/dery.html.

Devaney, M.J. '*Since at least Plato...' and Other Postmodernist Myths*. London: Macmillan, 1997.

Dobson, Michael. "Afterword: Shakespeare and Myth." In *Local and Global Myths in Shakespearean Performance*, edited by Aneta Mancewicz and Alexa Alice Joubin, 259–65. New York: Palgrave, 2018.

Dupuy, Jean-Pierre. *The Mark of the Sacred*. Translated by M.B. Debevoise. Stanford: Stanford University Press, 2013.

During, Simon. "The Historical Status of Postmodernism Under Neoliberalism." *Electronic Book Review*, 4 December 2016. https://electronicbookreview.com/essay/the-historical-status-of-postmodernism-under-neoliberalism/.

Durkheim, Émile. "Durkheim's Individualism and the Intellectuals." Translated by Steven Lukes. *Political Studies* 17, no. 1 (1969): 14–30.

Eagleton, Terry. *The Illusions of Postmodernism*. Oxford: Blackwell, 1996.

Enterline, Lynn. *Shakespeare's Schoolroom: Rhetoric, Discipline, Emotion*. Philadelphia: University of Pennsylvania Press, 2012.

Fedderson, Kim, and J. Michael Richardson. "*Slings & Arrows*: An Intermedial Adaptation." In *Outerspeares: Shakespeare, Intermedia, and the Limits of Adaptation*, edited by Daniel Fischlin, 205–29. Toronto: University of Toronto Press, 2014.

Fekete, John. *The Critical Twilight*. London: Routledge, 1977.

Felperin, Howard. "Political Criticism at the Crossroads: The Utopian Historicism of *The Tempest*." In *The Tempest*, edited by Nigel Wood, 29–66. Buckingham: Open University Press, 1995.

– *Shakespearean Representation: Mimesis and Modernity in Elizabethan Tragedy*. Princeton: Princeton University Press, 1977.

– *Shakespearean Romances*. Princeton: Princeton University Press, 1972.

Felski, Rita. *The Limits of Critique*. Chicago: Chicago University Press, 2015.

Fischlin, Daniel. *Canadian Adaptations of Shakespeare Project*. University of Guelph, 2007. Accessed January 2024. http://www.canadianshakespeares.ca.

Fiske, John. *Television Culture*. London: Methuen, 1987.

Fortier, Mark. "Two-Voiced, Delicate Monster: *The Tempest*, Romance, and Post-Colonialism." *Essays in Theatre* 15, no. 1 (November 1996): 91–101.

Frey, Erin. "Slings & Arrows." In *The Canadian Encyclopedia*. Historica Canada, online ed., 2013. Article published 16 January 2018. https://www.thecanadianencyclopedia.ca/en/article/slings-arrows.

Frye, Northrop. *Anatomy of Criticism: Four Essays*. Edited by Robert Denham. Vol. 22 of *The Collected Works of Northrop Frye*, edited by Alvin A. Lee. Toronto: University of Toronto Press, 2006.

– "Auguries of Experience." In *Visionary Poetics: Essays on Northrop Frye's Criticism*, edited by Robert Denham and Thomas Willard, 1–8. New York: Peter Lang, 1991.

– *Creation & Recreation*. Toronto: University of Toronto Press, 1980. Reprint, 1988.

– *Divisions on a Ground: Essays on Canadian Culture*. Edited by James Polk. Toronto: House of Anansi, 1982.

– *Fearful Symmetry: A Study of William Blake*. Princeton: Princeton University Press, 1947. Reprint, 2018.

Bibliography

- *Myth and Metaphor: Selected Essays, 1974–1988*. Edited by Robert D. Denham. Charlottesville: University of Virginia Press, 1990.
- *A Natural Perspective: The Development of Shakespearean Comedy and Romance*. New York: Columbia University Press, 1965.
- *Northrop Frye on Milton and Blake*. Edited by Angela Esterhammer. Vol. 16 of *The Collected Works of Northrop Frye*, edited by Alvin A. Lee. Toronto: University of Toronto Press, 2005.
- *Northrop Frye on Modern Culture*. Edited by Jan Gorak. Vol. 11 of *The Collected Works of Northrop Frye*, edited by Alvin A. Lee. Toronto: University of Toronto Press, 2003.
- *Northrop Frye's Notebooks on Renaissance Literature*. Edited by Michael Dolzani. Vol. 20 of *The Collected Works of Northrop Frye*, edited by Alvin A. Lee. Toronto: University of Toronto Press, 2006.
- *Northrop Frye's Writings on the Eighteenth and Nineteenth Centuries*. Edited by Imre Salusinszky. Vol. 17 of *The Collected Works of Northrop Frye*, edited by Alvin A. Lee. Toronto: University of Toronto Press, 2005.
- *Northrop Frye's Writings on Shakespeare and the Renaissance*. Edited by Troni Y. Grande and Garry Sherbert. Vol. 28 of *The Collected Works of Northrop Frye*, edited by Alvin A. Lee. Toronto: University of Toronto Press, 2010.
- "Romance as Masque." In *Shakespeare's Romances Reconsidered*, edited by Carol McGinnis Kay and Henry E. Jacobs, 11–39. Lincoln: University of Nebraska Press, 1978.
- *Words with Power*. New York: HarperCollins, 1992.
Frye, Northrop, and Helen Kemp. *The Correspondence of Northrop Frye and Helen Kemp*. Edited by Robert Denham. Vol. 1 of *The Collected Works of Northrop Frye*, edited by Alvin A. Lee. Toronto: University of Toronto Press, 1996.
Garber, Marjorie. *Academic Instincts*. Princeton: Princeton University Press, 2000.
Garbian, Keith. "The 1982 Stratford Festival." *Journal of Canadian Studies* 17, no. 4 (1982–83): 102–11.
Gebaur, Gunter, and Christoph Wulf. *Mimesis: Culture – Art – Society*. Oakland: University of California Press, 1995.
Gill, Glenn. *Northrop Frye and the Phenomenology of Myth*. Toronto: University of Toronto Press, 2006.
Goddard, Harold. *The Meaning of Shakespeare*. Vol. 1. Chicago: University of Chicago Press, 1951.
Grady, Hugh. *Modernist Shakespeare: Critical Texts in a Material World*. Oxford: Oxford University Press, 1991.

Graff, Gerald. *Literature Against Itself: Literary Ideas in Modern Society*. Chicago: Chicago University Press, 1979.

Graham, Kenneth J.E. "Soyinka and the Dead Dramatist." *Comparative Drama* 44, no. 1 (2010): 29–44.

Grossman, Marshall. "The Vicissitudes of the Subject in Northrop Frye's *Anatomy of Criticism*." *Texas Studies in Language and Literature* 24, no. 3 (1982): 313–27.

Guillory, John. *Professing Criticism: Essays on the Organization of Literary Study*. Chicago: University of Chicago, 2022.

Halliwell, Stephen. *The Aesthetics of Mimesis: Ancient Texts and Modern Problems*. Princeton: Princeton University Press, 2002.

Halpern, Richard. *Shakespeare Among the Moderns*. Ithaca: Cornell University Press, 1997.

Hamilton, A.C. *Northrop Frye: Anatomy of His Criticism*. Toronto: University of Toronto Press, 1990.

– "Northrop Frye as a Cultural Theorist." In *Rereading Frye: The Published and Unpublished Works*, edited by David Boyd and Imre Salusinsky, 103–21. Toronto: University of Toronto Press, 1999.

Hawkes, Terence. *Meaning By Shakespeare*. London: Routledge, 1992.

Hayes, Elliot, and Schonberg Michael, eds. *"The Tempest" as Directed by John Hirsch*. Toronto: CBC Enterprises, 1983.

Hazlitt, William. *Characters of Shakespeare's Plays*. Edited by J.H. Lobban. Cambridge: Cambridge University Press, 1908. Reprint, 2009.

– "On Shakespeare and Milton." In *Four Centuries of Shakespearean Criticism*, edited by Frank Kermode, 123. New York: Avon, 1965.

Headlam Wells, Robin. *Shakespeare's Humanism*. Cambridge: Cambridge University Press, 2005.

Hernstein Smith, Barbara. "Anthropotheology: Latour Speaking Religiously." *New Literary History* 47, no. 3 (2016): 331–51.

Hirsch, John. "Father Courage: An Interview with John Hirsch." By Robert Enright. *Border Crossings: The Exiled Imagination*, no. 4 (Fall 1988): 80–5.

– "Interview with John Hirsch." *Performing Arts in Canada* Winter (1965–66): 38–41.

– John Hirsch Fonds. University of Manitoba Archives, MSS 492 A2004–209.

– Sybil Shack Fonds. University of Manitoba Archives, MSS 152, PC 159, TC 104 A2002–56, A2004–31. Box 26.

Holland, Norman N. *The Dynamics of Literary Response*. New York: Oxford University Press, 1968.

Holmes, Jonathan, and Streete Adrian, eds. *Refiguring Mimesis: Representa-*

tion in Early Modern Literature. Herefordshire: University of Herefordshire Press, 2005.

Hunter, Ian. *Culture and Government: The Emergence of Literary Education*. London: Macmillan, 1988.

Hutson, Lorna. *The Invention of Suspicion: Law and Mimesis in Shakespeare and Renaissance Drama*. Oxford: Oxford University Press, 2007.

Hutt, William. "William Hutt, King of the Canadian Stage." Interview by CBC, 31 January 1962. https://www.cbc.ca/player/play/1704507249.

James, Henry. *The Portable Henry James*. Edited by John Auchard. New York: Penguin, 2004.

Jameson, Frederic. "The End of Temporality." *Critical Enquiry* 29, no. 4 (2003): 698–718.

– *The Political Unconscious: Narrative as a Socially Symbolic Act*. Ithaca: Cornell University Press, 1981.

– *Postmodernism, or, The Cultural Logic of Late Capitalism*. Durham: Duke University Press, 1991. Reprint, 2001.

– "Postmodernism, or, the Cultural Logic of Late Capitalism." *New Left Review* 146 (1984): 59–92.

Johnson, Samuel. "Preface to Shakespeare." In *The Plays and Poems of Shakespeare*, edited by A.J. Valpy, not paginated. New York: Worthington, 1885.

Kareda, Urjo. "Sold Out." *Toronto Life* 34, no. 11 (2000): 76.

Karim-Cooper, Farim. *The Great White Bard: How to Love Shakespeare While Talking about Race*. London: Viking, 2023.

Kennedy, Dennis. "Shakespeare and Cultural Tourism." *Theatre Journal* 50, no. 2 (1998): 175–88.

Kermode, Frank. "Hawkesbiz." Review of *Meaning by Shakespeare*, by Terence Hawkes. *London Review of Books* 15, no. 3 (1993): 9–10.

– *The Sense of An Ending*. Oxford: Oxford University Press, 2000.

Kierkegaard, Soren. *Works of Love*. Translated by Howard and Edna Hong. London: Collins, 1962.

Kleber, Pia. "Theatrical Continuities in Giorgio Strehler's *The Tempest*." In *Foreign Shakespeare: Contemporary Performance*, edited by Dennis Kennedy, 140–57. Cambridge: Cambridge University Press, 1993.

Klett, Elizabeth. "Shakespearean Authority and Emotional Realism in *Slings & Arrows*." *Early Modern Studies Journal* 5 (2013): 1–22.

Knausgaard, Karl Ove. *So Much Longing in So Little Space: The Art of Edvard Munch*. Translated by Ingvild Burkey. New York: Penguin, 2019.

Knelman, Martin. *A Stratford Tempest*. Toronto: McClelland and Stewart, 1982.

Knight, G. Wilson. *The Shakespearean Tempest*. Oxford: Oxford University Press, 1932.

Knowles, Richard Paul. "From Nationalist to Multinational: The Stratford Festival, Free Trade, and the Discourses of Intercultural Tourism." *Theatre Journal* 47, no. 1 (1995): 19–41.

– "Shakespeare, 1993, and the Discourses of the Stratford Festival, Ontario." *Shakespeare Quarterly* 45, no. 2 (1994): 211–25.

– *Shakespeare in Canada*. New York: Peter Lang, 2004.

Kostihova, Marcela. "The Myth of Shakespearean Authenticity: Neoliberalism and Humanistic Shakespeare." In *Local and Global Myths in Shakespearean Performance*, edited by A. Mancewicz and A. Joubin, 41–55. New York: Palgrave, 2018.

Kotsko, Adam. *Why We Love Sociopaths: A Guide to Late Capitalist Television*. Winchester: Zero Books, 2012.

Kott, Jan. *Shakespeare Our Contemporary*. London: Metheun, 1964.

– "*The Tempest*, or Repetition." *Mosaic* 10, no. 3 (1977): 9–36.

Kustow, Michael. *Peter Brook: A Biography*. New York: St Martin's Press, 2005.

Lamarque, Peter, and Stein Haugom Olsen. *Truth, Fiction, and Literature: A Philosophical Perspective*. Oxford: Clarendon Press, 1996.

Lamb, Charles, and Mary Lamb. *Tales of Shakespeare*. Leipzig: Bernhard Tauchnitz, 1863.

Lee, Alvin A., and Robert D. Denham, eds. *The Legacy of Northrop Frye*. Toronto: University of Toronto Press, 1994.

Lentricchia, Frank. *After the New Criticism*. Chicago: University of Chicago Press, 1980.

Lerer, Seth. *Shakespeare's Lyric Stage: Myth, Music, and Poetry in the Last Plays*. Chicago: University of Chicago Press, 2018.

Levin, Richard. "Bloom, Bardolatry, and Characterolatry." In *Harold Bloom's Shakespeare*, edited by Christy Desmet and Robert Sawyer, 71–80. New York: Palgrave, 2001.

Lewis, C.S. *An Experiment in Criticism*. Cambridge: Cambridge University Press, 1961.

Love, Heather K. "Close but Not Deep: Literary Ethics and the Descriptive Turn." *New Literary History* 41, no. 2 (2010): 371–91.

Lynch, Deidre Shauna. *Loving Literature*. Chicago: University of Chicago Press, 2015.

MacIntyre, Alasdair. *After Virtue: A Study in Moral Theory*. 2nd ed. Notre Dame: University of Notre Dame Press, 1984.

– *Marxism and Christianity*. London: Duckworth, 1995.

– *Secularization and Moral Change*. London: Oxford University Press, 1967.

Bibliography

- *Three Rival Versions of Moral Enquiry*. Notre Dame: University of Notre Dame Press, 1990.

Magnusson, Lynn. "Interruption in *The Tempest.*" *Shakespeare Quarterly* 37, no. 1 (1986): 52–65.

Martz, Fraidie, and Wilson, Andrew. *A Fiery Soul: The Life and Theatrical Times of John Hirsch*. Montreal: Véhicule Press, 2011.

Mazer, Cary M. *Double Shakespeares: Emotional-Realist Acting and Contemporary Performance*. Madison: Farleigh Dickinson University Press, 2015.

- "Sense/Memory/Sense-Memory: Reading Narratives of Shakespearean Rehearsals." *Shakespeare Survey* 62 (2009): 328–48.

McCoy, Richard C. *Faith in Shakespeare*. Oxford: Oxford University Press, 2013.

McCullough, Christopher J. "The Cambridge Connection: Towards a Materialist Theatre Practice." In *The Shakespeare Myth*, edited by Graham Holderness, 112–21. Manchester: Manchester University Press, 1988.

McGrath, Alistair. *The Intellectual World of C.S. Lewis*. Oxford: Wiley-Blackwell, 2014.

McLuhan, Marshall. *Understanding Media*. London: Routledge, 1964.

Merrill, Robert. "The Generic Approach in Recent Criticism of Shakespeare's Comedies and Romances." *Texas Studies in Language and Literature* 20, no. 3 (1978): 478–87.

Michaels, Walter Benn. *The Shape of the Signifier*. Princeton: Princeton University Press, 2007.

Monette, Richard. *This Rough Magic: The Making of An Artistic Director*. Stratford: Stratford Festival Canada, 2007.

Monta, Susannah B. "'It is requir'd you do awake your faith': Belief in Shakespeare's Theater." In *Religion and Drama in Early Modern England: The Performance of Religion on the Renaissance Stage*, edited by Jane Hwang Degenhardt and Elizabeth Williamson, 115–38. Aldershot: Ashgate, 2011.

Moore, Don. "Race, National Identity, and the Hauntological Ethics of *Slings & Arrows.*" In *Shakespeare and Canada: Remembrance of Ourselves*, edited by Irena R. Makaryk and Kathryn Prince, 97–109. Ottawa: University of Ottawa Press, 2017.

Mousley, Andy. *Re-Humanizing Shakespeare: Literary Humanism, Wisdom, and Modernity*. Edinburgh: Edinburgh University Press, 2007. Reprint, 2015.

Murdoch, Iris. *Metaphysics as a Guide to Morals*. London: Chatto & Windus, 1992.

- *The Sovereignty of Good over Other Concepts*. Cambridge: Cambridge University Press, 1967.

Newman, Peter C. *The Importance of Failure in the Canadian Psyche*. Stratford: Stratford Festival, 1985.

Noble, Denis. *Dance to the Tune of Life: Biological Relativity*. Cambridge: Cambridge University Press, 2017.

Norbrook, David. "'What Cares These Roarers for the Name of King?': Language and Utopia in *The Tempest*." In *Shakespeare's Last Plays*, edited by Kiernan Ryan, 21–54. London: Routledge, 1999.

Norris, Christopher. *What's Wrong with Postmodernism? Critical Theory and the Ends of Philosophy*. Baltimore: Johns Hopkins University Press, 1998.

Nuttall, A.D. *A New Mimesis: Shakespeare and the Representation of Reality*. New Haven and London: Yale University Press, 2007.

– *Two Concepts of Allegory: A Study of Shakespeare's "The Tempest" and the Logic of Allegorical Expression*. 2nd ed. New Haven: Yale University Press, 2007.

Orgel, Stephen. Introduction to *The Tempest*, by William Shakespeare, 1–92. Edited by Stephen Orgel. Oxford: Clarendon, 1987.

Ormesby, Robert. "'This Famous Duke of Milan of Whom So Often I Have Heard Renown': William Hutt at the Stratford and New Burbage Festivals." *Canadian Theatre Review* 141 (2010): 10–15.

Osborne, Laurie. E. "Serial Shakespeare: Intermedial Performance and the Outrageous Fortunes of *Slings & Arrows*." *Borrowers and Lenders* 6, no. 2 (2011): 1–8.

Parolin, Peter. "'What Revels Are in Hand': A Change of Direction at This Stratford Shakespeare Festival of Canada." *Shakespeare Quarterly* 60, no. 2 (2009): 197–224.

Parvini, Neema. *Shakespeare's Moral Compass*. Edinburgh: Edinburgh University Press, 2018.

Pechter, Edward. *Shakespeare Studies Today: Romanticism Lost*. New York: Palgrave, 2011.

Perreau-Saussine, Émile. *Alasdair MacIntyre: An Intellectual Biography*. Translated by Nathan J. Pinkoski. Notre Dame: Notre Dame University Press, 2022.

Pickstock, Catherine. *After Writing: On The Liturgical Consummation of Philosophy*. Oxford: Blackwell, 1998.

Pittman, Monique L. *Authorizing Shakespeare on Film and Television: Gender, Class, and Ethnicity in Adaptation*. Bern: Peter Lang, 2011.

Powe, B.W. *Marshall McLuhan and Northrop Frye: Apocalypse and Alchemy*. Toronto: University of Toronto Press, 2014.

Prendergast, Christopher. *The Order of Mimesis: Balzac, Stendhal, Nerval, Flaubert*. Cambridge: Cambridge University Press, 1986.

Bibliography

Prideux, Sue. *Edvard Munch: Behind The Scream*. New Haven: Yale University Press, 2005.

Rebhorn, Wayne. "After Frye: A Review-Article on the Interpretation of Shakespearean Comedy and Romance." *Texas Studies in Language and Literature* 21, no. 4 (1979): 553–82.

Ricoeur, Paul. "*Anatomy of Criticism* or the Order of Paradigms." In *Centre and Labyrinth: Essays in Honour of Northrop Frye*, edited by Eleanor Cook et al., 1–13. Toronto: University of Toronto Press, 1983.

– *Figuring the Sacred*. Minneapolis: Fortress Press, 1995.

– *Time and Narrative*. Vol. 1–3. Chicago: University of Chicago Press, 1983–84.

Righter, Anne. *Shakespeare and the Idea of the Play*. New York: Barnes and Noble, 1962.

Royster, Francesca T. "Comic Terror and Masculine Vulnerability in *Slings and Arrows*: Season Three." *Journal of Narrative Theory* 41, no. 3 (2011): 343–61.

Rozik, Eli. *The Roots of Theatre: Rethinking Ritual and Other Theories of Origin*. Iowa: University of Iowa Press, 2002.

Ryan, Kiernan. *Shakespeare's Universality: Here's Fine Revolution*. London: Bloomsbury, 2015.

Salter, Dennis. "Acting Shakespeare in Postcolonial Space." In *Shakespeare, Theory, Performance*, edited by James C. Bulman, 113–32. London: Routledge, 1996.

Sedgwick, Eve. "Paranoid Reading and Reparative Reading, Or You're So Paranoid You Probably Think This Essay Is about You." In *Touching Feeling: Affect, Pedagogy, Performativity*, 123–52. Durham: Duke University Press, 2003.

Selbourne, David. *The Making of "A Midsummer Night's Dream": An Eye-Witness Account of Peter Brook's Production from First Rehearsal to First Night*. London: Methuen, 1982.

Shakespeare, William. *As You Like It*. Edited by Juliet Dusinberre. London: Bloomsbury, 2006.

– *King Lear*. Edited by R.A. Foakes. London: Bloomsbury, 1997.

– *Macbeth*. Edited by Sandra Clark and Pamela Mason. London: Bloomsbury, 2015.

– *A Midsummer Night's Dream*. Edited by Sukanta Chaudhuri. London: Arden, 2017.

– *The Tempest*. Edited by Virginia Mason Vaughan and Alden T. Vaughan. London: Bloomsbury, 2011.

– *The Winter's Tale*. Edited by John Pitcher. London: Bloomsbury, 2010.

Shookman, Ellis. "Barthes's Semiological Myth of Brecht's Epic Theater." *Monatshefte* 81, no. 4 (1989): 459–75.

Sinfield, Alan. "Royal Shakespeare: Theatre and the Making of Ideology." In *Political Shakespeare: Essays in Cultural Materialism*, 2nd. ed., edited by Jonathan Dollimore and Alan Sinfield, 182–205. Manchester: Manchester University Press, 1985. Reprint, 1994.

Smith, Ian. *Black Shakespeare: Reading and Misreading Race*. Cambridge: Cambridge University Press, 2022.

Southard, Dylan. "Theatre on the Small Screen: 'Smash' Vs. 'Slings & Arrows.'" *American Theatre*, 26 January 2016. https://www.americantheatre.org/2016/01/26/theatre-on-the-small-screen-smash-vs-slings-arrows/.

Soyinka, Wole. "Shakespeare and the Living Dramatist." *Shakespeare Survey* 36 (1983): 1–10.

Stern, Tiffany. "(Re)historicizing Spontaneity: Original Practices, Stanislavski, and Characterisation." In *Shakespeare's Sense of Character: On the Page and from the Stage*, edited by Yu Jin Ko and Michael W. Shurgot, 99–110. Aldershot: Ashgate, 2012.

Stratford Festival. *Stratford Festival Souvenir Programmes*, 1975 and 1981–84.

Strier, Richard. *Resistant Structures: Particularity, Radicalism, and Renaissance Texts*. Berkeley: University of California Press, 1995.

Tallis, Raymond. *In Defence of Realism*. Lincoln: University of Nebraska Press, 1988.

Taylor, Charles. *Malaise of Modernity*. Toronto: House of Anansi, 1991.

– *A Secular Age*. Cambridge: Harvard University Press, 2007.

– *Sources of the Self: The Making of Modern Identity*. Cambridge: Harvard University Press, 1989.

Thomson, David. *Why Acting Matters*. New Haven: Yale University Press, 2015.

Tolkien, J.R. *Tree and Leaf*. Boston: Houghton Mifflin, 1965.

Tomko, Michael. *Beyond the Willing Suspension of Disbelief: Poetic Faith from Coleridge to Tolkien*. London: Bloomsbury, 2016.

Trussler, Simon. Introduction to *The Making of "A Midsummer Night's Dream": An Eye-Witness Account of Peter Brook's Production from First Rehearsal to First Night*, by David Selbourne, ix–xxx. London: Methuen, 1982.

Vogler, Christopher. *The Writer's Journey: Mythic Structure for Writers*. 3rd ed. Studio City: Michael Wiese, 2007.

Walton, Kendall L. *Mimesis as Make-Believe: On the Foundations of the Representational Arts*. Cambridge: Harvard University Press, 1990.

Bibliography

Wareh, Patricia. "'Base Respects of Thrift': *Hamlet* and *Slings & Arrows*." *Interdisciplinary Literary Studies* 17, no. 2 (2015): 264–88.

Warkentin, Germaine. "The Age of Frye: Dissecting the Anatomy of Criticism, 1957–1966." *Canadian Literature* 214 (2012): 15–23.

Warren, Roger. "Shakespeare at Stratford: The John Hirsch Years." *Shakespeare Survey* 36 (1986): 179–90.

– *Staging Shakespeare's Late Plays*. Oxford: Clarendon Press, 1990.

Weil, Simone. *The Need for Roots*. Translated by Arthur Wills. London: Routledge, 1952.

Wellington, Peter, dir. *Slings & Arrows: The Complete Collection*. Acorn Media, 2019.

Wilde, Oscar. *The Decay of Lying*. London: James R. Osgood, 1891.

Williams, Raymond. *Culture and Society, 1780–1950*. New York: Columbia University Press, 1958. Reprint, 1983.

Wimsatt, W.K., ed. *Northrop Frye in Modern Criticism*. New York: Columbia University Press, 1966.

Wood, James. *How Fiction Works*. New York: Farrar, Straus and Giroux, 2008.

– "Letter to the Editor." *London Review of Books* 12, no. 6 (22 March 1990). https://www.lrb.co.uk/the-paper/v12/n06/letters.

Worthen, W.B. *Shakespeare and the Authority of Performance*. Cambridge: Cambridge University Press, 1997.

Wright, Kailin. "'Who's There?': *Slings & Arrows*' Audience Dynamics." In *Shakespeare and Canada: Remembrance of Ourselves*, edited by Irene R. Makrayk and Kathryn Prince, 79–95. Ottawa: University of Ottawa, 2017.

Žižek, Slavoj. *The Fragile Absolute*. London: Verso, 2000.

Index

Adorno, Theodor W., 68
advertising, 46, 59–63. *See also* Baudrillard, Jean; Frye, Northrop; *Slings & Arrows*: Sanjay
anamnesis. *See* Plato
archetypes, 24, 27–30, 42–3, 70–2, 116–26. *See also* Brook, Peter; Frye, Northrop
Aristotle. *See* mimesis
Artaud, Antonin, 55–6
Atwood, Margaret, 19, 114

Barthes, Roland: anti-realism, 46, 54, 112–15, 127–40; Bertolt Brecht, epic theatre, 34–5, 63; death of author, 56–7; demystification, 57; parody/critique of, 129, 183; reader response, 82; structuralism, 183. *See also* Nuttall, A.D.
Bate, Jonathan, 8, 13, 125–6
Baudrillard, Jean: advertising, 38–9; aesthetic illusion, 33, 138; the simulacra, 53–64; television, 4–5; truth, 38
Baumander, Lewis, 166

Bennett, Sarah, 86
Bettelheim, Bruno, 73
Blake, William, 68–73, 76–7, 91, 111–12, 191–6. *See also* Coyne, Susan; Frye, Northrop
Bleak Mid-Winter, The, 29
Brecht, Bertolt. *See* Barthes, Roland; Brook, Peter; Hirsch, John
Bristol, Michael, 10–12, 21–2, 135–8, 151–6, 183
Brook, Peter, 6, 14; anti-realism, 34–5, 56, 186; audiences, 37, 39, 48; Bertolt Brecht, 34–5, 57; contemporary art scene, 170; deadly theatre vs holy theatre, 21–64; death of author, 56; demystification, limits of, 55–6, 130, 186; desacralization, 57–8; directing, 26, 165–70; enchantment, 22; *Hamlet* (Adrian Lester), 167; idealism, 56–7; living illusions/dead illusions, 15, 33–5, 47–8, 54–61; *Meetings with Remarkable Men,* 56; *A Midsummer Night's Dream* (1970), 49, 115; mimesis, 53–64, 131–2; misanthropist/

228

Index

nihilist (described as), 56; perennial elements in theatre, 30–1, 51; ritual, 57–8; sacred and secular, 54–8; stage vs screen, 51; Stratford (England), 39, 47–8; stripped-down productions, 49–51, 169–70; theatre as vocation, 4, 6, 32–3, *Threads of Time*, 77; *Tip of the Tongue*, 200n11; vital vs dead critic, 48
Bruster, Douglas, 25–6

capitalism, 3–18, 22, 43–5, 146–58, 183–5. *See also* Baudrillard, Jean; Halpern, Richard; Jameson, Frederic; Munch, Edvard
Cariou, Len, 193–5
Carroll, Lewis, 78
Chair, The (Netflix series), 32
Coleridge, Samuel Taylor: concrete vs general, 123; copy vs imitation, 36–7; poetic faith, 15–18, 21, 29, 32–52, 65–87; Shakespeare and mimesis, 3; *The Tempest*, 24, 27. *See also* Brook, Peter; Tomko, Michael
Cox, John D., 102
Coyne, Susan, 17–19, 32; art-life dialectic, 22, 67–8; conception for series, 3; holy theatre, 23; international communicability, 117; *Kingfisher Days*, 18–19, 65–87; *The Man Who Invented Christmas*, 107; mythopoeic sensibility, 65–87, 140

Day-Lewis, Daniel, 28, 132
Deleuze, Gilles, 128
Denham, Robert, 203n3, 204nn11–13

Derrida, Jacques, 82, 110, 138–9, 148
dialectic of conviction and malaise, 4–5, 21–31, 65–8. *See also* Shakespeare, William: *A Midsummer Night's Dream*
Dobson, Michael, 13
Don't Look Up (Netflix film), 53
Dupuy, Jean-Pierre, *The Mark of the Sacred*, 101
Durkheim, Émile, 14, 50, 55, 199n37

Eagleton, Terry, 161
Eliot, T.S., 75–6
emotional realism, 132–8
Enterline, Lynn, 133–4
ethics of limit. *See* Brook, Peter; Mousley, Andy; Pickstock, Catherine
Eyre, Richard, 203

Felperin, Howard, 126, 205n17, 206n41, 208n12
Fiske, John, 198n11, 203n23, 205n16
Foucault, Michel, 133, 151
Freud, Sigmund, 68–9, 72–3
Frye, Northrop, 14–15, 19; advertising, 61–4; anagogy, 78–9; *Anatomy of Criticism*, 92–3; art as vocation, 5; critiques of, 70–2, 204n12; *Divisions on a Ground* ("Culture as Interpenetration"), 117–21; *The Double Vision*, 84; *Fearful Symmetry*, 76–7, 91–2, 107; inspiration, 18; metanarratives, 15, 89, 110–15; *The Modern Century* (advertising), 61–3; *A Natural Perspective*, 17, 69–71, 103, 200n8, 203n1; origins

of theatre, 103; personality, theory of, 161; popular art, 17, 70–2; romance, 70–2, 89, 172, 205n29; *The Secular Scripture*, 98; Shakespeare, general interpretation of, 93, 110–12, 97–115; "The Stage Is All the World" (*Myth and Metaphor*), 106–13; Stratford, Ontario, at, 89, 106–12; *The Tempest*, 15, 84, 97–115, 190–6; visionary history, 140–1; *The Winter's Tale*, 74; *Words with Power*, 15, 81–2, 105–6, 137, 164

Fulford, Robert, 117

Goddard, Harold, 138
Goffman, Erving, 8–9
Gross, Paul, 28, 180–1
Guillory, John, 9, 199n36, 211n19
Gurdjieff, G.I., 56
Guthrie, Tyrone, 66

Halpern, Richard, 69–70, 85–6
Hamilton, A.C., 71
Hawkes, Terence, 67, 128, 147–53, 183
Hazlitt, William, 7, 108–9, 123–4
Hegel, G.W.F., 101
Heywood, Thomas, 3–4
Hirsch, John, 20; artistic director, Stratford, 89–90; biography, 89–90; Bertolt Brecht, 35–6; dialectical approach to art, 90, 94; fairy tales (influenced by), 73; parallels with Tennant, 26; rejection of formalism, 91; risk-taking, 90–1; "A Sense of Direction," 90; *The Tempest* (1982), 102–3, 187–96
Holland, Norman, 72

Hopkins, Gerard Manley, 75
humanism, 6. *See also* Brook, Peter; Coyne, Susan; Frye, Northrop; Hirsch, John
Hutson, Lorna, 133–4

Jameson, Frederic: bourgeois romance, 94–5; postmodernism, 40–3; *The Scream*, 40–2
Johnson, Samuel, 119–20
Jonson, Ben, 43

Kareda, Urjo, 19, 28–9, 140–5, 175, 199n29
Kermode, Frank, 88, 171–2, 176
Kierkegaard, Soren, 99–101, 193–5, 205n25
Knausgaard, Karl Ove, 45–6
Knowles, Richard P., 11, 162, 199n28, 202n6, 207–8n5
Kotsko, Adam, 155–6
Kott, Jan, 56, 104–5, 187–96

Lacan, Jacques, 53
Lamb, Charles and Mary, 69–72
Levin, Richard, 13
Lewis, C.S., 68, 76, 138, 199n36, 203n12, 209n4
locality/globality, 116–26
Love, Heather K., 8–9, 130

MacDonald, Ann-Marie, 180
MacIntyre, Alasdair, 198n15, 198n18; *Marxism and Christianity*, 96; *Secularization and Moral Change*, 96; *Three Rival Versions of Moral Enquiry*, 159–63; tradition, 156–7
Martin, Bob, 4, 172
Mazer, Cary M., 132–3, 199n26

McCoy, Richard C., 8, 138–9
McKinney, Mark, 4, 85
Meirelles, Fernando, 10, 117
metanarrative, 116. *See also* Frye, Northrop
mimesis, 3, 14–20, 44–5, 53–64, 114–39
mimetic rivalry, 26. *See also* Phillips, Robin
modernism (high), 19, 40, 54–5, 97
Monette, Richard, 11, 19, 28, 140–5, 177
Mousley, Andy, 8, 50, 201n26
Munch, Edvard, *The Scream*, 39–47, 153. *See* also Knausgaard, Karl Ove
Murdoch, Iris, 114, 151, 177

naturalism/realism. *See* mimesis
neo-liberalism. *See* capitalism
Newman, Peter, 121
Nietzsche, Friedrich, 39, 128, 159–62
Noble, Denis, 51
Nuttall, A.D., 129–32, 138, 197n3

Orgel, Stephen, 206n35
Osborne, Laurie E., 97

Parolin, Peter, 11
Pechter, Edward, 7–9, 138
Phillips, Robin, 19, 26, 85; mimetic rivalry, 200n7; Shakespirituality, 69; stripped-down productions, 50; theatre as vocation, 4; tradition, 120
Pickstock, Catherine, 58
Pirandello, Luigi, 99, 107
Plato, 3, 22; *anamnesis*, 76, 78–84; divine madness, 43; mimesis, 113; sophism, 33

poetic faith. *See* Coleridge, Samuel Taylor
postmodernism, 4–5, 97; anti-realism, 15–16, 34, 112–15; irony, 22, 60–4; media, 123. *See also* Baudrillard, Jean; Brook, Peter; Derrida, Jacques; Hawkes, Terence; Jameson, Frederic; Pickstock, Catherine; Prendergast, Christopher; *Slings & Arrows*: Darren Nichols; *Slings & Arrows*: Sanjay; Taylor, Charles
Powe, B.W., 112
Prendergast, Christopher, 114–15

Rampersad, Kimberley, 180
Ricoeur, Paul, 76–81, 109
risk, risk society, 38–9, 43–4. *See* also Weil, Simone
Romanticism, 5–6. *See also* Brook, Peter; Coleridge, Samuel Taylor; Frye, Northrop; mimesis; Munch, Edvard; postmodernism; Taylor, Charles
Ross (blogger), 54–5
Ryan, Kiernan, 8, 67, 124

second naïveté. *See* Ricoeur, Paul
secularism. *See* Brook, Peter; Jameson, Frederic; MacIntyre, Alasdair; Taylor, Charles
Shakespeare, William: *As You Like It*, 3, 21, 64; *Hamlet*, 3–4, 27, 32, 127, 167–70; *King Lear*, 27, 58, 171–82; Lady Macbeth (performing), 137; *Macbeth*, elementary school production of, 135–6; *Macbeth* and Geoffrey Tennant, 173–4; *Macbeth* and risk, 38, 59–60; Macbeth/Banquo relation

as parallel to Tennant/Welles, 27; *A Midsummer Night's Dream*, 22, 30, 34–42, 65–8, 88; race, 125 (*see also* Soyinka, Wole); *Romeo and Juliet*, 30, 46, 185–6; Sanjay's postmodernism, influence on, 32, 59; *The Sonnets*, 26; *The Tempest*, 83–4, 187–96 (*see also* Frye, Northrop; Hirsch, John; Kott, Jan); *The Tempest* and literary/dramatic imagination, 15–16, 39, 97–115; *The Tempest* and ship as metaphor of theatre, 24–7; *The Tempest* and Prospero, 60–1, 68; *The Tempest* and romance, 88; as frame for *Lear* in "The Promised End," 178; *Twelfth Night*, 175; *The Winter's Tale*, 74–6. *See also* Frye, Northrop

Slings & Arrows (episodes, characters, themes/forms): episodes 1.1–2, 21–31; episodes 1.1–5, 32–52, 146–58; episode 1.3, 46; episode 1.4, 161; episode 1.5, 167; episode 1.6, 26; episodes 2.1–6, 38–44; episode 2.2, 135–9; episode 2.3, 60–1; episode 2.5, 43; episode 2.6, 185–7; episode 3.1, 120–6; episode 3.2, 32; episode 3.4, 24–5; episode 3.6, 171–82; audio/aural elements, 18, 25–6, 61; Henry Breedlove (Geraint Wyn Davies), 31, 38; camerawork, 39–40, 51–2, 97, 163, 173–4; Claire (Sabrina Gredevich), 36; coloniality, 119–26; Anna Conroy (Susan Coyne), 184–5; Jack Crew (Luke Kirby), 122, 168; Basil Cruikshank (Sean Cullen), 24, 31, 48, 157–8; Cyril (Graham Harley), 27, 30, 122; Holly Day (Jennifer Irwin), 43, 61, 93, 122, 146–61; ending, 94, 171–82; Ellen Fanshaw (Martha Burns), 25–7, 121, 135, 179; Frank (Michael Polley), 30; Barbara Gordon (Janet Bailey), 121, 180; Charles Kingman (William Hutt), 13, 122, 171–82; Kate McNab (Rachel McAdams), 164, 167–8; Reg Mortimer (Julian Richings), 21–2, 54, 93; Nahum (Rothaford Gray), 180; Darren Nichols (Don McKellar), 9, 17, 46, 159–70, 183–5; Peter (David Alpay), 185–6; possessive individualism, 146–59; production challenges, 117–18; race, 123, 180 (*see also* Soyinka, Wole); reception, 10–11; Sanjay (Colm Feore), 32–3, 38, 44–7, 59–64; Sarah (Joanne Kelly), 185–6; satire in, 146–59; May Silverstone (Marcia Bennett), 28, 43; Richard Smith-Jones (Mark McKinney), 25, 43, 61; structure of series (narrative), 4–6, 171–82; Geoffrey Tennant (Paul Gross), 31–52, 119–26, 135–8, 165–70, 173–85; Lionel Train (Jonathan Crombie), 31, 184–5; Oliver Welles (Stephen Ouimette), 26–31, 32–3, 135–6, 168–9, 174–9. *See also* Shakespeare, William

Soyinka, Wole, 124–6

Stern, Tiffany, 134–5

Stratford Festival (Ontario): aesthetic critiques of, 28, 47–8, 152; diversity of, 180–1; ideological critiques of, 10–11, 162; relation to

Index

Slings & Arrows, 31, 59, 116–26, 140–5, 176–82; saviour syndrome vis-à-vis artistic directors, 30. *See also* Coyne, Susan; Frye, Northrop; Guthrie, Tyrone; Hirsch, John; Monette, Richard; Phillips, Robin

Strehler, Giorgio, 193–4

Taylor, Charles, 19, 55–6, 82–3, 96
theatre, as vocation, 4. *See also* Brook, Peter; Coyne, Susan; Frye, Northrop; Hirsch, John; Phillips, Robin
Tomko, Michael, 69, 200–1nn1–2
transcendence, 58

universalism, 16–7, 50, 67, 70–2. *See also* Frye, Northrop; Ryan, Kiernan

vernacular Shakespeare. *See* Bristol, Michael

Wardle, Irving, 192–4
Warren, Roger, 192–4, 204n5
Weil, Simone: the past, 169; risk, 44–5
Wellington, Peter, 9–10
White, Patrick Gordon, 180
Wilde, Oscar, 127–8
Wood, James, 150–2
Woolf, Virginia, 57